Praise for

YOU WILL BE MADE TO CARE

"The compassionate bullies of the Left have decided they must force you to shut up. My friend Erick Erickson exposes their unbelievable bullying so often ignored or excused by the media."

> —Mark Levin, host of *The Mark Levin Show* and author of *Men in Black*

"Erick Erickson is a brilliant thinker who knows how to deliver truth with punchy wit and without trigger warnings. This book explains to American Christians that ignoring the culture around us will not rewind us back to some safer place in the past. More than that, the book is a catalyst for thinking through a path forward for the years to come. Read this book and ponder how we can leave an inheritance for our children of liberty and justice, for all."

> —Russell Moore, president, Ethics & Religious Liberty Commission of the Southern Baptist Convention

"As William Penn, founder of Pennsylvania, so aptly stated: We will either be ruled by God, or we will be ruled by tyrants. We cannot let the tyrants win. This fantastic book is a huge leap toward victory!"

> —Brad Thor, #1 *New York Times* bestselling author of *Foreign Agent*

"Few more prophetic words have been spoken in our recent political discourse than 'You will be made to care.' Erick Erickson and Bill Blankschaen underscore in a convincing and justifiably alarming way that the Left is not looking for mere tolerance but to force social conservatives, indeed everyone, into submission to their ideology—prosecuting and persecuting along the way. You might not care about the agenda of social liberalism—but, menacingly, it cares about you. This is a must-read book."

> —David Limbaugh, *New York Times* bestselling author of *Jesus on Trial* and *The Emmaus Code*

"This urgently needed book lays bare the Left's plan to redefine the classic Christian views on sex and marriage as the legal equivalent of racism. Buy it. Read it. Blog it. Share it now before it's too late."

> —Maggie Gallagher, cofounder of the National Organization for Marriage, editor of ThePulse2016.com, and coauthor of *Debating Same-Sex Marriage*

"*You Will Be Made to Care* doesn't parse words. Threats to conscience and religious liberty abound. Inevitably, every Christian will be tasked with contending for the faith thtat was once for all delivered to the saints. *You Will Be Made to Care* is a trustworthy guide."

—Andrew T. Walker, director of policy studies, Ethics & Religious Liberty Commission

"Years ago, William F. Buckley Jr. urged fellow conservatives to call out 'Stop!' Today, Erick Erickson and Bill Blankschaen are crying out to the same movement, 'Wake up!' Among numerous other salutary concerns, one feels their passion for sanctified gender and sexuality throughout this vibrant, nimble, steel-spined book. Erickson and Blankschaen have succeeded in fashioning an easily applicable brand of cultural engagement. Now the need is this: for Christians to buy into this program and, like the Apostle Paul, own their citizenship through catalyzed faith."

—Owen Strachan, author of *The Colson Way* and president of the Council on Biblical Manhood and Womanhood

"Erick Erickson and Bill Blankschaen not only sound the alarm about the wildfire sweeping America in *You Will Be Made to Care*, but they explain why progressives do what they do and attack religious liberty. A stirring call to action, *You Will Be Made to Care* offers a practical roadmap for families, individuals, pastors, church leaders, and citizens to act while they still have time to experience a resurgence of faith, freedom, and liberty!

—Kelly Monroe Kullberg, author of *Finding God at Harvard*, founder of the Veritas Forum, and developer of the America Conservancy

"Many of the students who come through my college classroom want to avoid the great moral and social issues of our age, sitting on the sidelines with an attitude of 'Why should I care?' But as Erick Erickson and Bill Blankschaen point out, the sidelines are shrinking. Soon we will all be pressured into taking a stand. We will all be forced to 'care.' This book briefs readers on how to recognize typical strategies used to marginalize and discredit Christian perspectives in the public arena—and how to inspire a resurgence."

—Nancy Pearcey, professor at Houston Baptist University and author of *Total Truth: Liberating Christianity from Its Cultural Captivity* and *Finding Truth: 5 Principles for Unmasking Atheism, Secularism, and Other God Substitutes*

YOU WILL BE MADE TO CARE

YOU WILL BE MADE TO CARE

THE WAR ON FAITH, FAMILY, AND YOUR FREEDOM TO BELIEVE

ERICK ERICKSON AND
BILL BLANKSCHAEN

REGNERY
PUBLISHING
A Division of Salem Media Group

Regnery® is a registered trademark of Salem Communications Holding Corporation

Scripture quotations are from the ESV® Bible (The Holy Bible, English Standard Version®), copyright © 2001 by Crossway, a publishing ministry of Good News Publishers. Used by permission. All rights reserved.

Cover photo of Erick Erickson by Jonah Koch. Cover photo of Bill Blankschaen by Photography by Britton.

Cataloging-in-Publication data on file with the Library of Congress

ISBN 978-1-62157-474-3

Published in the United States by
Regnery Publishing
A Division of Salem Media Group
300 New Jersey Ave NW
Washington, DC 20001
www.Regnery.com

Manufactured in the United States of America

10 9 8 7 6 5 4 3 2 1

Books are available in quantity for promotional or premium use. For information on discounts and terms, please visit our website: www.Regnery.com.

Distributed to the trade by
Perseus Distribution
250 West 57th Street
New York, NY 10107

To Derek Thomas, Bill Davis, and John Sowell,
for guiding me in the science of living blessedly forever.
—Erick Erickson

To my children:
May your faith in God and your love of
Truth keep you forever free.
—Bill Blankschaen

CONTENTS

PART I

FIRST THEY COME FOR YOUR FAITH

CHAPTER 1

THE AUDACITY TO BELIEVE

Our faith journey isn't just about showing up on Sunday for a good sermon and good music and a good meal. It's about what we do Monday through Saturday as well, especially in those quiet moments, when the spotlight's not on us, and we're making those daily choices about how to live our lives.

—MICHELLE OBAMA[1]

K elvin Cochran always dreamed of becoming a firefighter. But Kelvin did more than dream. He rose to the pinnacle of his profession—serving as America's fire chief—before being blindsided by the city of Atlanta, which abruptly terminated his employment in 2015. Kelvin Cochran was fired for having the audacity to write a book about his Christian beliefs.

Chief Cochran's decorated career began humbly in Shreveport, Louisiana, where he grew up in a family that was abandoned by their father when Kelvin was quite young. His mother and five brothers and sisters survived on welfare and food stamps, living in a government project. Kelvin recalls times when his mother would have the children fill every pot and jug with water, knowing the water company would soon cut their family off. They had to light their home with candles when they could afford no electricity. And by the end of each month, his mother had only enough money to buy mayonnaise and bread. The six children would eat mayonnaise on toast for breakfast, mayonnaise sandwiches for lunch, and mayonnaise sandwiches again for dinner. If they wanted something sweet to drink, they had to make do with a couple teaspoons of sugar in a glass of water. "Poverty," Chief Cochran recalls, "was a terrible thing."

After church one Sunday afternoon, the family heard sirens in the alley outside their house. When Kelvin opened the door, he saw a big red Shreveport Fire Department truck. The house where the firefighters were battling to douse the flames belonged to Miss Katie across the street.

Seeing them in action that day sparked Kelvin's imagination: "When I saw those firefighters, I was smitten. All I ever thought about growing up from that point forward was being a firefighter, escaping from poverty, and wanting to have a family, because I realized how terrible it was not to have a daddy at home." When he shared his dream with grown-ups, they told him that "your dreams will come true if you go to school, treat other people like you want to be treated, respect authority, and have faith in God."

Those core principles, grounded in his Christian beliefs, guided Kelvin Cochran as his "childhood-dream-come-true-fairy-tale-career" took off. In 1981 he became one of the first African American firefighters in the Shreveport Fire Department. He was promoted to captain in just four years. He became an assistant chief of training after ten years and fire chief of the Shreveport Fire Department after just eighteen years of service. Cochran served faithfully in that role until he was recruited by Atlanta mayor Shirley Franklin to serve as fire chief for the largest city in the southeastern United States.

As fire chief for the city of Atlanta, Cochran oversaw more than 1,100 personnel serving in thirty-six fire stations across the city,

including some at the Atlanta airport. Managing a budget of about
$140 million, he was responsible for fire and rescue, field operations,
and any emergencies that were not law enforcement–related. His
duties included overseeing:

- Aircraft rescue firefighting at Hartsfield-Jackson International Airport, the busiest airport in the world;
- Special operations such as high-rise and waterway
  rescue; and
- Hazardous materials response teams—as three major
  interstates intersect in downtown Atlanta.[2]

Cochran was entrusted with tremendous responsibility, and he
served with such distinction in Atlanta that he came to the attention
of someone in Washington—newly inaugurated President Barack
Obama.

When the president nominated him to serve his country as the
U.S. fire administrator within the Department of Homeland Security
in August of 2009,[3] Chief Cochran answered the call to serve his
country. In short, he became the nation's fire chief, overseeing the
training of our nation's firefighters, educating for fire prevention,
establishing a national deployment strategy for natural disasters or
terrorist attacks, and coordinating the response of firefighters in the
event of national emergencies with FEMA.

Throughout his meteoric rise, it was Kelvin Cochran's Christian
faith that motivated him to serve and to excel.

From an early age, Kelvin's strong and prayerful mother followed
the biblical instruction to "train up a child in the way he should go."
As a young father, Cochran became active in his local church, serving
as a deacon, teaching children in Sunday school, and leading other
men to become better fathers and husbands. Cochran embraced the
Christian doctrine of vocation and sought to glorify God through

service to his fellow citizens. His faith guided him all the way to our nation's capital and the pinnacle of his profession.

After just ten months in Washington, D.C., Cochran got a visit from Mayor Kasim Reed of Atlanta, recruiting him to return to his previous position. In fact, he "begged"—the mayor's own word—the chief to return to lead the city's fire and safety efforts.[4]

Cochran returned to Atlanta in June of 2010 and continued to serve the city with distinction. After a winter storm paralyzed the city in January 2014, the mayor enlisted Cochran's expertise to coordinate emergency disaster response as incident commander.[5] And a few weeks later, with Cochran in the lead, the city weathered a second winter storm—with dramatically better results.

Under Kelvin Cochran's leadership, the Atlanta Fire Rescue Department celebrated as the Insurance Services Office raised "Atlanta's Public Protection Classification (PPC) rating to Class 1, indicating an exemplary ability to respond to fires."[6] The department also retained accreditation with the Commission on Fire Accreditation International (CFAI), an achievement earned by only two hundred fire departments in the world. Atlanta Fire Rescue was called "a model for innovative public fire protection practices" by the CFAI commission chair.[7] In fact, the Atlanta department experienced success story after success story with Cochran at the helm until—suddenly, a week before Thanksgiving 2014—everything changed.

All of Cochran's career success became irrelevant when he was targeted by gay activists who claimed that his Christian beliefs—the very ones that motivated him to serve with excellence for thirty-four years—now disqualified him from doing his job keeping Atlanta safe.

KICKED TO THE CURB AND MADE TO CARE
In November 2013 Chief Cochran had published a book titled *Who Told You That You Were Naked? Overcoming the Stronghold*

of Condemnation. The idea for the book came out of a men's Bible study examining the Genesis account of the Garden of Eden. As Cochran describes it:

> I asked them if they thought men today are still suffering from the consequences of what Adam did in the Garden of Eden. All of them without hesitation said, "Yes." I asked them to each share their stories of *why*. And as they shared, the question that God asked Adam, "Who told you that you were naked?" kept resonating in my spirit and in my mind. I was led to research the word *naked* because I felt that God was asking Adam more than *who told you that you don't have on any clothes*.[8]

Cochran's research led him to conclude that there were a lot of Christian men still acting as if they were "naked"—condemned—instead of living redeemed and restored lives as faithful fathers and husbands. So he wrote the book to share his findings and encourage Christian men with a basic expression of Christian beliefs.

Then without warning—nearly a year after he published his book—Cochran was called into a meeting with three members of Mayor Reed's administration and suspended without pay for thirty days pending an investigation. His alleged wrongdoing was publishing his religious beliefs about marriage and sexuality. On November 24, 2014, the mayor's Facebook page showed the following post:

> The contents of this book do not reflect the views of Mayor Reed or the Administration.... I was surprised and disappointed to learn of this book on Friday. **I profoundly disagree with and am deeply disturbed by the sentiments expressed in the paperback regarding the LGBT [lesbian,**

> gay, bisexual, and transgender] community.... Chief
> Cochran will be required to complete sensitivity train-
> ing.... I want to be clear that the material in Chief
> Cochran's book is not representative of my personal beliefs,
> and is inconsistent with the Administration's work to make
> Atlanta a more welcoming city for all her citizens—regard-
> less of their sexual orientations, gender, race, and religious
> beliefs.[9] [emphasis added]

All citizens, that is, except those whose religious beliefs happen to agree with the Bible instead of Mayor Reed's "personal beliefs." When Cochran was suspended, openly gay District 6 councilmember Alex Wan actually said, "[W]hen you're a city employee, and [your] thoughts, beliefs and opinions are different from the city's, you have to check them at the door."[10]

A month later, the investigation had found no wrongdoing and zero facts to support the claims of discrimination that had been hurled against the chief by the gay activists: "Reed officials found no evidence that Cochran treated lesbian, gay, bisexual and transgender employees unfairly during his tenure."[11] Investigators produced no evidence to support allegations that the chief was proselytizing at work, either.[12] In fact, the investigation produced no evidence of any policy violations whatsoever. And yet Chief Kelvin Cochran was unceremoniously fired, simply for his beliefs about marriage and sexuality, which were all consistent with historic Christian doctrine but were suddenly deemed to be bigotry so deplorable as to make him unemployable by the supposedly Bible Belt city of Atlanta.

Cochran's Christian faith shaped how he treated all people with respect and how he rose to the very peak of his profession. His commitment to live out his faith in his vocation and all of life is a reflection of historic Christianity. It is also a summation of Dr. Martin Luther King Jr.'s "Street Sweeper" speech: "Go on out and sweep streets like

Michelangelo painted pictures; sweep streets like Handel and Beethoven composed music; sweep streets like Shakespeare wrote poetry; sweep streets so well that all the host of heaven and earth will have to pause and say, 'Here lived a great street sweeper who swept his job well.'"

What Cochran did by living a life that consistently reflected his deeply held religious beliefs was no different from what Martin Luther King urged, and yet he wasn't even allowed to sit in the back of the bus. He was kicked to the curb.

Kelvin Cochran had dared to quote a passage from the Bible in his book! As part of a general call to "serve one another humbly in love" and to "love your neighbor as yourself," the Apostle Paul encouraged believers in Galatia to stay away from a number of sins, including any sexual activity outside of heterosexual marriage. All Cochran did, ever so briefly and in language you'd find in study Bibles across America, was to affirm the basic Christian teaching that gay sex, like heterosexual sex outside of marriage, is a sin.

So gay rights activists screamed loudly that he could no longer do his job. It wasn't enough for them to disagree with the chief's religious beliefs, or to explain why theirs were right. The activists offended by Cochran's religious beliefs had to destroy Kelvin Cochran's livelihood because these beliefs offended them.

Mayor Reed of Atlanta complied.

Chief Kelvin Cochran was made to care. And make no mistake, he will not be the last person who is. The Left is coming for your freedom to believe. The day is coming—sooner than you think—when you too will be made to care.

IT COULD HAPPEN TO YOU

What happened to Chief Cochran isn't an isolated incident. Across America over the last decade—and especially in the last few years—the attacks on religious liberty have intensified in what I can only describe as a war on our freedom to believe.

The examples are numerous—and multiplying.

Evangelical Christians **Jonathan and Elaine Huguenin** declined to photograph a same-sex ceremony based on their belief that marriage is a sacred union of a man and a woman. The New Mexico Human Rights Commission ruled that the Huguenins had discriminated on the basis of sexual orientation and ordered them to pay $6,637.94 in attorneys' fees.[13] The New Mexico Supreme Court upheld the ruling, with one justice claiming the Huguenins' loss of religious freedom was simply "the price of citizenship."[14]

Catholic Charities of Boston was forced out of adoption services because it would not abandon the clear tenets of the Christian faith and place children in the homes of same-sex couples.[15]

Two lesbian women asked the owners of an Oregon bakery, **Sweet Cakes by Melissa,** to bake a wedding cake for their same-sex commitment ceremony. When the business declined on religious grounds, the women filed a complaint under the Oregon Equality Act. The Labor Commission of Oregon ruled that Aaron and Melissa Klein, the owners of Sweet Cakes by Melissa, had violated Oregon's sexual orientation law. After being relentlessly harassed by gay activists who pressured vendors to stop doing business with them, the Kleins were forced to close their shop.[16] In July 2015, a state bureaucrat ordered the couple to pay $135,000 in damages and instructed them not to express their religious beliefs within the context of their business.

A same-sex couple received a marriage license in Massachusetts and asked **Jack Phillips,** the owner of Masterpiece Cakeshop, to bake a cake for a reception in Colorado. Phillips declined, citing his religious beliefs as the reason for refusing. The American Civil Liberties Union (ACLU) filed a complaint against him, arguing he had violated Colorado's public accommodation law. A judge ruled against the bakery in 2013, claiming that Phillips violated the law by declining service to the couple "because of their sexual orientation."[17]

Two men asked Arlene's Flowers and Gifts owner **Barronelle Stutzman** to arrange the flowers for their same-sex wedding ceremony. Stutzman had arranged flowers for the couple before, but she refused to help them celebrate their wedding, citing her "relationship with Jesus Christ"[18] and her belief that marriage is between one man and one woman. The Washington State attorney general filed a suit against Stutzman, arguing she had violated the state's sexual orientation law. But he didn't sue only Arlene's Flowers, Stutzman's business; he chose to sue her personally. The court ruled against Stutzman. For refusing to compromise her conscience, this seventy-year-old grandmother and her husband now face the loss of everything they own—including their dog.[19]

Jews Offering New Alternatives for Healing (JONAH), which offers faith-based therapy and counseling for those seeking to leave the homosexual lifestyle, was sued in New Jersey by plaintiffs supported by the radical progressive group Southern Poverty Law Center (SPLC). The suit claimed that homosexuality is fixed and immutable and that any person or organization, including religious nonprofits, that tries to help homosexuals overcome unwanted same-sex attractions is committing fraud. There are thousands of men and women who once identified as gay and are now living lives in conformity with their religious values, either married to someone of the opposite sex or single.[20] And yet a jury unanimously awarded $75,000 in damages in June 2015 after five of the six expert defense witnesses were barred from testifying.[21] JONAH will have to pay court costs as high as $3.5 million.

A devout Mennonite couple in Iowa, **Betty and Dick Odgaard**, declined a request to organize, facilitate, and host a same-sex ceremony in a seventy-seven-year-old church building in which they run an art gallery. The Odgaards refused on the basis of their religious beliefs, which include "the importance of living one's faith in all aspects of life." The Iowa Civil Rights Commission made them pay $5,000 in legal fees.[22] The Odgaards have since stopped providing all wedding services at the gallery.[23]

New Jersey's **Ocean Grove Camp Meeting Association**, a Methodist organization, stopped hosting weddings after the New Jersey Department of Civil Rights ruled it had discriminated against a lesbian couple. In 2007 it had declined the couple's application because homosexual unions violated Methodist doctrine.[24]

Citing her religious beliefs, **Aloha Bed and Breakfast** owner Phyllis Young declined to rent a room in her home to a lesbian couple when they told her they would only need one bed. Hawaii's First Circuit Court ordered her to stop discriminating.[25]

Jim and Mary O'Reilly, owners of Vermont's Wildflower Inn, stopped hosting weddings after being fined $30,000 for turning away a same-sex couple in 2010.[26]

A counseling student at Augusta State University named **Jennifer Keeton** refused to change her religious beliefs and endorse same-sex marriage and adoptions. The university ordered her to undergo a reeducation plan and prove to them that she had changed her religious beliefs in order to graduate. She refused. She sued to defend her religious liberty—and lost.[27]

Angela McCaskill, the chief diversity officer of Gallaudet University, was demoted after she signed a 2012 referendum petition regarding Maryland's same-sex marriage law. A federal court dismissed her discrimination lawsuit. As McCaskill's lawyer points out, her case demonstrates "people can have their livelihoods targeted for making a political statement."[28]

To ensure inclusion for gays, **Vanderbilt University** in Nashville, Tennessee, placed Graduate Christian Fellowship, a chapter of Inter-Varsity Christian Fellowship, on probation in an attempt to force it to drop the requirement that student leaders affirm its doctrinal and purpose statement. Altogether, according to the fellowship leader, "14 campus religious communities—comprising about 1,400 Catholic, evangelical, and Mormon students—lost their organizational status" for their refusal to compromise their religious beliefs.[29]

When the owner and two pharmacists at **Ralph's Thriftway** in Washington State refused to dispense abortion-inducing drugs, state regulators tried to force them to do so in spite of their religious objections and the fact that the drugs were readily available elsewhere. A 2012 federal court ruling eventually suspended the state regulations, which it found were designed "'primarily (if not solely)' to ban religiously motivated referrals while the state, at the same time, permits pharmacies to refrain from stocking and delivering drugs for 'almost unlimited' business, economic, and convenience reasons."[30] But the verdict was overturned by the Ninth Circuit, and now the only recourse for Ralph's is an appeal to the Supreme Court.

The University of California–Hastings denied campus recognition to the **Christian Legal Society** because CLS would not accept members who did not adhere to the society's religious principles. In 2010 the U.S. Supreme Court agreed with UC Hastings that every student organization must admit any student who desires to join. Even the *Los Angeles Times* argued in a 2010 editorial that the decision "actually undermines diversity by making every student group potentially interchangeable in its membership."[31]

In Illinois the **Evangelical Child and Family Agency (ECFA)** had contracted with the state for decades to provide foster care services. In 2011, however, a new state civil union law,[32] coupled with an existing sexual orientation policy, effectively forced private agencies to license unmarried, cohabiting couples—including same-sex couples—as foster care parents in order to keep state contracts. Because the ECFA believed it was in the best interest of every child to be in a home with a married father and mother, they and many other faith-based organizations were forced to stop serving over two thousand children.[33]

And the list goes on. There are many more such examples of the war on our freedom to believe. And they almost all have one theme in common—sex. Nearly all these cases involve sexual orientation or sexual behavior—the "pelvic issues," as they've been called, that fascinate the Left. Progressives are rabidly committed to expanding the freedom to express oneself sexually without consequences and without criticism. In fact, their right to feel good about their sexual expression trumps your right to express your beliefs about it. You are required to approve and even help them celebrate—or you can lose your job, your business, your chosen career, your home, and even your dog. The sexual revolution ideology of the 1960s means that personal feelings outweigh the transhistorical truths that have fostered the flourishing of all humanity.

They aren't winning every single case, of course, at least not yet. There are a handful of examples, including some truly egregious attempts to compel Christians to engage in speech that contradicts their beliefs, in which religious liberty has prevailed—for now.

For example, **Hands On Originals**, a Kentucky T-shirt company owned by Christians, refused to print gay-pride designs for a local homosexual group. The group filed a complaint with the Lexington-Fayette Urban County Human Rights Commission, which ruled the company discriminated against homosexuals. But in April 2015, the Fayette Circuit Court overruled the commission, determining that the company did *not* discriminate when it declined to print the shirts.[34]

Eastern Michigan University settled a case with **Julea Ward**, a Christian counseling student who had declined to affirm the homosexual lifestyle in a counseling session. When a federal court ruled in favor of Ward because "Ward's professors ejected her from the counseling program because of hostility toward her speech and faith," EMU reinstated her to the university and paid her $75,000.[35]

These are the forces of diversity and tolerance, arrayed against the "anti-gay" "haters" on the Christian side of the issue.

But where are the actual examples of attacks on the rights of gays—to earn a living, to own a business, to finish a college degree, to create and maintain organizations defined by their beliefs, or to work as a pharmacist, baker, or photographer? No sexual identity, no amount or degree of even the most "transgressive" sexual expression makes you unfit for those rights in America today. No right-wing Christian zealot is trying to take them away. The Left cries "discrimination" against homosexuals and makes wild comparisons to Jim Crow laws—a logically incoherent comparison that insults the great civil rights leaders of the twentieth century. But no one can point to any real incident in which a person has been denied service because of his or her sexual orientation. Refusing to help celebrate a gay wedding or to provide a bed in one's own home for lesbian sex is simply not the same thing as discrimination against persons. It's simply a refusal to be drafted onto the opposing side. An objection to being *made to care.*

Sonny Bunch of the Washington Free Beacon has written that he does not think I am quite right to say *You will be made to care.* Instead, he thinks it should be *You will be made to shut up.*[36] I would suggest that Bunch is simply stopping short of realizing the other side's end game.

Yes, along the way to making people care, many of us will be made to shut up. In fact, we see that is the initial play with the Left. The fire chief in Atlanta referred to homosexuality as a sin and lost his job. Phil Robertson of *Duck Dynasty* quoted Scripture, and the Left tried to drive him from the airwaves. The Benham Brothers are evangelical Christians who had their TV deal canceled for offending the gay mafia. Yes, Christians and all those who question political correctness will be made to shut up. But that is only the halfway point.

Particularly on the issue of gay marriage, gay rights activists want the entire veneer of normal. They want the whole package, complete with your stamp of approval. They want to have their cake and eat it too—and they want you to bake it for them. The Christian florist must be forced to provide flowers for gay weddings. Everyone who appears in the media must enthusiastically celebrate homosexuality and gay marriage. Pastors will be forced to marry gay couples. After all, weddings normally happen in a church.

For those of you who say this will never happen, just wait. It won't be long. Gay marriage was also never going to happen. More than one employee of major Fortune 500 companies has already told me about being "strongly encouraged" to participate in gay-pride events. Corporate employees are required to complete surveys, with their names on them, asking intrusive questions about their views of gay rights. Eventually, you will be made to care. Once the gay mafia has established that everyone agrees with it because all other voices have been made silent, those of you still thinking that you do not have to pick a side or that you can compromise and nuance your position will have to take a side. The time for choosing is closer than you think. You will be made to care about gay marriage one way or the other, and if you care the wrong way, good luck finding or—as Kelvin Cochran discovered—keeping a job.

Sonny Bunch is right that you will be made to shut up. But then you will be made to care.

THE ONE THING WE NEED NOW

I talk to a lot of people. It's what I do. As the editor of RedState for ten years, current editor of The Resurgent (TheResurgent.com), and host of the most listened to talk radio program in Atlanta, *The Erick Erickson Show*, I talk to a lot of conservatives and Christians—candidates, cultural leaders, and common folk who are just tired of fighting. After decades of culture wars, failed leadership in both parties, and almost eight years of a progressive president committed to fundamentally transforming America, there's a sense that we are no longer slouching toward Gomorrah, as Robert Bork famously put it, but rushing headlong toward inevitable decline.

The compassionate bullies on the Left who disguise their tyranny as a call for tolerance want to make you think you are alone. They want you to think your beliefs are the freakish manifestations of an archaic faith. But you are not alone. Though you feel as if you're the only one left fighting for your beliefs in a culture that has lost its mind. Though you see what seems to be a cultural wildfire burning across our land. Though you hear nothing but negativity from a press that serves as the lackeys of the Left. Take heart, my friend. You do not stand alone. There is hope.

This book is not intended for political insiders. For far too long, conservative Christians in America have looked to Washington for solutions that should have come from their own humble obedience to God. We hoped for a Supreme Court ruling instead of obeying the commands of the Supreme Being. If you're not an avid fan of politics, don't worry. Our focus will not be on political solutions. Because if we have learned anything from the success of the homosexual agenda, it is that the late Andrew Breitbart was right: "Politics is downstream from culture."[37]

The key to fighting and winning this war for the freedom to believe can be found in one word, which we will unpack more fully later in this book. We need a *resurgence*. Now is not the time for quitting. Now is the time for engaging culture strategically with an understanding of the times in which we live and a reinvigorated faith in God. Now is the time for building up our own faith and intentionally surrounding ourselves with a community that shares our beliefs. These may well be "times that try men's souls," but as Thomas Paine also noted, "Tyranny, like hell, is not easily conquered."[38] Although

Jesus Christ conquered hell nearly two thousand years ago, overcoming tyranny is still a work in progress. And it is our privilege to take part in the struggle. Such times can produce a new generation of heroes because they offer an opportunity for clarity, authentic community, and courageous leadership. As my friend Kevin DeYoung reminds believers, "The world needs to see Christians burning, not with self-righteous fury at the sliding morals in our country, but with passion for God."[39]

I'm not into whining and complaining. There are a lot of those kinds of books out there, if all you want to do is make some noise. I'm more interested in making a difference. In this book I'm not only going to educate you as to the extent of the problem but also explain why progressives must insist on silencing all opposition. I'm going to reveal not only how the Left is destroying marriage, but also why marriage matters for human flourishing. And I will be challenging not only our political, cultural, and religious leaders (especially those within evangelical Christianity), but also you—as a believer, as a parent or grandparent, and as a citizen—to respond to this challenge to your faith. It is time for brave men and women (the only two gender categories we need, thank you) to stand up, step up, and start moving forward to defend our freedom to believe—*before* we, and those we love, are made to care.

CHAPTER 2

THE COMING WILDFIRE

Americans need to understand that the endgame of the
LGBT rights movement involves centralized state power—
and the end of First Amendment freedoms.

—DAWN STEFANOWICZ[1]

Mount de Sales Academy is a Catholic school in Macon, Georgia.

Until May 21, 2014, the school employed a band teacher who is openly gay. The Catholic Church's doctrinal position is that identifying oneself as gay is not, in and of itself, a sin. Rather, it holds that engaging in sex outside of marriage is a sin.[2] Marriage is a sacrament in the Catholic Church—a sacred bond between one man and one woman.

The Catholic school in Macon does not approve of people teaching there if they've violated the sacraments of the church. Even heterosexual teachers who get divorced are generally let go. The band teacher wanted to get married to another man—a step that would knowingly violate a sacrament of the church. As a result, the Catholic school dismissed him. It is true that the school administration botched their handling of the dismissal. A Catholic Church bishop had to get involved to insist that Catholic doctrine be adhered to.[3]

According to the mid-Georgia newspaper the *Telegraph*, the teacher felt discriminated against because "he didn't want to conform to gender stereotypes." So the Obama administration told the Catholic Church that it must treat gays and divorced heterosexuals differently from the way Catholic dogma dictates, that the new era of sexual orientation trumps religious beliefs:

> An investigation by the U.S. Equal Employment Opportunity Commission has determined "there is reasonable cause to conclude" that fired Mount de Sales Academy band director Flint Dollar was discriminated against because of his sexual orientation.
>
> The determination letter, dated Jan. 30, goes on to say that the commission will try to "eliminate the alleged unlawful practices by informal methods of conciliation."
>
> If a settlement isn't reached, the EEOC may file a lawsuit against the private school in Macon or issue a "right to sue" letter.[4]

Note that the Catholic Church did not refuse to employ the man for identifying as gay, although it could have made a sound theological argument for doing so. The school is a private, religious institution that exists for the purpose of educating students in a manner consistent with Catholic teaching. Yet it did not turn him away. It was only when the teacher chose to do something he knew the church could not approve that the church acted in a manner consistent with its beliefs.

What the Obama administration and the Left in general seem incapable of understanding is that there can be no compromise for people of faith on issues of morality. Matters of right and wrong cannot be resolved by "informal conciliation." Augustine of Hippo, one of the greatest Christian thinkers of all time, frames the issue rather neatly: "Right is right even if no one is doing it; wrong is wrong even if everyone is doing it."[5] For the Catholic Church and all who take their faith seriously, there can be no compromise on matters of conscience and no negotiations about right and wrong—no matter what opinion polls or Supreme Court justices may say.

I'm an evangelical Protestant, not a Catholic. But we are all in the same fight as Christians to defend our right to free exercise of our religion. I find it more than a little ironic that this story of religious discrimination appeared in the *Telegraph* on the very same day that Georgia Republicans voted down the Religious Freedom Restoration Act in Georgia. Not only Protestant believers such as Kelvin Cochran but also Pope Francis and the Catholic Church will be made to care. Venerable institutions that have served as pillars of Western civilization will not be exempt from the coming American nightmare.

In fact, the ordeal of making them care has already begun.

ENEMIES OF THE HUMAN RACE

Christians will be made to care—either for the world or for truth. There can be no neutrality on this issue. That should come as no surprise to any believer. Jesus himself said, "Whoever is not with me is against me, and whoever does not gather with me scatters" (Matt. 12:30). It is the nature of those who love darkness to despise the light. It is the nature of unrighteousness to suppress the truth. It is the nature of evil to seek to destroy all that is right and good in the world. Even as the Dark Lord Sauron was not content to be confined to Mordor in Tolkien's Middle Earth, so evil seeks to eliminate the peaceful Shires of our world. Archbishop Charles Chaput of Philadelphia, a man widely respected by Christians of all denominations, explains why:

> Evil talks about tolerance only when it's weak. When it gains the upper hand, **its vanity always requires the destruction of the good and the innocent, because the example of good and innocent lives is an ongoing witness against it.** So it always has been. So it always will be. And America has no special immunity to becoming an enemy of its own founding beliefs about human freedom, human dignity, the limited power of the state, and the sovereignty of God.[6] [emphasis added]

Lest you think *evil* is too strong of a word to describe the present wave of attacks on our freedom of conscience, consider this: if you believe, as all of humanity has done throughout history, that marriage is a sacred bond between a man and woman, the Supreme Court has declared you to be, according to Justice Antonin Scalia, *an enemy of the human race.*

In his June 26, 2013, dissenting opinion in *United States v. Windsor*, Scalia claims that Justice Anthony Kennedy and his colleagues did just that by belittling and demeaning the opposition as they overturned the Defense of Marriage Act (DOMA):

> But to defend traditional marriage is not to condemn, demean, or humiliate those who would prefer other arrangements, any more than to defend the Constitution of the United States is to condemn, demean, or humiliate other constitutions. To hurl such accusations so casually demeans *this institution.* In the majority's judgment, any resistance to its holding is beyond the pale of reasoned

disagreement. To question its high-handed invalidation of a presumptively valid statute is to act (the majority is sure) with *the purpose* to "disparage," "injure," "degrade," "demean," and "humiliate" our fellow human beings, our fellow citizens, who are homosexual. All that, simply for supporting an Act that did no more than codify an aspect of marriage that had been unquestioned in our society for most of its existence—indeed, had been unquestioned in virtually all societies for virtually all of human history. It is one thing for a society to elect change; it is another for a court of law to impose change by adjudging those who oppose it *hostes humani generis*, **enemies of the human race.**[7] [emphasis added]

Justice Scalia was quoting an old Latin phrase whose origins go back to the Roman Empire. According to the Roman historian Tacitus, when Nero persecuted the Christians as his scapegoats for the burning of Rome in 64 AD, the Christians, who were "killed by dogs by having the hides of beasts attached to them, or...nailed to crosses or set aflame, and, when the daylight passed away...used as nighttime lamps" were "convicted not so much for the crime of burning the city, but for hatred of the human race" (*odium humani generis*).[8] Does that sound familiar—the idea that Christians are "haters"? At the end of the second century AD, the Christian writer Tertullian defended Christians against the charge that they were the enemies of the Roman princes and people, of the human race (*hostes...generis humani*), of gods, emperors, laws, and customs, and even of all nature.[9] Another familiar idea—maybe you've heard the phrase "born that way"? As Tertullian argued, the Romans preferred to call Christians "enemies of the human race" when they are really just "enemies of human error."[10] If he had been writing in English, he might have said that Christians hate the sin but love the sinner.

In more modern times, "enemies of the human race" was a legal term applied to slavers and pirates (a similar phrase was applied to evil magicians in ancient Roman law)[11] to denote that such persons were outside the protection of the laws. Which is exactly where Christians will soon be—if we can't be *made to care.*

Still not convinced? The *New York Times,* the most powerful newspaper in America, signaled its support for reading Bible-believing Christians out of acceptable society with a column by Frank Bruni that captures the spirit animating much of the LGBT movement and its allies. Christians have not chosen this war, but make no mistake—it is a war. And religion itself must be made to care. Here are the relevant excerpts of Bruni's argument:

> [H]omosexuality and Christianity don't have to be in conflict in any church anywhere.
>
> That many Christians regard them as incompatible is understandable, an example not so much of hatred's pull as of tradition's sway. Beliefs ossified over centuries aren't easily shaken.
>
> But in the end, the continued view of gays, lesbians, and bisexuals as sinners is a decision. It's a choice. It prioritizes scattered passages of ancient texts over all that has been learned since—as if time had stood still, as if the advances of science and knowledge meant nothing.
>
> It disregards the degree to which all writings reflect the biases and blind spots of their authors, cultures and eras.[12]

Got that? Today, we have special access to the truth that St. Paul, the authors of the Bible, the Fathers of the Church, and virtually every Christian in history until around 1970 believed to be true. And not only do we know they were wrong, we have the duty to make those who still believe in clear scriptural teaching and the reliability of authoritative tradition repent of their heresy. Bruni continues, "So our debate about religious freedom should include a conversation about **freeing religions and religious people from prejudices** that they needn't cling to and can indeed jettison, much as they've jettisoned other aspects of their faith's history, rightly **bowing to the enlightenments of modernity**" [emphasis added].[13]

According to Bruni, you must be liberated from your own religious beliefs and made to bow to the beliefs of others who are more enlightened. To help make the case, Bruni points to liberal evangelical professor David Gushee as evidence that not all who call themselves Christians embrace the core beliefs of Christianity: "Conservative Christian religion is the last bulwark against full acceptance of L.G.B.T. people."[14]

By "full acceptance," it is important to understand, Gushee and his friends on the Left do not mean kindly speaking the truth to those the church deems to be engaging in sinful behavior. Full acceptance will arrive when the "bulwark" of "conservative Christian religion" has been removed and Christians are made to demonstrate full approval of gay behavior. Having defined people of faith—and Christians in particular—as the enemy, the one obstacle standing between the LGBT activists and cultural hegemony, what do they propose to do about it? Bruni explains:

> [Jimmy] Creech and Mitchell Gold, a prominent furniture maker and gay philanthropist, founded an advocacy group, Faith in America, which aims to mitigate the damage done to L.G.B.T. people by what it calls "religion-based bigotry."
>
> Gold told me that **church leaders must be made "to take homosexuality off the sin list."**
>
> **His commandment is worthy—and warranted.**[15]
> [emphasis added]

Not must be "persuaded," but must be "made." Not won over, but compelled. Forced. Christian, you must be forced not just to change your behavior, but to change what you believe. You must be made to give your approval.

Yes, this is evil—regardless of who is advancing or defending it. And we should not shy from saying so.

When former secretary of state and presidential candidate Hillary Clinton gave the keynote address at the Women in the World Summit in New York City in April 2015, she spoke of advancing "reproductive rights"—a.k.a. abortion. Clinton said, "Laws have to be backed up with resources and political will.... And deep-seated cultural codes, **religious beliefs** and structural biases **have to be changed**" [emphasis added].[16] You see, it's not just about a single issue, such as gay marriage. It's about progressive bullies who believe they know what you should believe better than you do. Their agenda is simple—use whatever means necessary, including the hammer of government, to force their beliefs on you.

We have a columnist in the *New York Times* saying the religious must be forced to change their views, quoting a millionaire intending to use his money to make it so. We have a Supreme Court majority fostering intolerance toward people of faith. We have the leading presidential candidate for the Democratic Party saying that religious beliefs "have to be changed." America, we have a problem.

Another powerful politician once made similar statements expressing his frustration with religious leaders for standing in the way of societal progress. He gave key Christian leaders this warning. I quote him exactly, except that I have substituted "same-sex marriage" for the different issue he was demanding the churches get on board with, and "America" for the country where he was in power: "The Church must get used to the teachings about same-sex marriage. Just as the Catholic Church couldn't prevent the earth from revolving around the sun, so Churches today cannot get rid of the indisputable facts connected with same-sex marriage. If you cannot recognize these, history will simply leave you behind."

When two of the church leaders told him that their faith left no choice but to serve as loyal opposition, the politician retorted, "You are not my most loyal opposition, but traitors to the people, enemies of the nation and the destroyers of America." To which our own Supreme Court might well add *hostes humani generis*—enemies of the human race.

The politician who made those statements? Adolf Hitler.[17] The year? Nineteen thirty-five. The country he referenced? Not America, but Germany. The issue he insisted that church leaders support was not same-sex marriage, but "blood and race." At the time, many Germans believed that Hitler's ideas offered an enlightened way forward for society through eugenics. Nazi race politics spread like a wildfire, in spite of moral opposition in Germany and around the world. Hitler attacked the church and people of faith when they refused to redefine sin to conform to the spirit of the age.[18] But after the horrors of the Holocaust, Hitler's theories have been scientifically debunked, his actions declared morally bankrupt, and his name tossed onto the trash heap of history where it belongs.

And the church still stands.

I am not equating homosexuals with Hitler or his evil ideology, which targeted homosexuals as well as Jews, gypsies, and any Christians who dared to resist him. I am only pointing out that history can show us what happens when the force of government is used to coerce Christians and other people of faith to abandon their beliefs in favor of the latest cultural fad. And it is not good.

In other words, we have seen this trend before: to isolate and destroy those who refuse to approve of that which they believe to be morally wrong. We know how this story ends. It does not end well for those individuals whose religious freedoms are incinerated by the ideological wildfire of the day—and it's a disaster for all of society.

AND SO THE WILDFIRE BURNS

Every once in a while, a society succumbs to a cultural wildfire—and loses its mind. It does things that future generations look back on and wonder, *How could they have possibly thought that was a good idea?* Back in the sixteenth century, when the Dutch controlled trade and commerce around much of the known world, the people who brought us wooden shoes began to substitute tulip bulbs for money.[19] That's right. The bulbs you plant in the ground that produce flowers in the spring became the preferred currency of the day instead of gold, silver, and precious metals. For a while, the tulip bulb bubble was huge. Everyone used these plants you can find at any garden center today to conduct business. In short, people lost their minds. No doubt many thought using plants in place of gold was nuts, but they went along with it because everyone else was doing it. But then the tulip bubble burst—and the world returned to reality.

American society finds itself now in the early stages of something similar. A cultural wildfire has begun to burn. To most Christians and conservatives, it seems that society has lost its mind, attempting to play God by redefining gender and abolishing marriage. Many people of faith have been trying to ignore the signs of smoke from this wildfire in the hopes that it will just go away. Others have been trying to avoid the heat by being nice, hoping that a little compromise would keep the flames at bay. Still others have thought all that would be required to extinguish the flames was a kinder, gentler, more winsome voice. But the accommodation of evil never achieves the desired end; it only increases the inevitable cost of victory.

We have already seen how Jack Phillips of Masterpiece Cakeshop in Colorado has been made to care by this wildfire burning through our culture. The details of the case are chilling.

For years Phillips served both gay and straight customers equally. But when a gay couple insisted that Phillips bake a custom wedding cake for them in 2012, Phillips declined. According to an administrative law judge who reviewed the case, "Phillips believes that decorating cakes is a form of art, that he can honor God through his artistic talents, and that he would displease God by creating cakes for same-sex marriages." And get this: Phillips offered to sell the couple a cake he had already made that they could then customize as they desired. They refused, insisting that he be made to decorate it for them.

Phillips made his faith priorities clear: "I'm a man who is devoted to following Jesus Christ. He's the one that's in charge of all this.... It's not up to the courts to decide what marriage is. It's up to God to decide that. If we are living in obedience to Jesus Christ and the teachings of the Bible we are on the right side of history—no matter what they say."[20]

On August 13, 2015, the Colorado Court of Appeals ruled Phillips must make cakes for gay weddings if he is to make any cakes at all. His attorney Jeremy Tedesco said, "Government has a duty to protect people's freedom to follow their beliefs personally and professionally rather than force them to adopt the government's views."[21] Some have cried discrimination, claiming that Phillips is a hater who refused service to homosexuals. But that is not what happened. He was happy to sell the gay couple a cake *that he had made*—but that was not enough. They insisted that he give his seal of approval to their ceremony by using his baking artistry to create and decorate a customized cake that would celebrate their relationship. They insisted that he violate his conscience. And the government agreed. To add insult to injury, the court ordered that his entire staff undergo training in the state's policies—including his eighty-eight-year-old mother. Reeducation camp for bakers has come to America.

Some of you may still be wanting to wish the wildfire away, dismissing what's happening in our culture as isolated to specific industries that are directly related to wedding ceremonies. But the wildfire will not be contained there. Over time, the gay rights movement will move to pushing Christian pastors to marry gays who—like most people—want to get married in churches. Over time, the Left will move to push religious schools to abandon standards on sexuality. Already universities such as Gordon College are falling out of favor with their local governments and institutions for maintaining traditional values. Gordon College has had a long-standing collaboration with the Peabody Essex Museum in Massachusetts, for example, but when the college requested a "religious exemption" from President Barack Obama's executive order prohibiting "discrimination" over sexual orientation, the museum ended its collaboration with Gordon. And Mayor Kim Driscoll of Salem, Massachusetts, canceled a contract with the college.[22]

Over time, progressives will continue to insist that religious institutions lose their tax-exempt status. Over time, Bible-believing churches will be labeled as hate groups, and orthodox Christianity will be forced out of the public square. In time, the state will intervene to "protect" children from parents who want to raise them as orthodox, Bible-believing Christians. A parent's belief in one-man-one-woman marriage will be viewed as a negative factor in custody decisions—even though study after study confirms that the healthiest place for children to grow up is in a stable home with a mom and a dad who are their biological parents.

The "hate crime" label will be used more frequently against Christians and all people of faith. In fact, it has already been used that way in Canada—to silence discussions about homosexuality, gender, and marriage. Writing this book would be a hate crime in Canada. Dawn Stefanowicz is a Canadian, the child of a gay parent, who warns of the Orwellian consequences of Canada's federal mandate for same-sex marriage in 2005, just over a decade ago:

> In Canada, it is considered discriminatory to say that marriage is between a man and a woman or that every child should know and be raised by his or her biological married

parents. It is not just politically incorrect in Canada to say so; you can be saddled with tens of thousands of dollars in legal fees, fined, and forced to take sensitivity training.... Over and over, we are told that "permitting same-sex couples access to the designation of marriage will not deprive anyone of any rights." That is a lie.[23]

Even thinking Christian thoughts about marriage can get you in trouble in Canada. Just ask Esau Jardon, a Christian jeweler in Canada who actually did create engagement rings for two lesbians. The couple, by their own account, were pleased both with the rings and the service they received. They even referred friends to Jardon's store. But then they became angry when a friend visited the store and saw a sign supporting traditional marriage. The couple argued that Jardon's beliefs had "tainted" the rings he created. I. Kid. You. Not.

Jardon made what seems a sane case for equal protection under the law: "When I walk on Church Street in Toronto, where I am right now, and I see [LGBT rainbow flags], and I see a lot of signs and a lot of things on public property, I don't have a problem with them. I accept it. **I chose to come to Canada...and we accept the whole package.... I don't discriminate against that, nor do I come and tell them to take them down. For the same reason, I ask to have the same respect in return, especially when it's in my own business**" [emphasis added].[24]

But after the progressive bullies mobilized, threatening to make his life a living hell, Jardon refunded the couple's money.

Writer Rod Dreher offers this accurate assessment of the principle at work here: "You must not only bake the cake, or arrange the flowers, or make the ring; you must hold the correct opinion when you do it."[25] In other words, it's not only about making the Christian shut up, but making him care.

And in America we're just a few years behind Canada. The prohibition on religious tests in our Constitution is being replaced in practice with the enforcement of a secularism test. Soon people of faith will not need to bother applying for certain jobs, political appointments, or elected office. Christians are the new bigots because our God said, "Go and sin no more," and dared list homosexuality as one of those sins. Ultimately, over time, two thousand years of Christianity will be treated as the deviant lifestyle. You will be forced to pick a side. If you remain true to your God, you will be outside the bounds of acceptable conduct. If you pick the wrong side, you will be punished. Gay rights activists cannot show you tolerance or treat you equally. Your faith, which claims that homosexuality is a sin, must not be allowed to remain in the public square. And in the fervent quest for the veneer of complete normalcy for homosexual relationships, your beliefs cannot be allowed to stand.

But there is good news: Christianity is growing worldwide, even in places like China and Saudi Arabia. And the religion that withstood Nero and Hitler, and even now withstands ISIS, can withstand a bunch of angry people in comfortable shoes who need rainbow stickers on their cars to tell us who they are.

The resurgence is already under way. And it is led by the One who cannot fail: "The wicked plots against the righteous and gnashes his teeth at him, but the Lord laughs at the wicked, for He sees that his day is coming" (Ps. 37:12–13).

CHAPTER 3

OUR FIRST FREEDOM

Religious freedom is the proverbial canary in the coal mine.
When you hear it, when it's compromised, it's a warning
that our other civil liberties are sure to follow.

—KRISTEN WAGGONER[1]

When Elaine and Jonathan Huguenin, the owners of Elane Photography whom we met briefly in chapter 1, declined to use their artistic talents to photograph a lesbian commitment ceremony, they thought they were exercising their most basic constitutional rights. Elaine explained simply that "the message a same-sex commitment ceremony communicates is not one I believe."[2] Mrs. Huguenin and her husband declined to provide their services because they are Christians and believe Holy Scripture, and the orthodox tenets of their faith tell them that marriage is between a man and a woman.

In an act of spite and retribution, one of the lesbian women filed a discrimination claim to punish Mrs. Huguenin for adhering to her religious beliefs. The photographer expected her freedom of speech and her free exercise of religion to be protected. New Mexico is, after all, still in America. But in an alarming decision, the New Mexico Supreme Court ruled that Christians, Muslims, Orthodox Jews, and others like the Huguenins must occasionally surrender the faithful practice of their religion if they are to participate in American culture. The words of Justice Richard Bosson's concurring opinion should alarm every reasonable American: "At its heart, this case teaches that at some point in our lives all of us must compromise, if only a little, to accommodate the contrasting values of others.... That compromise is part of the glue that holds us together as a nation, the tolerance that lubricates the varied moving parts of us as a people.... In short, I would say to the Huguenins, with the utmost respect: **it is the price of citizenship**" [emphasis added].[3]

In the name of tolerance, Mrs. Huguenin can be compelled by state power on pain of punishment to provide her artistic services against her orthodox religious beliefs, which have been held by Bible-believing Christians and Jews for several thousand years. The complaining party is under no obligation to simply tolerate one woman who disagrees with her and find someone else who is happy to provide the service she wants. The Left's tolerance only flows one way. David Cortman, senior counsel for Alliance Defending Freedom (ADF), gives this grave warning: "A government that forces any American to create a message contrary to her own convictions is a government every American should fear."[4]

The U.S. Supreme Court declined to hear the Huguenins' case.

THE INDISPENSABLE CONDITION

I believe people should be free to live and work according to their faith without fear of being punished by government. Apparently, that belief makes me some kind of radical on the lunatic fringe these days.

After all, it's not as if our country was founded by people fleeing religious persecution from the government. Oh, wait. It was. The first people who came to this land were *religious refugees*, which is why our freedom of religion is often called the first freedom. They believed religious freedom to be a basic human right deserving protection under the law.

Our freedom of religion is also often called the first freedom for another very simple reason—it comes first in our Bill of Rights. Last year at the 2015 RedState Gathering in Atlanta, I interviewed nine of the Republican presidential candidates at the largest gathering of presidential candidates in Georgia's history. When I asked them about the importance of defending religious liberty, several pointed to the position of the First Amendment in the Bill of Rights as evidence of the importance of our freedom of religion. And they were right—as far as they went. Religious freedom is the first freedom protected by those ten critical amendments, without which the Constitution itself would never have been ratified. For those who need a refresher or were the product of Common Core schooling, the First Amendment reads as follows: "Congress shall make no law respecting an establishment of religion, or prohibiting the free exercise thereof; or abridging the freedom of speech, or of the press; or the right of the people peaceably to assemble, and to petition the Government for a redress of grievances."

The Bill of Rights clearly places the first and highest priority on keeping government from restricting religious liberty. On that basis alone, most of the religious liberty cases Christians are losing in America today should not stand, because they involve people simply seeking to live out their religious beliefs in ways that none but the most vindictive would view as offensive. But if we stop at that reasonable conclusion, we miss the deeper reality of what is at stake for human flourishing. The language used in the Bill of Rights protects the free *exercise* of religion, not just our freedom to believe in it. In other words, the Constitution guarantees us the right to act outwardly on what we believe inwardly to be true. It is that freedom to think and believe within that is, in fact, our first freedom. All other freedoms depend on the right to live according to what we believe to be true and right—that is, according to our conscience. For that reason, freedom of conscience is our first freedom.

It turns out Jiminy Cricket wasn't too far off when he advised Pinocchio, "Always let your conscience be your guide."[5] Our nation's founders agreed. The free exercise clause protects our right to live out what we believe to be true about life and the universe. It guards our freedom both to think and to act according to the dictates of our conscience. In *Palko v. Connecticut*, U.S. Supreme Court Justice Benjamin Cardozo described the foundational place held by our freedom of conscience:

> Of that freedom [of thought and speech] one may say that **it is the matrix, the indispensable condition, of nearly every other form of freedom.** With rare aberrations a pervasive recognition of that truth can be traced in our history, political and legal. So it has come about that the domain of liberty...has been enlarged by latter-day judgments to include liberty of the mind as well as liberty of action.[6] [emphasis added]

Liberty of the mind means no one should ever be forced to convert or die. No one should be forced to embrace the popular thinking of the day about marriage, which goes against the entire history of civilization. No one should be forced to change his or her beliefs to graduate from a university. No one should be forced to recite secular doctrines about marriage to get a job.

And yet here we are.

Liberty of action follows closely behind liberty of mind. No one should be punished by the government for refusing to act in a way that violates his or her conscience. No one should be forced by the government to participate in any activity that he or she believes to be morally wrong. Atheists should not be compelled to pray in public school. Muslim T-shirt makers should not be compelled to print shirts with Muhammad cartoons on them. Black bakers should not be compelled to bake cakes for the KKK. And Christian florists should not be compelled to design flower arrangements for ceremonies that sanction what they believe to be sinful.

And yet here we are.

When Jason Carter, nephew of President Jimmy Carter, ran for governor in my home state of Georgia in 2014, he said, "When the government doles out rights, it should do it equally." There's a reason Carter lost. Rights come from God, not the government. Our freedom of conscience is a fundamental right—what the Declaration of Independence refers to as an *inalienable* right. We are "endowed by our Creator" with the liberty to think, reason, and believe. The government doesn't give us our freedom of conscience, and the government can't legitimately take it from us—though many governments throughout the history of humanity have tried.

James Madison, who is often referred to as the father of the Constitution, declared our freedom of conscience to be our most treasured possession and demonstrated why any just government must defend it impartially:

> **Government is instituted to protect property of every sort;** as well that which lies in the various rights of individuals, as that which the term particularly expresses. This being the end of government, that alone is a *just* government, which *impartially* secures to every man, whatever is his *own*....

> ... Conscience is the most sacred of all property; other property depending in part on positive law, the exercise of that, being a natural and unalienable right.[7] [emphasis added]

When it comes right down to it, our freedom of conscience is what makes the First Amendment worth defending. If we are not free to believe, then we have no religion to exercise. If we cannot think our own thoughts, we have no speech that is truly ours. If we are not free to assess the powers that be, there is no freedom of the press, no matter how many cable channels we may enjoy. And what's the point of assembling if we're all required to embrace the same beliefs anyway? You can forget about private property or gun rights if you're not free to think capitalistic thoughts or believe some things are worth dying for. Kristen Waggoner, senior vice president of legal services with Alliance Defending Freedom, explains why this first freedom is indispensable: "The right of religious freedom is an inalienable right. It's not an American invention; it's a free, political right; it's a universal human right. And it gives everyone, the religious and the non-religious, the freedom to explore the meaning of life, the purpose of why they're here, the fundamental questions. And most importantly, it gives us the right to live as if those answers we've found are actually true. And that's what's at stake right now" [emphasis added].[8]

Apart from a vigorous defense of our first freedom—our freedom to believe—all other freedoms fail. And that's why the Left, a relatively small group in society wishing to shift culture outside of millennia of accepted norms, seeks not only to silence those who disagree but also to compel them to approve.

Christians and other people of faith are raising the alarm now because we see that what is beginning to happen here is already well under way in Europe and Canada. Far too many cultural, political, and church leaders both in those places and here have chosen compromise over conscience, cautious silence instead of courageous speech, and indifference rather than decisive action. Christians, by definition, cannot be silent. Christ compels us in the Great Commission to *go forth and teach*. Christianity is a religion of the city square. And yet there are a lot of people, perhaps even you, straddling the fence, saying, *Well, this really doesn't affect me. It doesn't affect my life; it doesn't affect my family; it doesn't affect my marriage.* Some have even taken the next step, saying simply, *I. Do. Not. Care.*

But the Left will allow no fence sitting. Many say we should have *legal* gay marriage, but not have *religious* gay marriage. Even if that were an option Christians would be willing to approve, the Left would not honor the distinction. You may not care that God calls sex outside of heterosexual marriage *sin*, but the world surely does. Look at what happened to Pastor Louie Giglio of Passion Church in Atlanta. He had to excuse himself from honoring President Obama at his second inauguration because of the outcry from progressives over his orthodox Christian beliefs on gay marriage.[9] It was just more evidence that you may choose to ignore the problem for now, and in so doing sit on the sidelines, or give aid and comfort to the allegedly open-minded and tolerant who want to redefine marriage and restrict rights under the guise of ensuring equal rights. But the sidelines are shrinking more every day. Soon they will be gone.

Like so many other tyrants throughout history, first they will come for *your* faith. Then they will force you to care about *their* faith. For in spite of its constant complaints about Christians and the Kingdom of God, the Left does not desire a faith-free society. Progressives want you to embrace their beliefs instead, to worship at the altar of a different higher power, one more compatible with their own secular religion and the Kingdom of Man.

Consequently, you will not be permitted to keep your head down and mind your own business. Barring a significant change in the direction of our culture, one day soon, the world will make you care.

Your church will be accused of discrimination should it refuse to perform a same-sex wedding. Many churches will lose their tax-exempt status. For Christians like me, the costs of sharing the gospel will go up. You may not believe me. You may think I am being hyperbolic. But the history of the world shows that events ultimately come to a head. They boil to their essence. And at that point, you will be made to choose between conscience and compliance.

"MAYBE PROGRESS SHOULD LOSE FOR ONCE"

The problem we're facing today in America is that a small group wishes to shift culture outside of a millennia of accepted norms on issues such as the structure of family, the sanctity of life, the definition of marriage, and even fundamental biological realities like gender. They have decided that the way we have structured society for all of human history doesn't matter anymore, because their way is better. They've reached this conclusion based on emotions and not facts, on a slavish fascination with what they call progress rather than a healthy respect for the wisdom guarded by tradition. They believe they can become as gods, redefining good and evil, both for themselves and for the rest of us who lack their alleged enlightenment.

Their ideology skews far to one side of the spectrum, hence my referring to them as the Left. They call themselves progressives today, partly because of their commitment to moving forward to what's next and new, and partly because other terms such as "liberals," "socialists," and "Marxists" have become unpopular—and for good reason. The failed liberal policies of the last fifty years have caused the Left to rebrand, returning to the "progressive" label it used in the early twentieth century—before its policies failed back then.

Change of the status quo is central to the thinking of those on the Left, and cries of *revolution* are never far from their lips. But revolution without a clear moral compass and respect for tradition produces only anarchy and chaos. What progressives are doing now more resembles the French Revolution of the 1790s than America's principled War for Independence a few years earlier. The French cries for liberty, fraternity, and equality disguised an anarchist desire to throw off all authority and celebrate the autonomous self, freed from all the restraints of morality and history. It did not end well for the thousands who lost their heads in the bloodbaths that followed or for the millions who were subjugated by the dictator Napoleon.

Yet progress, we are told, is inevitable. We who believe marriage to be a sacred covenant between a man and a woman are vilified by those on the Left as being on the wrong side of history. But just because ideas are new doesn't mean they're any good. It wouldn't be the first time that *the spirit of the age* proved to be a demon in disguise. Progress is not always what it appears to be.

Last summer I saw the film *Jurassic World*, a return to what seems to be the never-ending story of arrogant engineers tearing down genetic barriers in order to create new and improved dinosaurs. Needless to say, it doesn't go well. A lot of people get eaten. But at one point, a memorable exchange takes place between Vic Hoskins, the security chief who wants to use dinosaurs as weapons, and Owen Grady, a dinosaur whisperer who has trained them. When Grady resists the plan to weaponize dinosaurs, Hoskins states matter-of-factly, "Progress always wins." To which Grady replies, "Maybe progress should lose for once."[10]

Exactly.

The Left's rush to embrace all that is new—in defiance of warnings from nature and nature's God—reminds me of another scene from *Jurassic Park*, the original film featuring Jeff Goldblum as Dr. Ian Malcolm. As park founder John Hammond defends the rush to re-create dinosaurs, Malcom interrupts with this warning: "[Y]our scientists were so preoccupied with whether or not they *could* that they didn't stop to think if they *should*."[11]

That's always how it is with the Left.

The rest of us know that *new* doesn't always mean *right*. *The latest* doesn't mean *the wisest*. And only a fool would arrogantly dismiss moral traditions that have held sway across religions, continents, and all of recorded time—and insist that everyone else agree with them.

"THE DEMOCRACY OF THE DEAD"

The wisdom of King Solomon warns us not to shift boundaries put in place by those who've gone before us: "Do not move the ancient landmark that your fathers have set" (Prov. 22:28). Those boundaries are there for good reason, and the consequences of moving them—of ignoring what G. K. Chesterton called "the democracy of the dead"— will be real and painful.

An English theologian and Christian apologist of the early twentieth century, Chesterton used the phrase "democracy of the dead" to highlight the value of tradition to democracy. He warned of discriminating against those who've gone before us:

> Tradition means giving a vote to [the] most obscure of all classes, our ancestors. It is the democracy of the dead.... **Tradition refuses to submit to the small and arrogant oligarchy of those who merely happen to be walking about.** All democrats object to men being disqualified by the accident of birth; tradition objects to their being disqualified by the accident of death. **Democracy tells us not to neglect a good man's opinion, even if he is our groom; tradition asks us not to neglect a good man's opinion, even if he is our father.**[12] [emphasis added]

For people supposedly preoccupied with equality, progressives sure are quick to discriminate against opinions held by those who don't happen to be alive at the moment. In truth what they want is not equality for the many, but superiority for the "enlightened" ideas for an elite minority of those who happen to be "walking about today." It is an oligarchy we see reflected in their dependence on the courts to enforce their agenda.

Not surprisingly, most of today's progressive movement leaders got their start in the 1960s sexual and cultural revolution, which was all about discarding their parents' opinions on faith and family. They act now as if the world began with their own birth. Such arrogance is hazardous to the health of any free society because it leads not just to contempt for history, but to efforts to erase it from memory.

We witnessed progressive attempts to whitewash history in the wake of the tragic shooting in Charleston, South Carolina, on June 17, 2015. To hear the commentary from the Left afterward, one might be forgiven for thinking the Confederate battle flag had shot and killed nine people that day—instead of a hate-filled man-child trying to start a race war. The flag was not really the issue; the outcry against it was just the natural result of the Left's constant agitation against everything associated with the traditional American way of life. They do not like it. And they especially do not like the South, where faith and freedom thrive. A few days after the shooting, Thomas H. Crown correctly predicted what would happen next—and why:

> The next, logical step after erasing the Battle Flag of the Army of Northern Virginia from even polite mention will be to scrub the names of these men, these Americans, who fought bravely and with cowardice, with valor and with dishonor, from the memorials they currently enjoy.... This will not stop the mad and the evil from slaughtering

innocents for a thousand awful reasons, but it will allow us a moment to preen over those who cannot punch us in the face as we deserve, and for the America of today, that's a pretty damned good feeling.[13]

As if on cue, protesters began demanding the removal of monuments deemed unacceptable by the kings and queens of tolerance. (Forgive me if there are other gender categories for royalty in which I am unversed.) In New Orleans, the mayor requested and two local commissions voted to remove four monuments to Southern leaders. If the city council declares them to be a public nuisance, the statues will be destroyed.[14] Many other local governments are doing the same thing.

But the madness doesn't end with wiping away history above ground. Oh, no. The Memphis City Council voted in July 2015 not only to remove a monument of Confederate General Nathan Bedford Forrest but to dig up the dead bodies of the general and his wife and kick them out of their resting place in a city park.[15] Apparently, coercing the living to comply is not enough for bullies on the Left.

Even the dead must be made to care.

The arrogant lunacy of the Left seems to know no bounds. Even in the heart of the South, fraternities and sororities caved to pressure and banned the wearing of that most vicious item of clothing—the hoop skirt. That's right. The hoop skirt. If you're planning to attend any theatrical productions at the University of Georgia, you won't see any more Southern belles in ante bellum dresses like Scarlett O'Hara's in *Gone with the Wind*. Such sights "constitute a choreography of exclusion," according to author Elizabeth Boyd, who claimed the restrictions don't go far enough: "If UGA and other Southern schools really want to lead, they will not only ban the hoop; they will also go after the belle.... They will just say to hell with the belle."[16]

Bye-bye, Scarlett. You may have survived the Civil War, but the Left won't let you keep Tara. As it turns out, tomorrow will *not* be another day. Even Rhett Butler, frankly, will be made to give a damn.

As Hillary Clinton put it, deep-seated beliefs must be changed. You will be forced to embrace the latest trends in fashionable morality or be branded a bigot. You will be forced to design flowers for a ceremony that violates your conscience as your "price of citizenship." The progressive plan is as simple as it is contradictory: force you to comply with their beliefs in the name of tolerance but offer no such tolerance for the majority of people in America, who disagree with them. They hide their tyrannical agenda behind cries for compassion, love, and acceptance, which is why I call them *compassionate bullies*. They somehow manage to look kind and caring—while kicking the crap out of your conscience.

CHAPTER 4

THE
COMPASSIONATE
BULLIES

They're trying to frighten you, they're trying to scare you, and if we don't stand up, then that's exactly what they're going to do.... If we don't start standing up for our Constitution and for our rights, our beliefs, there's going to be nothing to stand up for.

—BARRONELLE STUTZMAN[1]

F
ew people would ever suspect that the gracious grandmother who runs Arlene's Flowers in Richland, Washington, began her life on Alcatraz. When Barronelle Stutzman was still quite young, her father worked on the prison rock as a guard before the family moved to Washington and put down deep roots in the community there. But it wasn't until she was twenty years old that Barronelle Stutzman found true freedom within when she realized something critical was missing from her life—she needed a personal relationship with Jesus Christ.

Until that point in life, Barronelle had been what she calls a "token Christian," justifying whatever she wanted to do by wearing the Christian label. From that point on, however, her life changed. She began to learn how to live out her faith consistently in every area of her life—including her floral business. Barronelle bought Arlene's Flowers from her mother, who had developed Alzheimer's, and she has worked at the business for more than forty years.

Barronelle makes it clear to any prospective employee that Arlene's Flowers is God's business, and she treats it as such. Everyone is invited to join in prayer at the shop every morning. Good customer service is not just good business but a way to show the love of Christ to everyone who enters through her doors. She builds authentic friendships with customers out of her love for God. One such relationship took an unexpected turn in 2013 when a customer she had served for nearly a decade asked her to design the flowers for his same-sex wedding. Barronelle had provided him with flowers for years, and she knew he identified as gay. She had designed flowers for both this man and his partner to celebrate anniversaries and birthdays. But as Barronelle describes it, "My religious conviction and my belief is that marriage is between a man and a woman, and that was where I had to draw the line. Designing for a birthday or anniversary is totally different from a wedding…to be a part of it and participate—I just could not do that. I would be dishonoring Christ."[2]

When her customer inquired about flowers for the ceremony, Barronelle explained her beliefs to the customer as lovingly as she could. The customer said he understood, that his own mother had expressed similar thoughts. They continued to talk about his wedding plans. After Barronelle referred him to three other florists, they hugged and parted ways. And the seventy-one-year-old grandmother thought the story was over. But the enemies of conscience on the Left saw an opportunity to send an ominous, threatening message to Barronelle and anyone who shares her beliefs.

To the best of Barronelle's understanding, the customer's partner posted angry comments on Facebook alleging that the couple was refused service. The phones at Arlene's Flowers began ringing off the hook with hate calls and even death threats. The story went viral, catching the attention of Bob Ferguson, the attorney general of the state of Washington. Then, in an unprecedented move, Ferguson took the initiative to file a complaint charging that Barronelle had violated the Washington Consumer Protection Act and Washington Law against Discrimination. Later, the ACLU filed a lawsuit on behalf of the couple, and the two lawsuits have been joined. Never in the history of Washington State had the attorney general filed a lawsuit against an individual or business owner for a violation of the laws against discrimination without going to the Human Rights Commission first. Barronelle's attorney Kristen Waggoner, senior counsel with Alliance Defending Freedom, explains more about the vindictive nature of the state's action against Stutzman:

> The Attorney General's action is unprecedented. The State and ACLU not only sued her business, Arlene's Flowers, and put the 40-year business in jeopardy that was built by Barronelle and her mother, but they seek to take this 70-year-old grandmother's personal assets, potentially her home, her retirement, everything she owns, to pay attorney's fees and costs if she loses the case. And it's unnecessary. If this were about wanting to set clear legal precedent, all he would need to do is file the lawsuit against her business. This is a punitive attempt to absolutely ruin her, personally and professionally, just because she will not use her artistic talents to promote same-sex marriage.[3]

You read that right. The attorney general of the state of Washington and the ACLU are suing not only this God-fearing grandmother's floral business, but also her, personally, for everything she's got. If she loses the case, attorney's fees are expected to run well into seven figures, meaning her shop, her house, her retirement savings—

even her dog—must go to satisfy the overlords of the Left. After having left Alcatraz so many decades ago, Barronelle finds herself in a prison of a different sort now for refusing to compromise her faith.

After nearly two years, a county judge ruled that Barronelle had broken the law and was liable to pay fines, costs, and attorney's fees for the two lawsuits. The attorney general had asked for $2,000, the maximum fine allowed under the Washington statute. But after taking a lot of heat for the vengeful way he was coming after Barronelle, Ferguson made her a settlement offer. If she would pay the full fine plus just one dollar in attorney's fees and agree to stop "discriminating," then he would drop the suit. Barronelle flatly refused the offer. "Basically, they're trying to bribe me to do something that is totally against my religious beliefs," Barronelle said. "My freedom is not for sale."[4]

In April 2015 Barronelle's legal team appealed the ruling. In June ADF asked the Washington Supreme Court to review the case. Waggoner captures the essence of the problem: "Americans oppose unjust laws that strong-arm citizens to express ideas against their will. Barronelle and numerous others like her around the country have been more than willing to serve any and all customers, but they are not willing to express any and all messages. A government that forces any American to create a message contrary to her own convictions and surrender her livelihood is a government every American should fear."[5]

Meanwhile, Barronelle has stopped providing floral arrangements for weddings altogether. She says she would serve the gay couple again if they walked into her shop today, just not in any way that would require her to violate her conscience. This soft-spoken yet courageous florist says she knows the case is bigger than her own interests: "When a government comes in, tells me how to think, how to act, or takes everything I own and destroys me because I disagree, then we certainly don't live in a free America. This is about everybody's right to believe and act on their beliefs, not just mine.... It's me today, but it will be you tomorrow. You cannot sit this one out."[6]

Like the witch in *The Wizard of Oz* who terrorizes the Munchkins, who only want to be left alone to live a simple life, these progressive radicals cackle at Barronelle and Christians like her: *We will make you care about what we care about. We will punish you for believing differently than we do. We will make your life a living hell, take your business, your retirement savings, your house—and your little dog, too!*

THE JIHADISTS OF AMERICAN CULTURE

Under the guise of compassion and caring, the Left attacks a helpless grandmother, trying to force her to approve of that which she cannot in good conscience endorse. All the while, it claims it is acting in the best interest of society, acting on behalf of all those poor same-sex couples who can't get flowers for their ceremonies—except that they can. They can even get flowers from Barronelle for anything other than a wedding. In spite of the lawsuits and vindictive bureaucrats, she says she still thinks of her former customer as a friend and would happily sell him flowers if he walked into her shop tomorrow. Meanwhile, both her former customer and the State of Washington are trying to take everything she has for not bowing at the altar of sexual sin.

But these radicals want to look like they care as they force their views on others. It's what bullies do. That way other people think better of them and they sleep better at night, assuaging any guilt they may feel for giving nightmares to genteel grandmothers. The progressives' compassionate bullying reminds me of the catchy slogan for Monsters, Inc., in the Disney Pixar film of the same name: "We scare because we care."[7] For example, the very people who support Planned Parenthood's butchering and selling of baby body parts also advanced the disaster of Obamacare *because they care for children.* The same people who insist that *The Vagina Monologues* be permitted on college campuses also set up "safe zones" to restrict free speech *because students must be protected from harmful ideas*—like marriage being between a man and a woman. They outlaw incandescent light bulbs so we can use only toxic mercury *because they care about polar bears and penguins with happy feet.*

Around the country, progressive bullies have attacked Christians for daring to put their faith ahead of the pet causes of those who feign compassion while destroying life-giving liberties. What we are seeing is a scorched-earth, take-no-prisoners approach as the wildfire burns across our land. It is not enough that Christians be quiet. Christians must be silenced *and* punished. Their faith cannot be respected. Legislation that ensures people are free to live and work according to their faith without fear of being punished by government must be stopped and decried as discrimination.

In Denmark, France, San Bernardino, and elsewhere, we have seen Islamic extremists take lives because of the Islamic extremists' beliefs. They do not want tolerance. They do not want pluralism. They do not want to show respect for the views of others. They will take life as revenge for being offended. There will be no magnanimity. There will be no mercy. In taking life, the Islamic extremists want to create a public spectacle. They want not just revenge for perceived wrongs, but also to make others fear—and to think twice before doing the same. They want to silence others and drive them from the town square. They use death and violence to do it.

Thankfully, unlike the radical jihadists, progressive activists have not turned physically violent for the most part. Instead, they are intent on *compassionately* crushing any who disagree with them. Unlike the Islamic jihadists, they will not kill, but they will destroy. They won't cut your head off, but they will destroy your reputation so that you are afraid to show your face in public. They won't burn down your home, but they'll take the homes, businesses, and life savings of any who defy them. They will use the tools of the state and mob action—fear and intimidation—to make it happen. They threaten, scare, and make public examples of those who disagree in order to send a message that dissent is hazardous to your emotional, mental, and financial health. There will be no magnanimity, and there will be no mercy. There will be no going down the street to another florist, baker, pharmacist, venue operator, or photographer. Any who defy them are labeled bigots and driven to the fringes of society.

They will viciously attack those who disagree with them because they tire of the debate, which they never wanted to begin with. They have no interest in explaining or defending their beliefs. They want victory and know the only way to get it is to silence, isolate, and destroy any who get in their way. The progressive activists who yell *bigot* at those who disagree with them are the jihadists of American culture. But unlike the jihadists—who don't care if everyone approves of their destructive ways—it's important to progressives that they appear to be kind as they mercilessly crucify you for your faith.

Crushing legal action and punitive lawsuits are one way the Left punishes those who refuse to recant their faith. Death threats and harassment are other tactics the Left employs to make you care. That's what happened to Memories Pizza in Indiana after the state passed its own version of the federal Religious Freedom and Restoration Act (RFRA). A reporter in need of a story stuck a camera in the faces of Crystal O'Connor and her father, Kevin, owners of a small-town pizza shop. She asked them a hypothetical question—what would they do if a same-sex couple asked them to cater a wedding ceremony? The O'Connors said they would never deny anyone service on the basis of sexual orientation, but they would decline to sell pizzas for a same-sex wedding ceremony because of their religious beliefs.[8] Key word: *would*. No one had asked them to cater a wedding. No customer had walked away displeased and claiming, as in other cases, that he or she had been emotionally raped by the ordeal. Nothing. Memories Pizza doesn't even cater weddings. I. Kid. You. Not.

Yet the URL to the original story at the time of this writing still lists the headline as: "rfra-first-business-to-publicly-deny-same-sex-service."[9] Truth be damned. The national media ran with the story, and the backlash from progressive bullies began. Death threats, calls to burn the shop to the ground,[10] incessant phone calls with fake orders, and endless harassment of all sorts forced the owners to shut the doors of the business for more than a week.[11] The shop has now reopened, but the message was received loud and clear—state your religious beliefs at your own risk.

When conservatives set up a fund on the website GoFundMe.com to help Memories Pizza cover costs as it stayed closed, progressive bullies harassed GoFundMe. Alix Bryan, an employee of CBS's Richmond, Virginia, affiliate, filed a complaint with the Internet fund-raising company alleging that the fund-raising campaign for Memories Pizza was fraudulent—"just in case," as she tweeted.[12] The progressives could not stand others standing with Memories Pizza. "Are you kidding me? Indiana pizzeria raises $17k in an hour by being bigoted?"[13] tweeted Alix Bryan. In fact, the Memories Pizza fundraiser, spearheaded by conservative radio host Dana Loesch, raised more than $842,000.[14]

WHY THE LEFT MUST MAKE YOU CARE

There is one key reason that those on the Left must force their beliefs on the rest of us. It's really very simple. If they didn't force their craziness on us, we would never embrace it. Deep down, they know that to be true. Progressive thinking doesn't work in the real world. Its beliefs are inconsistent with all of nature. It requires us to believe things that we know do not fit with the reality we experience every day. It is completely at odds with what we know to be true about ourselves.

Andrew T. Walker, coauthor with Eric Teetsel of *Marriage Is: How Marriage Transforms Society and Cultivates Human Flourishing*, describes the truth of the matter:

> Philosophical liberalism is built on lies about human nature. It is built on this truth that humanity is at root and at heart good, and the problem is that society tramples on otherwise good individuals. And so we ought to correct society by leveling the playing field altogether. That notion of inherent goodness, biblically speaking, is false and wrong. Liberalism is by nature coercive because it is built on a system of anthropological falsehoods. And for falsehoods to be taught and to gain acceptance in pop culture, they have to be mandated.... [L]iberalism succeeds by suppressing truth, and you suppress truth by codifying those lies into law.[15]

Most of us are honest enough with ourselves to admit we are sinners, that we fall short of being the person we know we should be. We recognize that human nature is broken. Different religions speak about the flaws in humanity in different ways, but as a Christian I have no problem using the same word God uses to describe us even though He loves us—*sinner*. The word literally means *one who falls short of the mark*, of the holy standard defined by the God who created us. In the political arena, conservatives recognize that we are all defective at some level, and so our system of government must include both accountability through checks and balances and religious virtue that transforms us from within.

I am a conservative because I am a Christian. I know that we are all sinners, and so I want those in charge to have strictly limited powers over the rest of us. But progressives base their entire system on the belief that humanity is essentially good—it is only the environment in which people live that causes them to do bad things. They think that if they can change our environment, they can change our nature. Consequently, progressives view everyone as victims of oppressive forces of all sorts—greedy corporations, hypocritical church leaders, backward parents, the archaic institution of marriage, evil Republicans, and Christianity itself. Nothing is ever your own fault. If you experience difficulty in the world, it's because someone has done it to you. It is the aim of the Left to free you from these supposed oppressors who restrict your ability to be your naturally wonderful self. After all, if we are all essentially good, life should improve significantly once these restrictions are removed.

But in fact every single one of us knows this to be a lie. Because we know ourselves to be, on our best day, less than angelic.

P. Andrew Sandlin, president of the Center for Cultural Leadership, describes this dynamic of the Left's perpetual drive for liberation from the forces that are keeping us from the perfect lives just within our grasp, if only they can slay every last oppressor:

> St. George devoted his life to killing dragons, and when he'd killed them all, he lost his life's passion, so he invented new dragons. St. George, you see, *needed* his dragons. In the same way, the political left began by killing the dragon of arbitrary state authority, but quickly moved on to slay alleged arbitrary church authority and fascist authority and, more recently, Caucasian authority and family authority and paternal and maternal authority and capitalist authority and, in these last decades, male and "heterosexual" authority. The left are liberators eternally in search of the oppressed whom they must liberate. They are on one huge liberation crusade, and if there are no oppressed, they must invent

them.... The broader agenda is social liberation of all kinds, and Western leftist elites differ from Lenin and Mao only in degree and in methods employed, not in principle. Mao used the end of a gun barrel; Western elites use public schools and major foundations and TV and art and music.[16]

The Left's utopian lies are not new. We've seen them before. But they don't line up with what we know to be true about the human experience. And because they are in conflict with reality, it takes an awful lot of compulsion to make them work—or, rather, to keep up the futile attempt to make them work.

Ed Morrissey, cultural pundit and editor of *Hot Air*, points out that the dream of utopia never has worked and never will:

[W]hat they think they are doing is making a brave new world by imposing top-down mandates on people for behavior. It's clearly a Utopian impulse. They have a view of what a perfect world would be like, and the only way to get there is to control people's minds and control people's thoughts. It goes beyond actions. It goes into speech...if you're thinking a certain way, it's wrong.

Those are the types of things that you get with Utopias. Communism was a form of Utopianism. With Communism it was always, *Well, come the Revolution, everything will be better. Come the Revolution, and everything will sort itself out.* But people are not perfect little cogs in perfect little machines. They never are; they've never been that way. Those types of systems are set up for failure because that isn't how human beings operate.[17]

The Christian faith especially has always resisted such delusions of perfection. Christians naturally oppose schemes for making the world a better place simply by eliminating God and freeing each of us to discover and celebrate our "authentic self." From the beginning of Scripture, we read of our fall from right relationship with our Creator and of His loving plan to become one of us, to die to restore us in spite of our ongoing struggle against Him. The gospel of Jesus Christ requires us to put our trust in someone other than ourselves. It demands repentance—both acknowledging our guilt and embracing God's wisdom instead of our own. The Apostle Paul is considered by scholars, both within and without the Christian church, to be among the brightest intellects of all time. He may not have been familiar with twenty-first-century cultural dynamics, but when he wrote his letter to believers in Rome he described very accurately those who choose to believe man-made lies over what is clearly revealed by both Scripture and nature itself. He didn't have to watch CNN or surf the Internet to know about the tendency we all have to resist the authority over us and choose to live a lie instead. So Paul talks about those who have "exchanged the truth about God for a lie and worshiped and served the creature rather than the Creator" (Rom. 1:25). Consequently, he warns, "[T]hey became futile in their thinking, and their foolish hearts were darkened. Claiming to be wise, they became fools…." (Rom. 1:21–22).

It is no coincidence that most of the animus from the Left is focused on Christianity. Christians have always been at the forefront of calling out the utopian dream for what it is—nonsense. The truth is this: if the Left did not force people to support its worldview, if it did not force them to be indoctrinated with progressive ideology, if it did not mandate approval for unnatural behaviors, few people would naturally follow such self-destructive thinking. Left to our own devices, few of us would find the lies of the Left to be a solid foundation on which to build our lives. The Left must force you to care; otherwise, most of us simply would not comply.

For example, a basic understanding of biology demonstrates that man and woman were made to go together. The history of the world shows what happens when people are left to themselves—men and women marry. It's what they do. It's how the human species continues to populate the planet and produce stable societies. Homosexual behavior is not normal. Simple statistics tell us that any behavior in which only 4 percent of the population (at most) participates is, by definition, not the norm.[18] But anyone who refuses to endorse same-sex marriage is derided and denounced as a bigoted hater and forced to comply with a delusional concept of marriage.

The Left's bullying tactics are not restricted to the issue of same-sex marriage, though. That is simply the latest front in its assault on freedom. It's applying the same pressure to those who believe the rather obvious truth that there are only two genders—male and female—and not the more than eighty you can choose on Facebook.[19] We used to view people who were confused about their gender with compassion. We recognized that they needed therapy. Now we must affirm them or be scorned as evil discriminators oppressing Bruce Jenner as he tries to discover his allegedly authentic self.

Progressives use the force of government to take money from those who work to give it to those who refuse to do so. No one would naturally do that and think it a good idea. Because we recognize our fallen nature, we innately know that a handout culture does more harm than good. So the Left must mandate the redistribution of hard-earned wealth to others as an act of compassion. It must use the force of government to fund abortion, because if progressives came to your door selling "I kill babies and sell their spare parts" T-shirts, you probably wouldn't buy one. The Left must use the force of government to withhold water from the farmers of California's central valley, turning what was once America's breadbasket into a dust bowl. No one in his or her right mind would ever do such a thing. It must force us to embrace the top-down educational standards of Common Core even though it's obvious that parents—not bureaucrats in Washington—are best positioned to direct the education of their own children.

If those on the Left did not force us to care, most of us would dismiss them as looney and go on about our lives. So it should come as no surprise that progressives resort to coercive tactics. The use of force is standard operating procedure for philosophies that lack the moral and logical fortitude to stand on their own. If you can't convince someone through persuasive arguments and sound reason, apply pressure. History abounds with examples of oppressive ideologies that were supposed to magically usher us into a new era of enlightened living—if only we did as we were told. None of them ended well for the common person, like Barronelle Stutzman, who is simply trying to live a life grounded on core values of faith, family, and freedom.

Her ordeal has been and will continue to be a painful one. She could have walked away from all of it by paying the one-dollar fine and compromising, but her beliefs were not for sale. Barronelle refused to cave to the compassionate bullies—not unlike another creative person who walked the earth some two thousand years ago. He too faced stiff opposition from those who claimed to be acting in the public's best interest. He too faced severe consequences for not compromising what He knew to be true to fit the spirit of the age. His sacrifice at the hands of those bullies is what inspires Barronelle—and millions of others today.

History remembers those compassionate bullies who "crucified the Lord of glory" (1 Cor. 2:8) only as the hypocrites they were—Pharisees—but it recalls the name of the humble carpenter from Nazareth quite differently.

CHAPTER 5

THE
ANTIRELIGION
RELIGION

What we're watching emerge in this country is a new kind of
paganism, an atheism with air-conditioning and digital TV.
And it is neither tolerant nor morally neutral.

—CHARLES J. CHAPUT[1]

E very town in America should be so lucky as to have a grocery
store like Ralph's Thriftway. When Kevin Stormans's grandfa-
ther Ralph started the family business in 1944, such stores were
the hub of every community in America. Even today, in an era of
impersonal mega-superstores, the two family-owned stores in Olym-
pia, Washington, still thrive as part of the fabric of the local economy.
Visitors to Ralph's Thriftway find the original one-stop-shopping
experience with everything from sushi to Starbucks, from Subway to
seafood, from a pharmacy to a full-service deli. They find organic
produce from local growers, the sweetest treats from local bakers,
and the best products from local vendors. Shoppers can even mail
letters or have a license renewed while picking up Chinese for dinner.

61

They always find a friendly face and a warm, family atmosphere so typical of the family businesses that once formed the backbone of the American economy.

But what they won't find are abortion-inducing drugs in the store's pharmacy. And for that sin of omission, the Stormanses are being made to care.

It started back in 2006 when a customer visited the pharmacy and asked for "Plan B" birth control medication. Kevin Stormans recalls, "We didn't carry it. We never had a need to; nobody asked for it. And, frankly, at that point in time I didn't even know what it was."[2] After being told that the pharmacy had no demand for the product, the customer called Kevin and became irate—at which point Kevin figured he'd better find out what the fuss was all about. "I started checking into it and realized that one of the possibilities of this product is that it is life-terminating. After the egg is fertilized, [Plan B] can prevent it from implanting. We talked about it as a family and said that's not something we can support...that's not a product we're going to carry."[3] Kevin and his family made the decision never to stock Plan B or any other medication with abortion-inducing properties in their pharmacy. When the angry customer called again, Kevin cited his religious beliefs as the reason his pharmacy would not carry the product. Hate mail, picketing, and angry phone calls ensued. The governor of Washington even joined in the boycott, canceling her long-standing account with the store. At one point, business dropped by 30 percent because of the bullying.[4]

Then the Washington State Board of Pharmacy told Kevin that the regulations governing referrals had recently changed. They insisted the pharmacy carry the drugs or close. The Stormanses chose a third option and sued to defend their freedom to live consistently with their beliefs.

What they didn't know at the time was how Planned Parenthood had collaborated with the governor to change the regulations to discriminate against people of faith. But they were going to find out.

Under the new regulations, a pharmacist could no longer refer a customer to another pharmacy for religious reasons. And yet the state allowed pharmacies to refer customers for any other reason—religion alone was singled out for discrimination.

The Stormanses' case finally came to trial in federal court in 2012. Kristen Waggoner, senior vice president of legal services for Alliance Defending Freedom, describes what happened next:

> After a twelve-day trial, the court found that the regulations were intended "primarily (if not solely) to target religious objectors" to Plan B and Ella. Even the chairman of the Board of Pharmacy testified that nothing had changed in the practice of pharmacy in Washington State after these regulations became effective, *except* religious referrals were banned. Pharmacies continue to refer for business, economic, and convenience reasons, but they are not permitted to do so for religious reasons. In fact, ten times more pharmacies declined to stock Plan B for business reasons than for religious reasons, and 98 percent of all pharmacies either stocked Plan B or had an effective referral mechanism in place to ensure customers received the drug.
>
> The trial court entered over a hundred pages of detailed findings on the evidence. He addressed all of the state's and Planned Parenthood's arguments. Planned Parenthood said, *We need this regulation to make sure customers have access to drugs.* The court sifted through all of the evidence in great detail and held that *there is no problem with access to any drug anywhere in the state.* There is not *one* woman in Washington State who has been denied Plan B or Ella due to a pharmacist's religious objection. You can buy these drugs on the shelf next to

Tylenol now. The trial court heard from twenty-two witnesses, most of whom were with the Board of Pharmacy,
and reviewed thousands and thousands of documents. It
concluded that there was no question the state was allowing
pharmacies to refer patients many times a day for convenience reasons or to increase their profit. The sole purpose
of the regulations was to force pharmacists with religious
objections to Plan B out of pharmacy.[5]

The federal trial court ruled that the regulations were "riddled
with exceptions for secular conduct, but contain[ed] no such exceptions for identical, religiously motivated conduct."[6] But Planned Parenthood, the same organization that profits from the dissecting of
unborn children, insisted that religious referrals must be banned. They
appealed to the Ninth Circuit Court of Appeals. Incredibly, the Ninth
Circuit overturned the initial trial court decision despite the fact that
no new evidence was presented. Waggoner calls the Ninth Circuit's
ruling "alarming":

> In our jurisprudential system, when a trial court holds a
> trial and hears multiple witnesses firsthand, and then
> makes findings of facts about the testimony and evidence,
> the appellate is only supposed to reverse those findings if
> it concludes that the findings clearly contradict the evi-
> dence. They did not find that here. They ignored the stan-
> dard of review. Instead, they essentially just decided the
> case on a record that they created themselves.
>   It's alarming for three significant reasons. *First*, it is the
> first time in the history of our nation since the time of the
> Quakers when we have forced someone to participate in the
> taking of human life. That's what's at issue here. It's the first
> time we have not protected providers, either legislatively or

judicially, from being forced to potentially participate in taking human life. *Second*, the rationale from the Ninth Circuit's decision can apply with equal force to surgical abortions. This rationale could potentially apply to a doctor who doesn't want to perform an abortion, even a late-term abortion. Under the court's rationale, the doctor could be forced to do so if a law were passed and applied to all doctors. That's a chilling and unprecedented ruling. *Third*, in terms of how our judicial system is supposed to work, the court had an end and it didn't seem to care as much about the means to get there. That is deeply disturbing, particularly for those who have believed in the American system of law and justice.[7]

The fate of the Stormanses' multigenerational business now hangs in the balance, as their last legal hope is the U.S. Supreme Court.

Two other pharmacists in Washington who have also suffered at the hands of these secularist priests joined their case. One of them, Margo Thelen, already lost her job.[8] Her employer had allowed her to refer the few Plan B customers, as she has done for years, until the regulation became effective. Another pharmacist, Rhonda Mesler, the sole breadwinner for her family, has been told by her employer that she will lose her job or need to transfer to another state if the latest ruling stands.[9] It wasn't so long ago that people crossed oceans to come to America so they could exercise their religious beliefs freely. Now they're having to leave their homes in America behind if they refuse to aid in the taking of human life.

Kevin, Margo, and Rhonda have been brought before the secular inquisition. Their beliefs have been declared heretical by the secular clergy in flowing black robes. They must bow or be excommunicated from civil society. "[The present] assault on conscience extends beyond homosexuality to other issues," Waggoner warns.

This assault on the conscience is not because people can't get what they need or want. Access in all of these cases is undisputed. It's about political ideology and an attempt to force people of faith, who contribute to the common good, out of the marketplace. We may not draw the line where the Stormans family did, or we may not draw the line where the florist or the baker does, but we all have lines. A law that forces the Stormans family to cross their line will eventually require all of us to conform at some point.

The creed of the Left is clear: convert or be destroyed.

RELATING TO FREAKS AND BIGOTS

In the previous chapter, I explained a key reason the Left relies on coercion to advance its agenda. But there is another reason worth considering, and it is this: progressives pressure religious people to conform to their own ideology because they find it difficult to understand religious belief in the first place. They embrace a system of beliefs that can best be described as *secular* because they think their way of looking at the world has no religious or spiritual basis. I disagree with their self-assessment (for reasons we'll explore in subsequent pages), yet their secular perspective helps explain some of why they struggle to relate to people standing on religious convictions.

Dr. Russell Moore is the president of the Ethics & Religious Liberty Commission of the Southern Baptist Convention, the nation's largest Protestant denomination, and author of *Onward: Engaging the Culture without Losing the Gospel*. He explains the *why* behind the disconnect:

> [M]any secular progressives don't understand religious conviction at all. It's not simply that they're opposed to

religious conviction—they don't understand what it's like to be motivated by religious principles. So, if one thinks about, for instance, the case of the Little Sisters of the Poor or Hobby Lobby, when it comes to being mandated to purchase abortion-inducing drugs and devices, many of the people who are pushing this think there must really be some other motivation. People must really be motivated by economic interest or some sort of political interest because they really don't understand what it means for the Little Sisters of the Poor to say, "We think we're going to be accountable at Judgment for the way that we handle our money and our insurance here."[10]

Thus many on the Left assume something other than faith motivates people to take principled stands—the concept of eternal accountability is one they refuse to contemplate. And so they think that our beliefs can be changed by applying the right pressure. They cannot comprehend anyone being motivated by a faith so deep that nothing can move it. They see no need for God or the Bible and dismiss those who do as superstitious slaves who need to be liberated from their captivity to an ancient mythology. From the perspective of the secular progressives, the only merciful thing to do is to correct the religious zealots and discourage others from following in their errant ways. When the florist refuses to recant, they dismiss her as a freak they can't understand, a bigoted hater in need of punishment and corrective therapy. When the pizza shop owner repeats millennia-old Christian beliefs, they "cry havoc and let slip the dogs of war."[11]

WE ARE ALL PEOPLE OF FAITH

But more than a simple misunderstanding is behind the attacks on Christians and people of faith. At its core, the war on our freedom to believe is nothing short of a religious war. It is the waging of a radical jihad, a holy war by one religion—secularism—upon all others. The fact that most secular progressives do not think of themselves as people of faith doesn't make their beliefs any less religious. One definition of religion is "a pursuit or interest to which someone ascribes supreme importance."[12] The interest to which secularists give supreme importance is that there be no god permitted in the town square to question their own truth claims. They have essentially created their own god and put their faith in the absence of any god other than themselves. At the end of the day, we are all people of faith, as my coauthor, Bill Blankschaen, explains in his recent book *A Story Worth Telling: Your Field Guide to Living an Authentic Life*:

> When it comes right down to it, we are all "people of faith," even the most devout atheists. Where the Christ-follower believes in the supernatural revelation of truth by an infinite Creator, the atheist believes in his own assessment of the nature of reality and the impossibility that God could exist and reveal himself in various ways. The professing atheist cannot prove that there is no God based on what he or she sees, senses, and feels, but he or she acts *as if* this belief were true. The atheist walks by faith just as a Christian does, but with a radically different focus.[13]

The same is true for the secular progressive who thinks he is not religious—and therefore wants to exclude all religious beliefs from the public square. The question is not *Do you have faith?* but *Who or what is the object of your faith?* There's really no such thing as an atheist. Atheists are people who don't believe in God. But they do believe in some god substitute. They worship something. It may be themselves, it may be the planet, it may be some cause, but everyone has a god. Just not everyone has the right God. Everyone claims someone or something as the voice of final authority in his or her life, the standard by which to measure what is true and right and what is false and evil. Blankschaen uses a simple paradigm to capture the three basic options we all face for choosing our voice of ultimate authority:

> **Yourself.** You rely ultimately on your own understanding to guide your story. That's not to say you don't consult others, but you depend on your own conclusions, usually what you can see, sense, or feel, as the ultimate authority for making sense of the universe and your place in it.
>
> **Others.** You are acknowledging that you are not qualified to exercise ultimate authority in this universal tale. Yet you think someone, or a collection of someones, just might be.... At the end of the day, your trust still focuses on people, just like yourself, who have flaws and limited understanding....
>
> **God.** I am talking about the self-existent One, the God who is and who is not silent. God needs neither anyone nor anything in order to be, yet God chose to create all things, including us, to craft a story worth telling, a story that would become the standard for measuring every other story. This God did not leave us to wonder about him, but revealed himself to us personally, indirectly through what he created and directly through the written word that we now call the Old and New Testaments. But he didn't stop there. As evidence of his infinite genius, he introduced a plot twist: He became one of us in order to restore the relationship that had been shattered by our lack of faith in him. The Creator became part of his creation; the Master of all became a humble servant, in order to reconcile his enemies to himself. By his sacrifice, we find new life—by faith. He became the

hero that each of our stories desperately needs. And now he invites us to align our story with his.[14]

The secularist chooses one of the first two options above, believing in a reality that is ultimately defined by his or her own reasoning even though he or she knows that reasoning to be limited and faulty.

THE INCONSISTENT RELIGION

Another definition of religion is "the worship of the superhuman, or of a controlling power."[15] For secular progressives, that controlling power is ostensibly science. But in reality it is more the worship of self, with personal feelings acting as the controlling guide for their system of faith. Notice how on the one hand, they appeal to science when it comes to predictions of catastrophic climate change, with chants of *The science is settled!* and threats to excommunicate from polite society all who disagree with their new scientific creed. On the other hand, they believe you can somehow shape your own gender—something for which there is no scientific support whatsoever. It is a belief driven purely by emotion—and, as important as appeals to science may be for secularists, feelings trump science in the hierarchy of the secular church. The belief that people are born gay is another doctrine about which the Left is adamant and for which there is no scientific evidence. And yet when it comes to God, progressives revert back to science: because science cannot put the Almighty in a test tube to be studied empirically, He must not exist. And anyone who believes that He exists must be silenced, shunned, or treated as inferior. Never mind that in the whole of human history, only a tiny minority of people have rejected the idea of the Divine. There is a deep arrogance in the Left's self-righteous pretension, when you consider that the fairest polling on the subject shows most people tend to believe in something greater than themselves. The idea that this life is all there is and we can only look forward to rotting in the grave may be popular among people in the West today, but it isn't what the majority believe world-wide. It isn't what a majority throughout history have believed either. Incidentally, the people who have believed in an afterlife, and particularly in a day of judgment, are usually the people trying to leave this world a better place than they found it. Meanwhile, the greatest death cults in history have been those that claimed to be free from religious beliefs and trumpeted the wonders of science instead.

Secularism, you see, is the antireligion religion. While secularists steadfastly seek to diminish the religious beliefs of others, they promote their own religious beliefs with great zeal. Secularists claim that Christians, Hindus, Muslims, Jews, and others should not be allowed to speak in the town square, because they are peddling their religion. But progressives have their own sacraments, including abortion. They have their own liturgies, including acceptable books that people should have to read. They have their own beliefs about sexuality. They have their own beliefs about what happened at the origin of all things. They want those beliefs taught as undisputed facts in schools and all other views silenced or denounced as myths. They are essentially modern book burners. They would prefer that the Bible and other books of faith and traditional worldviews be removed in favor of their own. Instead of reading the Bible to children, as was done in America's schools for centuries, we must read *Heather Has Two Mommies*. Instead of worshiping at the altar of God, as our first president did *during a session of Congress*,[16] we must be made to worship at the altar of Planned Parenthood via congressional funding. Instead of believing in a Creator who is separate from His creation and yet sustains it, we are to believe a god is present in all of us and to worship nature at the First Church of the Environmental Protection Agency.

The absurdity of the modern secular religion may be most clearly demonstrated by this contradictory belief that requires more faith than most can muster: whom you sleep with is something you're born with, but whether you're a boy or a girl is something you can decide for yourself.

ZEALOTS FOR THEIR FAITH

Progressives like to portray Christians and others who openly acknowledge their faith as zealots to be feared, as if those who take their beliefs seriously represent a hazard to healthy society. But Christians are not the ones seeking to eliminate and silence those with whom they disagree. Quite the opposite. It is radical jihadists who seek to destroy those who offend them.

When *Charlie Hebdo*, a French satirical and secular magazine, published comics depicting the Islamic prophet of Muhammad, terrorists responded with two attacks, one in 2011 and another in 2015. They killed twelve people in the latest attack, including the editor of the publication.[17] The terrorists were offended. They were offended by a publication that criticized their religion. And so they sought revenge.

They had to destroy the people who did it. But you need to understand what the destruction was about. The destruction of their enemies had to be done as a public spectacle and in a public way so that others would think twice before insulting Muhammad again. They had to destroy them with no mercy. They could show no grace. They could show no humility. They could not stop until the offender was vanquished. They had to destroy the publisher in such a way that not only would others think twice before doing the same in the future, but others would so fear being completely destroyed that they would silence themselves. In fact, the terrorists hoped to set up a dynamic in which everyone would clamor for others to be silent as well, lest they themselves might in some way be hurt. They hoped to persuade any potential critics of Muhammad to excuse themselves from the town square instead of expressing their beliefs about the terrorists' religion.

They believe that the views they want to silence are not worthy of ever being spoken. They're not ideas anyone should consider. Those who express them must be punished; they must be vanquished; and everyone else must know that the same thing could happen to them as well.

And that's the exact same dynamic—thankfully, minus the physical violence—that explains the secularists' campaign against Christian belief. They do the only thing they know how to do—bully and intimidate and marginalize anyone who dares criticize their religion. They go to the mayor of Atlanta and demand that he kick Chief Kelvin Cochran to the curb for expressing his religion. They insist the pharmacists in Washington be made to sell abortion-inducing drugs for questioning a sacrament of the secular religion. They demand that a florist be made to pay all she has for refusing to submit to the progressive dogma of the day. They insist the baker must be made to design cakes—conscience be damned.

Say what you will, intimidation works. *Charlie Hebdo* has said it will no longer print images deemed offensive to Islam.[18] Message received. And when Pamela Geller hosted a contest to draw images of Muhammad in Texas, it was Geller—not the terrorists who attacked her—who received the greatest outrage from the Left.

And while we can be profoundly grateful that the penalties imposed by the antireligion religion do not rise to the level of death and bodily mayhem, intimidation also works when we're talking about career-ending harassment and financial ruin. Public theologian Dr. Brian Mattson distills the essence of the antireligion religion:

> This is, at its heart, a religious war against God.... In Psalm 2, the Psalmist asks a question: "Why do the nations rage, and the peoples plot in vain? The kings of the earth"—*a political term, by the way*—"take their stand against the Lord and against his anointed. Let us break

their chains, they say. Let us loose their fetters." So the rulers of this earth in rebellion against God see God's order as chains that are just tying us down. [They think that] if only we could break those chains and loose those fetters, we could spread our wings and fly. I believe there really is a spiritual, cosmic war going on here in our culture—whether we see God's design as good, as He declared it in the creation week, or whether we see it as chains and fetters tying us down.[19]

It is not a choice between religion or no religion. It is only a question of whether one religion will be permitted to dominate the public square and silence all others.

According to the secularist creed, everyone must be made to check his or her religion at the gate of the town square—or pay the consequences. Everyone, that is, except the secular progressives themselves, zealots of the antireligion religion.

All others will be made to care.

CHAPTER 6

FAITH IN A BOX

For the sake of human progress, the best thing we could possibly do would be to diminish, to the point of eliminating, religious faiths.

—E. O. WILSON, HARVARD UNIVERSITY
EVOLUTIONARY BIOLOGIST[1]

I magine telling a Christian pastor he could preach, but not refer to the Bible. Or restricting a Muslim imam to counseling wayward souls only if he didn't encourage a change in behavior. Or what if a rabbi could only give marriage advice as long as he didn't mention the words *right* and *wrong*? If religious beliefs were confined by such restrictions, what good would they do anyone?

Christianity has a long history of ministry within the walls of America's penal system. A prominent example of someone in prison who found a new direction in life thanks to Christians is Chuck Colson, the one-time Nixon operative who started Prison Fellowship after his life was transformed by Christ behind bars. Christians and other people of faith have always been willing to go where no one else would go to reach the people dismissed as being nothing but trouble. They have always been active in ministering to inmates of all ages, but especially to juvenile offenders whose lives can be redirected by the timely application of truth and a message of hope, healing, and forgiveness.

But truth—particularly certain principles found in the Bible—is no longer allowed in Kentucky's juvenile justice system. If pastors want to do prison ministry, they must check their faith at the gate.

At least one pastor is unwilling to do so. David Wells,[2] a pastor at Pleasant View Baptist Church, had his access to prison ministry revoked by the Kentucky Department of Juvenile Justice in July 2015 when he refused to sign a document promising not to call homosexual behavior sinful. Pleasant View Baptist had been active in ministry at the prison for thirteen years before the pastor was kicked out for having the audacity to apply his faith in his prison ministry. Mat Staver, Liberty Counsel founder, points out the lunacy of the new policy: "Many juveniles are in DJJ custody because of sexual crimes. David Wells must be able to discuss what the Bible says about matters of sexuality with the juveniles he is trying to help. To remove the Bible from a pastor's hands is like removing a scalpel from a surgeon's hands. Without it, they cannot provide healing."[3]

Well, healing is not what officials think these inmates need. In a letter from his bureaucratic overlords—bearing the Orwellian title "The Justice and Public Safety Cabinet"—whose mission, it seems, is to protect inmates from caring Christians, Wells was informed that his religious beliefs would keep him from serving as a—wait for it— religious services volunteer. It appears from the letter that only secular zealots need apply for that position:

> Please be advised that your participation as one of our
> Religious Services volunteers must conclude. We sincerely

appreciate your years of service and dedication to the youth served by this facility.

However, due to your decision based on your religious convictions that you cannot comply with the requirements outlined in DJJ Policy 912, Section IV, Paragraph H, regarding the treatment of LGBTQI youth, I must terminate your involvement as a religious volunteer serving the youth in this facility per policy DJJ Policy 112, Section IV, Paragraph H, (8).[4]

DJJ Policy 912 IV(H), "Sexual Orientation and Gender Identity," requires that volunteers "shall not refer to juveniles by using derogatory language in a manner that conveys bias towards or hatred of the LGBTQI community. DJJ staff, volunteers, interns, and contractors shall not imply or tell LGBTQI juveniles that they are abnormal, deviant, sinful, or that they can or should change their sexual orientation or gender identity."[5]

There's a whole lot of crazy going on in that regulation, but the upshot is that the only way any religious services volunteer—other than a secularist—can ever set foot in those halls again is to compromise what he or she believes, because every major religion views those behaviors as sinful. Most disturbing is how religious expression is labeled as "derogatory" and even the implication that such behaviors are not normal—and they are not—is deemed biased and hateful. If Kentucky bureaucrats are looking for bias and bigotry, they need go no further than their own regulations restricting the free exercise of religion and speech.

Another pastor at Pleasant Valley Baptist Church described the real-world impact of the restrictions: "We're dealing with juveniles who have been prostituted since they were infants because their mothers needed money for drugs, or who have been sodomized all their lives. They feel like this is the only life they've ever known. Under this policy, we can't even go in there and read the Bible to them to give them a message of hope."[6]

David Wells refused to have his faith crammed into the box created for it by the Left. I shudder to think who will be there now to counsel imprisoned young people in need of life direction. Bruce Jenner? Stacy Floden, director of communications and program services for the Department of Juvenile Justice, had the shameless audacity to claim, "These requirements foster an open and inclusive culture within the department's programs...."[7] Unless, of course, you happen to believe God might have something to say about issues of gender and sexuality. In an ironic twist, it is the Christians whose faith is being locked out to protect those who are locked up—from the Bible.

WHAT GOOD IS CHRISTIANITY ANYWAY?

I'll bet you didn't know that the rubber used in automobile tires once led to the elimination of more than ten million people. But it did, until Christians did something about it.

The horror began deep in the heart of Africa when King Leopold II of Belgium joined the colonial land rush in 1885 and acquired the territory now known as the Democratic Republic of the Congo. When John Dunlop developed the pneumatic tire, Leopold declared all rubber in the Congo to be property of the state—*his* property. And to satisfy the growing demand for rubber, the king's agents turned to rape, murder, cannibalism, slavery, and mutilation. By one account, ten million native people vanished from the region in just fifteen years.[8] In one particularly gruesome episode, hungry native troops who were not permitted to use bullets to hunt for food—only to protect the rubber trade—hunted for food anyway and then cut off the hands of living people in an attempt to prove the bullets had been used to kill people instead. Horrific.

The cry from the Congo should have been heartbreaking, but no one heard it. The king's agents went to great lengths to conceal the evil being done to build his wealth. But there was one group of people who told the world of the evil—Christian missionaries. In spite of threats and the very real danger posed to themselves and their families, they spoke up and worked tirelessly to end this evil genocide. When the Reverend Joseph Clark lectured at Harvard University to push for an end to the genocide in the Congo, the *Harvard Crimson* reported, "[King Leopold's] sole aim is to drive the natives to their limit in gathering India rubber for his consumption, and the instances of cruelty on the part of soldiers to gain this end are barbarous beyond belief. Not only are their bodies mutilated, but they are frequently killed and eaten by the native soldiers in the employ of Leopold."[9] Clark's wife, Alice Seeley Harris, served as secretary of the Anti-Slavery Society (later Anti-Slavery International) and traveled throughout Europe and America. Her "shocking photos revealed to the world the horrendous truth of slavery in the Congo and helped bring public pressure and international scrutiny to the situation faced by its people."[10] Many other missionaries joined the effort, crossing the ocean with Bibles in their hands and returning with photographs and stories that would save millions from destruction.

Christians like these missionaries are not the exception, but the norm. Throughout the history of the world, Christians have consistently spoken up in the face of evil when all others choose to be silent. They do so because their faith demands it. Christians are not the only people of faith to do good, but as they have lived out their faith in the town square, they have accomplished some of the greatest good the world has ever known—from the end of King Leopold's genocide in the Congo to the abolition of slavery. But now the Left insists they be silent. The secularists demand that every religion but their own be banned from public discourse. Progressives believe the world would somehow be a better place if they could only get religious freaks like you to put your faith in a box on a shelf in your hall closet.

They are wrong.

BLAMING CHRISTIANITY

In response to an ISIS killing video in early 2015, President Barack Obama chose to equate Christianity and Islam, suggesting that critics of those atrocities needed to get off their "high horse" because many evil things—the Inquisition, the Crusades—had been done in the name of Christianity.[11]

I would feel better about the president's exegesis on matters of faith if I were convinced he had faith in anything other than himself and his secular beliefs. After all, he sat in the Reverend Jeremiah Wright's church for twenty years listening to black liberation theology,[12] a radical and racist ideology far removed from mainstream Christian discourse. Since then, the president has eschewed any regular faith practices. After Obama mocked Christians in 2008 as bitterly clinging to guns and religion,[13] no one should be surprised he got his history of Christianity wrong.

What is even more troubling, however, is *how* he got his history wrong. The Crusades, which he blamed on Christians, were actually a response to the Islamic invasion of the Holy Land and brutal persecution of Christians. While there certainly were atrocities—as there have been in every war in world history—the Crusades were launched for a justifiable and good reason.

And history is full of good brought about by Christianity. Neither slavery nor Jim Crow laws would have been ended but for the adamant voices of Christians. Famously, William Wilberforce, a member of the British Parliament, dedicated his life to ending slavery because he believed that his Christian faith demanded it of him. Wilberforce had considered withdrawing from Parliament because of his devout faith, thinking that the public square was no place for someone committed to living a life of holiness. But his friend Prime Minister William Pitt persuaded him otherwise. Pitt challenged Wilberforce by asking this question: "If a Christian may act in the several relations of life, must he seclude himself from them all to become so? Surely the principles as well as the practice of Christianity are simple, and lead not to meditation only but to action."[14] What Pitt was saying is this: Christianity requires you to live out what you believe, not pull back and keep your faith in a box. It calls you not only to private prayer but to public action.

Fortunately, Wilberforce responded to Pitt's words and put his faith into action—as Christians do every day across America to make our country a better place. And his actions—which ultimately resulted in the abolition of the heinous slave trade—inspired other Christians whose moral efforts liberated slaves around the world and laid the foundation for ending slavery in America. The United States became the only country to ever fight a war with itself to end slavery. In his bestseller *What's So Great about Christianity*, Dinesh D'Souza describes the unique contribution of Christians to ending slavery:

> Christians were the first group in history to start an anti-slavery movement. The movement started in late eighteenth-century Britain, spread to other parts of Europe, and then gathered force in the United States, where the economy of the South was heavily dependent on slave labor. In England, William Wilberforce spearheaded the campaign that began with almost no support and was driven entirely by Christian convictions, a story effectively told in the film *Amazing Grace*. Eventually Wilberforce triumphed, and in 1833 slavery was outlawed in Britain. Pressed by religious groups at home, England then took the lead in repressing the slave trade abroad.[15]

In the era of Jim Crow here in the United States, it was Christians, including Dr. Martin Luther King Jr., who again gave a moral voice to the movement to end segregation—a wrong, it should be noted, that, just like gay marriage, was mandated to be the law of the land by the U.S. Supreme Court (in *Plessy v. Ferguson* in 1896).

There are countless examples of the unparalleled benefits the world has derived from Christians applying their faith to public life. Rights for women, ownership of private property, limits on government power, access to education for all, protections for children—just to name a few of the ways our society thrives thanks to Christian beliefs. The fact is this: Christianity has been the greatest force for moral good the world has ever known. Not that it hasn't had its flaws, to be sure; some people claiming to act in the name of Christ have indeed committed evil deeds. But you don't see Christian missionaries beheading the unconverted and abusing women as ISIS does. Instead, Christians offer clean water and teach the equal value of all—including homosexuals, whom radical jihadists toss from tall buildings. Even Friedrich Nietzsche, famous for claiming God is dead, admitted that Christianity pioneered the radical idea that all men are created equal.[16] D'Souza explains how the idea of freedom for all, though it hasn't always been perfectly applied, rises from Christian theology:

> [T]he modern idea of freedom means the right to express your opinion, the right to choose a career, the right to buy and sell property, the right to travel where you want, the right to own your own personal space, and the right to live your own life. This is the freedom we are ready to fight for, and we become indignant when it is challenged or taken away.
>
> This modern concept of freedom we inherit from Christianity. Christianity emphasizes the fact that we are

moral agents. God has freely created us in His own image, and He has given us the power to take part in His sublime act of creation by being architects of our lives. But God has also granted to other human beings the same freedom. This means that in general we should be free to live our lives without interference from others as long as we extend to others the same freedom. My freedom to swing my fist has to stop at your nose.[17]

What progressives fail to understand is that their own freedoms—which they are now making use of to abuse and bully Christians—exist in the first place primarily because of the influence of Christianity. By trying to cram Christianity into a sacred box, they are restricting their own freedom to disagree with Christians, or anyone for that matter.

FREEDOM OF RELIGION, NOT WORSHIP

A favorite tactic of the Left is to affirm your right to believe whatever you want—as long as you don't live your life based on your beliefs. You can have your sacred beliefs as long as you keep them in your sacred box. What you can't have is the freedom to act on your beliefs. Thus President Obama and officials in his administration have repeatedly used the phrase "freedom of worship" as opposed to "freedom of religion" when discussing the freedom our Constitution protects—in spite of the fact that a unanimous Supreme Court opinion said that wording is not accurate.[18] Author and speaker Ashley Samelson McGuire points out the problem:

To anyone who closely follows prominent discussion of religious freedom in the diplomatic and political arena, this linguistic shift is troubling.

The reason is simple. Any person of faith knows that religious exercise is about a lot more than freedom of worship. It's about the right to dress according to one's religious dictates, to preach openly, to evangelize, to engage in the public square. Everyone knows that religious Jews keep kosher, religious Quakers don't go to war, and religious Muslim women wear headscarves, yet "freedom of worship" would protect none of these acts of faith.[19]

By "freedom of worship," they mean that you are entitled to your beliefs in a safe haven for one hour on a weekend, but otherwise you must put them away in a box and conform to their views. You can believe anything you want in your sacred space on Sunday, but don't try living it in their secular world on Monday. What they're essentially saying is that you're no longer allowed to be defined by your faith. You can be defined by sexual orientation—or whatever gender you choose this week—but you cannot be defined by your deeply held religious beliefs.

But what I believe to be true determines what I do. Beliefs always produce actions—or they are not real beliefs. Secularists expect people of faith to treat religious beliefs as Captain Barbossa in *Pirates of the Caribbean* treated the rules of Pirates' Code: "They're more like guidelines, really."[20] The Left thinks Christians can set their faith aside when they leave church on Sunday. They think Jews should keep their beliefs in the synagogue and Muslims should set aside their doctrines as they leave the mosque. They fundamentally misunderstand the nature of religious beliefs even as they seek to "fundamentally transform America" with religious beliefs of their own.

It is more than a little ironic that they claim to be doing what is good for society by removing Christians from the town square. Followers of Jesus Christ living out their faith in public life have produced—and continue to produce—some of the greatest good the world has ever seen. The secularists' track record is not so good. Secular leaders who sought to silence Christians in the twentieth century produced a death toll in excess of one hundred million.

An example from Nazi Germany may help us understand how a secular movement to ban faith from public discourse can be a precursor to greater evils. Yes, I am bringing the Nazis into this discussion—because the parallels are strong. Progressives in the West today are outraged by any comparison to the Nazis—perhaps because their behavior often overlaps with that of Hitler's followers. (Planned Parenthood's thrifty repurposing of the byproducts of their genocidal activities is one striking example. Besides collecting huge piles of the hair and other bits of their victims for various economic uses, the Nazis supplied live subjects to medical researchers. Given our better technology for preserving human tissue, Planned Parenthood has been able to profit from selling baby parts from abortions to research labs.)

In 1935 Hermann Göring, premier of Prussia and head of the Prussian Gestapo, warned local governors to make sure clergy were kept in line as they engaged in public service: "It has to be fundamentally understood that all priests who are employed in the public service—**as for instance in giving religious instruction in public schools**—will be expected not merely to avoid any possible negative attitude towards Nazism in their teaching, but also like all other members of the public service to commit themselves positively on Nazism's behalf, and thus stand without hesitation in Nazism's service. **Only then can Nazism allow the priests to participate in religious education of young people**" [emphasis added].[21]

Note that clergy were allowed to teach religion—the area in which they were supposedly the experts—*only if* they endorsed the views of the secular government.

Like the pastor in Kentucky who must check his faith at the door of the prison if he is to serve as a chaplain, the clergymen in Nazi Germany were told that they could only participate in public service if they submitted to the secular spirit of the age. J. S. Conway, author of *The Nazi Persecution of the Churches*, describes what happened next: "The consequences of non-compliance were soon apparent. The Governor of Hanover Province shortly afterwards ordered his civil service employees to submit to him written statements promising that they would give up membership of any denominational professional organization to which they belonged, and would withdraw their children from denominational youth organizations."[22]

The clergy in Germany in 1935 didn't just have to be silent. They had to cut professional ties and pull their children from church organizations. They had to remove any evidence of the sacred to preserve their livelihood. And today in America, the Kentucky clergyman— who, unlike the priests who taught religion in Nazi Germany's public schools, is not even paid by the government—must sign a statement promising not to question the government's position even though it conflicts with his religious beliefs. *The Nazi Persecution of the Churches* quotes the Nazi governor of Hanover Province explaining away his party's blatant violation of conscience: "It is not intended to exercise any pressure on conscience by this measure, for **those who believe that they cannot follow this directive are hereby notified that they must withdraw from any further participation** in the rebuilding of the State" [emphasis added].[23]

In other words, no one is forcing you to violate your conscience— if you don't want to comply, leave. Find another career. Whatever. Just don't participate in public life. Don't volunteer to help troubled youths in Kentucky's juvenile detention system.

Under the Nazis, most clergy caved: "Faced with the alternative of dismissal from their posts or obedience to the behest of their Nazi superiors, few men were ready to give up their livelihood.... But for the Nazis that was not enough. **The only sphere in which they were prepared to tolerate Church activity was in purely spiritual matters** concerned with the next world" [emphasis added].[24]

It is human nature to seek the path of least resistance. So it is not surprising that clergy would choose their jobs over their religious beliefs. Disappointing, perhaps, but not surprising. But note well that their compromise only emboldened their persecutors. In Nazi Germany, religious beliefs would ultimately be tolerated only in private spiritual matters, and as long as they had no connection with the physical world. Only Christians willing to keep their faith out of the public conversation were permitted to participate in the public life of the society—for a while.

So it is with all such secular oppressors. The Kentucky pastor is being required to set aside his Christian beliefs when helping troubled youths, as if matters of morality, sexuality, relationships, and life purpose were no longer areas that religion should address. Am I the only one thinking that if our faith doesn't inform these issues, what good is it?

The Christian view of reality has always been radically opposed to this split thinking. Scriptures espouse a worldview that sounded heretical to the secular world of Jesus's day—claiming that how we live our lives in the physical realm is just as important to God as what we believe in the spiritual realm. When God, the infinite but personal Spirit, became a man in the person of Jesus, He forever validated the connection between the two realms. The imagined walls between physical and spiritual, private and public, sacred and secular all fell down, leaving only a simple gospel of grace and forgiveness with comprehensive implications for all of life, including sexuality, marriage, family, and the limits of human government.

That is not to say that a Christian view of reality should be forced upon any individual. Not at all. But orthodox Christians cannot put their faith in a box and somehow separate what they believe from how they live in the world every day. If they could, slavery would still be the norm today. My Christian faith affects how I do my job every day; it shapes how I interact with my neighbor; it motivates me to treat those I disagree with as people made in the image of God—even if I think they're nuts. And it requires me to speak the truth in love no matter what any secular government may say. It moves me to be a happy warrior, not trying to be offensive, but boldly speaking truth to those who seek to split reality and confine my faith to a sacred box so they can advance their own faith in the public square.

I love people too much to stand idly by and let that happen. I stand with the saints whose countercultural message turned the ancient secular world upside down. They stood in humble defiance against Rome, the most powerful government in the world, because they owed their allegiance to the One who is Truth, not those who believed truth could be redefined to fit their own needs and to advance a secular gospel.

CHAPTER 7

WHAT THE HELL ARE THEY THINKING?

Of all tyrannies, a tyranny sincerely exercised for the good of its victims may be the most oppressive.... those who torment us for our own good will torment us without end for they do so with the approval of their own conscience.

—C. S. LEWIS[1]

What a bunch of left-wing lunatics!

It's easy to hear of the outlandish attacks against people of faith and conclude that society has lost its mind. In many ways, it has. And it would be easy to simply dismiss the Left as a bunch of lunatics, crazies on the fringe with whom we can never connect. Truth be told, some of them *are* nuts.

But as much as I love to talk politics, life is more than politics. As believers in Christ, we are called to take the Good News to all people, to love our enemies, and to pray for those who persecute us (Matt. 5:44). To do that effectively, we need to understand what motivates secular progressives to do what they do so that we can connect over a cup of coffee, chat while our children play T-ball, or talk about life as we borrow a cup of sugar from our neighbors.

I hear a lot of anger directed at the Left and even at those on the Right who don't respond with as much passion as some think they should. I've received my share of it, as well, from fellow believers. I understand the frustration with political leaders who say one thing to get elected, then sell out their principles once in office. I get the exasperation as our president tramples on the law to advance his divisive agenda. I relate to the desire to push back hard on those who seek to restrict our freedom to believe. But it is important as believers that we not give in to the temptation to do unto others as is being done to us. Jesus certainly didn't erupt in outrage when being led to the cross. Stephen didn't cite legal precedent as the bullies of his day pummeled him with stones. Both prayed for forgiveness for their accusers. As Dr. Russell Moore explains, Christians must treat those with whom they disagree with love: "We don't demonize them. We speak to them, with an alternative vision of what it means to love and to cherish every human life, in our families and in our laws."[2] And if you do not understand what they are thinking, what motivates them, how can you ever have a meaningful conversation about life?

I know it is difficult, perhaps even painful, to do, but let's delve into the mind of the secular progressive to see if we can understand better why he perceives Christians not as a blessing but a curse.

There are at least three key things progressives think that help explain why they view people of faith, and Christians especially, the way they do. I'm not saying all progressives are consciously aware of their own thought processes. I wouldn't say all Christians are, either. Nor do all three things apply equally to all. In fact, the number of people on the Left who consistently think these things decreases as we move down the list. But let us make an effort to be like the sons of Issachar in the Old Testament Chronicles who "had understanding of the times, to know what Israel ought to do" (1 Chron. 12:32).

REASON NUMBER ONE: THEY THINK THEY KNOW BETTER THAN GOD

At the heart of the Christian faith is a basic understanding: "We all like sheep have gone astray. We have turned everyone to his own way" (Isa. 53:6). "None is righteous, no, not one; no one understands; no one seeks for God" (Rom. 3:10–11). We are all sinners. I join with the Apostle Paul in competing for status as chief among them. There but for the grace of God, go I. The Fall plunged us all into darkness and corrupted to the deepest levels our ability to do good.

I mentioned earlier that the Left's view of humanity leads it to believe in utopian fantasies inconsistent with human nature. But it's important to understand that none of us likes admitting we are sinners in need of grace and forgiveness. None of us enjoys acknowledging that we are fundamentally flawed. And none of us jumps at the chance to admit that we are not in charge of the universe. The problem began all the way back in Eden when our first parents chose to "be like gods" and make their own rules for how the universe would function. God said *this*, but I think *that*. Every one of us has been doing the same thing ever since. We have all been born into the world seeking to be autonomous, a law unto ourselves. We want to do what *we* want to do, and so we rebel against our Creator. We shake our fist at the Almighty and dare Him to stop us. Until He does, and then we whine about how unfair and unkind He is to us.

The fact that progressives think they know better than God should come as no surprise to Christians, for it is the experience common to us all. That's why we need the gospel of Jesus Christ to free us from our slavery to sin and our own destructive desires. The Apostle Paul explains in Romans 1:16–21:

> For I am not ashamed of the gospel, for **it is the power of God for salvation to everyone who believes,** to the Jew first and also to the Greek. For in it the righteousness of God

is revealed from faith for faith, as it is written, "The righteous shall live by faith."

For the wrath of God is revealed from heaven against all ungodliness and unrighteousness of men, **who by their unrighteousness suppress the truth.** For what can be known about God is plain to them, because God has shown it to them. For his invisible attributes, namely, his eternal power and divine nature, have been clearly perceived, ever since the creation of the world, in the things that have been made. **So they are without excuse.** For although they knew God, they did not honor him as God or give thanks to him, but **they became futile in their thinking, and their foolish hearts were darkened.** [emphasis added]

Far from giving us a reason to ridicule those who seek to destroy believers, Paul reveals why we should care about them. It is the fallen nature of humanity not only to run from our Creator but to suppress the truth our Creator wired into us—namely that this is His world, and it runs best when it runs His way. When we insist on living life in our own way, we end up with empty lives devoid of true fulfillment. The end result is futile thinking and darkened hearts—lives that don't make sense and that hurt a lot. Christian thinker and cultural observer Os Guinness says, "The sad fact is that without truth and virtue, those who proclaim freedom and set out to do what they like often end up not liking what they have done."[3]

The bottom line is this: the reason most on the Left oppose people of faith is that they are simply doing what comes naturally to them. I don't mean that as an insult but as an observation about our shared and fallen human condition. What we need the most, we want the least. We want to be as gods, a role for which we're spectacularly ill-equipped.

REASON NUMBER TWO: THEY THINK
THEY ARE DOING GOOD

When we remove God from authority over our lives, it's not as if we can leave a vacuum. Because we are all finite beings, we must replace Him with another system of beliefs—a religion of our own making. For help in explaining the belief system of progressives, I turned to noted cultural Christian apologist Nancy Pearcey, author of *Finding Truth* and *Total Truth*. "If you do a scientific study of religions," she points out,

> the only thing they really have in common is that they say *something* is the ultimate reality. They all disagree on what that something is. Philosophy also says *something* is the ultimate reality and that *something* shapes everything else.... And in that sense **you could call any philosophy a religion in the sense that it puts something in the place of God. It has a God substitute....** Insofar as it is a complete system, it's got to start with something. You can't start thinking without a starting point, without proposing something as that ultimate, self-existent, eternal reality.[4] [emphasis added]

For most on the Left, their religion is postmodernism, a form of secularism. If we can understand how postmodernism came to be and what it views as the ultimate authority, we can better understand why it is that progressives think they are doing good when they try to silence people of faith.

In order to make some sense of their thinking, we need to rewind a few centuries to pick up the story line. Stick with me. What we discover will explain a lot of the Left's animus toward believers. In the late 1700s, as America was finding its way after gaining its independence, European thinkers known as the Romantics were staging a revolution of a different sort, a revolution of the mind. They were reacting to the Industrial Revolution and its extreme emphasis on science, to the view of man as little more than a cog in a machine. As is often the case, they reacted against one extreme by embracing another. The Romantics embraced the nonphysical world of ideas and feelings and ended up adopting a kind of pantheism. They sought connections through a shared worship of nature. Pearcey explains:

> When the Romantics first proposed a kind of pantheism, they accepted the notion that in a sense our mind creates reality, which is very postmodern. That our mind creates reality goes back to Immanuel Kant, who essentially said the universe as we experience it is the universe constructed by our minds. Maybe there's an objective universe out there, but we can't know it. The only universe you and I can know, the only world you and I can experience, is the one that's constructed by our minds. But the Romantics didn't want it to be the individual mind; it was this pantheistic mind. And **that pantheistic mind expresses itself through the community and its experience, through its laws, through its morality, its language, its social relationships**, and so on.[5] [emphasis added]

The German philosopher Hegel took the Romantics' pantheist idea a step further and offered a spiritualized version of evolution. Pearcey puts it this way: "The difference is that Hegel applied the concept of evolution not to biology but to the world of ideas. His claim was that all our ideas—law, morality, religion, art, political ideals—result from the gradual 'actualization of the Universal Mind' over the course of history. **Everything is caught up in a vast historical process**

advancing toward a final perfect state. For many people, the law of historical progress functioned as a substitute for divine Providence" [emphasis added].[6]

Exactly. *Progress*. In place of a transcendent God who made and governs all things, Hegel opened the door for the worship of an impersonal force that connects and animates all things as it drives historical progress. Based on his perspective, therefore, progress, by definition, must always be good—no matter where or how it might lead us—because it is an expression of the divine.

Of course, few but the most radical environmentalist whackos openly advocate the worship of nature today. Hegel's thinking was secularized and made more palatable over time. Pearcey explains how Hegel's ideas morphed over the last two centuries:

> Hegel took a kind of pantheism that was popular among the Romantics and he changed it. Typically, pantheism is not evolutionary; it doesn't change. The spiritual essence that's supposed to be at the core of all reality is stable in eastern pantheism, for example. But he proposed that there's a Spirit—what he called the Absolute Spirit—that evolved in and through the world. And so, he was the first person to really say that pantheism can be evolutionary. As this pantheistic god evolves through history, it throws up all these different cultures, and it incarnates itself in various cultures. It started out as a pantheistic idea that then became secularized. Instead of the Absolute Spirit, the spirit was *Geist* (Hegel was German); it kind of got secularized to *the zeitgeist* ... or the spirit of the age.... Consequently, **we're all driven by the Spirit of the Age.**[7] [emphasis added]

I realize I am condensing into a few paragraphs what could fill volumes on the history of philosophy, but essentially the postmodernist progressives—those seeking to impose their beliefs upon the rest of us—do so because they have embraced the forces of cultural progress as their ultimate authority, their Absolute Spirit.[8] The ideas that animate us right now in this present age—whatever they may be—are evidence of that progress and thus must be championed; conversely, tradition is what stunts our growth as a culture and keeps us stuck in the societal stone age. Thus the postmodernist mind places supreme importance upon the forces of cultural change, which it believes to be moving us inevitably toward a better place.

There is a reason why so many of us feel as if the Left is intent on overturning everything Western civilization has thought to be true. It is—and it *must* be, in order to keep up with what it believes to be the progress of history. The postmodern god—the Spirit of the Age—requires it of progressives. Their religion calls them to reject the sin of tradition. Their Gospel of Societal Evolution calls all men, women, and every other gender in between to repent of their resistance to progress. Their faith demands that they leave behind established truths and follow the *zeitgeist* to usher in "a brave new world."

When we see ourselves according to this Gospel of Societal Evolution, we begin to understand why so many on the Left attack Christians with such passion. They view us as the ones standing in the way of the forces of progress that will surely bring salvation for all. From their perspective, we are the ones standing in need of redemption. We are the ones leading wayward souls astray with our ancient and heretical myths. As an unknown source put it, *Truth sounds like hate to those who hate truth.* We view the Left as making power grabs—oppressing grandmothers, pharmacists, and undergrads—and yet that is exactly how it views us for refusing to bend to cultural evolution. Because we dare to speak truth as if it is unchanging, progressives view us as imposing our beliefs about truth onto them. In their minds, we are the aggressors. And the best thing they can do for cultural progress is to make us care.

REASON NUMBER THREE: THEY THINK YOUR BELIEFS CAN CHANGE

We've seen that Russell Moore has pointed out how people on the Left struggle to understand deeply held religious beliefs because they think they have none of their own. As we've also seen, they do in fact have religious beliefs, but even those beliefs are based on the assumption that all things are in a constant state of transition.

Because change is essential to its own belief system, the Left expects Christians and all people of faith to change their beliefs as well. Throughout history, however, the people of God have never proved particularly good at modifying their beliefs to align with the Spirit of the Age. When the Babylonians insisted that all bow to the king as god, three young men refused to comply and were sent to the fiery furnace. They emerged unharmed (Dan. 3:25). When the Medes and Persians insisted that all comply with laws forbidding prayer to Yahweh, Daniel ignored them and was introduced to a den of hungry lions. He emerged unscathed (Dan. 6:23). When a wicked official manipulated the king to commit genocide, Esther risked everything to unmask the evil. The official received the ignoble death due him (Esther 5–10). When the Sanhedrin flogged the Disciples and told them to speak no more of Jesus, they went away praising God for the opportunity to suffer in His name (Acts 5:41). The stoning of Stephen only prepared for the conversion of Saul, the greatest enemy of the early church—who became its greatest missionary (Acts 7:59). Even when Nero lit his garden with the living bodies of believers, Christians didn't waver in their beliefs.

It is secularism and its postmodernist garb that will prove to be the blip in the history of the universe, not Christianity. What we are witnessing now is an aberration, the latest attempt by the Kingdom of Man to supersede the Kingdom of God. Like previous attempts, tracing all the way back to Babel, it too will fail. The only question is, at what cost? How extreme will be the pain? What will be the damage to the institutions of the family, the church, and government? And how high will be the body count?

In *Big Problems, Bigger God,* pastor Steve Smothermon bluntly says what most Christians believe about being expected to change our beliefs to conform to the secular *zeitgeist*: "Today we blur the lines and tolerate everything. Either we're to accept it all or be labeled as intolerant. Frankly, I don't care how many people label me; I only care how God labels me. If I listen to what the world tells me, truth is the new hate speech. If I speak truth today, even to some Christians, they freak out.... But political correctness is just another word for cowardice. It isn't only robbing us of freedom of speech in America; it's eliminating our access to the truth. And without truth, we have no hope of finding a better life."[9]

Amen.

CHAPTER 8

PASTORS, PRIESTS, AND POWERLESS PULPITS

Neither in earlier time or today has the party the inten-
tion of waging any kind of war against Christianity.... But
we will ensure the purging from our public life of all those
priests who have mistaken their profession and who ought
to have been politicians and not pastors.

—ADOLF HITLER, SEPTEMBER 11, 1935[1]

"It certainly is going to be an issue."

So said Obama administration solicitor general Donald Verrilli to Supreme Court Justice Samuel Alito during oral arguments for *Obergefell v. Hodges* in April of 2015. Justice Alito had asked if Christian organizations could lose their tax-exempt status if they refused to recognize gay unions as marriage. Verrilli added, "I don't deny that."[2]

No one familiar with the scorched-earth tactics of the Left should be surprised.

The legal recognition of gay marriage is not the end game. Christianity itself must be made to care. Churches, religious private schools, private universities, and charitable organizations will be forced to give up their tax-exempt status or embrace Sodom writ large. President Obama's solicitor general all but admitted it to the Supreme Court.

Already, in the previous year, the president of the United States had taken a position before the Supreme Court to the left of the American Civil Liberties Union. The Obama administration had argued in court that there is no "ministerial exception" in the law allowing churches to define who is and is not a minister and what are and are not a minister's duties. The president asserted that the government should have the right to define which church employees count as ministers. Four years ago, everyone would have said such a position was nuts. The ACLU still says it is nuts. The Supreme Court shot the administration down in a unanimous 9–0 ruling.[3] Yet that's the anti-clergy position that the president argued and his administration still maintains.

And now they want to take the tax-exempt status of religious organizations that do not bend the knee to the secular Spirit of the Age. The people telling pastors and church leaders not to worry about losing their tax-exempt status are the same ones who said same-sex marriage would never happen. It's coming. It's only a matter of *when*, not *if*, the Left forces the issue.

But let's be candid, shall we? As important an issue as losing tax-exempt status would be for some churches, it is a damn shame if the threat of losing tax-exempt status is what it takes to get the attention of pastors and priests in pulpits across America. My friend Dr. Brian Mattson sums up the reality of it: "It's a sad commentary on the state of the American church that we only wake up and care when they go for our pocketbooks."[4]

For far too long, pastors have been asleep at the wheel, allowing our culture to drift into secularism without raising the alarm from the pulpit. At the founding of our country, ministers and clergy were the fiercest defenders of freedom because they recognized the true source of all freedom and the evil inherent in tyranny of all sorts.

Sermons on issues affecting public life were commonplace. In the decades leading up to the American War for Independence, sermons laid the cultural groundwork to justify the need for action. Issues such as the repeal of the Stamp Act, overreach in government power, science, current events, astronomical discoveries, the death penalty, and changes in marriage laws were common topics for sermons. Ministers were among the first to call for resistance to the king's tyranny and even among the first to pick up a musket to defend those freedoms granted by God to us all.

But not anymore. Instead we get sermons on "Five Tips for Achieving a Fulfilling Life" and books about how to make every day a Friday—while a cultural wildfire burns around us. Sermons that apply Scripture and transhistorical truth to the cultural issues of the day are rare and deemed out of bounds by many Christians. I'm sure few readers can recall the last time their pastor, or any pastor, attempted to explain the cultural shifts that have rocked our society over the last half century. And I'll bet you've never heard a sermon on the vital importance of religion to public virtue and thus to the preservation of our freedoms in America.

Pastors have remained silent as morality has collapsed. When was the last time you heard a sermon decrying the family-destroying evil of divorce, or one explaining that *all* sexual immorality outside of marriage—not just homosexual behavior—is sinful, and calling on everyone to repent? For that matter, how often do you even hear pastors use the word *repent* anymore? One reason for their silence is that many of them—and other leaders within their own churches—have struggled with the same issues. They have guilty secrets of their own, or they have looked the other way instead of dealing with immorality among their peers. They don't go there for fear that they might disqualify themselves or rock the boat in their own congregations.

Don't misunderstand me. I love pastors. I'm a seminary student myself, and I preach on occasion. Ministers of the gospel have a challenging calling, shepherding the souls of Christ followers. But it is a calling, not a recommendation. The terms are nonnegotiable—complete obedience to Christ and His Word no matter what resistance you encounter. And you will encounter resistance. You cannot follow after Christ and remain safely on the sidelines. Many pastors have attempted to stay on the sidelines for far too long, hoping the action will pass them by so they can keep munching on their popcorn and soaking up the sun while sipping Diet Coke in the bleachers. What they've failed to realize is that the sidelines in America have been shrinking. The secularists have become bolder and more aggressive because they sense the church is weak and vulnerable. And they are right. Everyone is now fair game. Secularists could tackle anyone at any time. Just ask the florist, the baker, the clerks of court, the prison chaplain, the justice of the peace, the pharmacist, the counselors, the students, the professor, the teacher, the television personality, the jeweler, the coach—and the list goes on. There is no more room left on the sidelines for spectators. Everyone is on the field. Anyone could be hit at any time. But only a few pastors seem to realize that the rules of the game have changed.

The Left will not tolerate dissent. And history tells us that pastors will be among the first who must be silenced if they do not silence themselves first. We are engaged in a war of religions, of competing systems of beliefs that have consequences in the real world. Let's face it: the gracious gospel of Jesus Christ is a continuous assault against the graceless secular religion. They cannot let it stand. So, yes, pastors and priests in America need to wake up and start planning for the day when their churches no longer have nonprofit status. Given the willing support of the media, the lackeys of the Left, it will become increasingly difficult for judges who base their rulings on the prevailing Spirit of the Age to justify giving a tax break to an institution vilified as bigoted and homophobic. But more important, pastors had better start preparing themselves and their congregations to minister faithfully in a secular culture that is becoming increasingly hostile to truth. I hope I'm wrong, but the progressives have momentum on their side. The attacks on pastors and churches will come sooner than we think.

WHY PASTORS HAVE FAILED TO LEAD

The truth is that pastors and priests alike have contributed to the irrelevance of organized religion in the United States. Christianity was already abandoning sound doctrine in the early part of the twentieth century as progressives infiltrated the mainline denominations. In an effort to preserve what they perceived as the fundamentals of the faith, well-meaning evangelical Christians focused on the basics, to the neglect of a robust world- and life view. As a reaction to the immorality and cultural upheaval of the 1960s, most Christian leaders who remained committed to God's Word focused on personal piety and the importance of living right before God as an individual, not as a culture. Many embraced an anti-intellectualism that discouraged deep thinking about cultural issues and an eschatology that promised an escape with Jesus's prompt return: "Why polish brass on a sinking ship?" Many pastors, the products of liberal seminaries and universities, embraced the split thinking we touched on earlier. They thought of the world as divided between private (the realm of personal faith in God) and public (the realm of shared secular culture), or as the two spheres came to be known in Christian circles, between the *sacred* and *secular*.

Yet as society crumbled around them, some church leaders realized that God holds us responsible for our behaviors, not just individually but corporately as a nation. And so they began trying to influence politics through efforts like the Moral Majority or the Christian Coalition—but without the intellectual or theological underpinnings that had supported Christians in public life for centuries.

Essentially, they threw a Hail Mary pass, hoping to salvage an increasingly secular culture by putting the right people in the end zone, a.k.a. Washington, D.C. It was a top-down approach that, while well intentioned, forgot that politics is downstream from culture. As a result, many pastors and believers put their faith in getting certain candidates who supported "family values" elected, passing constitutional amendments, or nominating the right Supreme Court justices. (Let's not forget that Anthony Kennedy and David Souter were two of those "right" justices.)

The end result of their efforts was this: they won a few elections but lost the culture—and turned off a lot of people to Christianity in the process. As a reaction to the political excesses, many pastors and Christian leaders ran the other way. Some, like Shane Claiborne and the New Monastics, chose to focus solely on personal piety, simple living, and compassion for others, as if that were the extent of what it means to follow Christ. They embraced the banner of "social justice" (as if justice were not social by definition) and partnered with progressives to attack the evils of capitalism and pursue a utopia on earth with a God sticker slapped on it. Many pastors today have followed their lead and partnered with progressives to bring about heaven on earth by using the force of government to make people care about the causes they think people should care about. "Being Christian doesn't make you immune to Utopianism," says Ed Morrissey. "Doctrinally, it really should; but it doesn't, because Utopianism is a very, very seductive philosophy.... We're called to make the world better. But there's a difference between improving the world by personal acts of *caritas* and trying to perfect the world by imposing restrictions on other people that eliminate their ability to choose for themselves the path of salvation."[5]

Meanwhile, others, especially pastors at many of the megachurches in Protestant circles, chose to stop talking about any issues that might be deemed offensive to a secular culture. Instead, they set out to convince unbelievers that the new generation of Christian was a kinder, gentler believer. And so seeker-friendly churches were born in the hope that a winsome voice that didn't mention sin would draw everyone to Jesus. The strategy did draw large crowds; however, the seeker-friendly Jesus didn't have much to say to them. Because this strategy put butts in the pews, many churches in America followed this lead, hoping to be the next big thing in ecclesiastical circles. In doing so, pastors traded truth for Twitter followers, television appearances, bestseller lists, and speaking gigs at conferences—and now we're all paying for it.

One consequence of the seeker-friendly approach is that we have a lot of people in the pews who are only there for the show. And those who do believe often have little to no understanding of their faith and its implications for all of life. We've done a great job of attracting the hungry, but we've denied them access to the miraculous loaves and fishes that will put meat on their spiritual bones. Compared with previous generations, most Christians today have no grasp of the basic doctrines of the faith, the content of Scripture, or the history of the church. That fact is especially ironic given our unprecedented access to study tools for spiritual growth with the rise of the Internet. Consequently, today's believers are especially vulnerable to the secular Gospel of Societal Evolution. Even pastors who know the truth don't preach it, because they think their congregation can't handle it. But if that is true, it's more a poor reflection on the pastor than on the people entrusted to his care. Shepherds are supposed to guide the flock where they need to go to ensure they are fed. Instead, what we have today is a hungry church with a wimpy faith because pastors don't teach them the whole counsel of God. Pastors tell their followers that they need Jesus, but not enough preach on what should happen after they've found Him.

I must confess to being surprised when, on the Sunday after the *Obergefell* decision, so many evangelical pastors and churches made statements from the pulpit affirming God's definition of marriage. I had expected the silence to continue. But I was wrong. Perhaps, just perhaps, the church is beginning to awaken from her cultural slumber and is ready for her pastors to lead her once again.

"SPEAK THE WORD OF GOD WITH BOLDNESS"

When the Apostles and early Christians were threatened by the tyrants of their day, they responded with courage and set the example for pastors to follow today:

> When they were released, they went to their friends and reported what the chief priests and the elders had said to them. And when they heard it, they lifted their voices together to God and said, "Sovereign Lord, who made the heaven and the earth and the sea and everything in them, who through the mouth of our father David, your servant, said by the Holy Spirit,
> 'Why did the Gentiles rage,
> and the peoples plot in vain?
> The kings of the earth set themselves,
> and the rulers were gathered together,
> against the Lord and against his Anointed'—
> for truly in this city there were gathered together against your holy servant Jesus, whom you anointed, both Herod and Pontius Pilate, along with the Gentiles and the peoples of Israel, to do whatever your hand and your plan had predestined to take place. And now, Lord, look upon their threats and grant to your servants to continue to speak your word with all boldness, while you stretch out your hand to heal, and signs and wonders are performed through the name of your holy servant Jesus."

And when they had prayed, the place in which they were gathered together was shaken, and they were all filled with the Holy Spirit and continued to speak the word of God with boldness. (Acts 4:23–31)

When the Protestant Reformation occurred (I'm simplifying here), Martin Luther needed an explanation for why the pope need not wield the power of the sword. He focused on the idea of the two kingdoms—there is God's kingdom in Heaven, over which the church presides here on earth, and there is God's kingdom on earth, over which civil authorities preside. John Calvin picked up the two kingdoms doctrine and ran with it.

Over time, however, the doctrine has become corrupted, and many Protestant pastors now hide in a cowardly way behind a bastardized version of it, insisting that pastors should make no commentary about civil society. In other words, pastors should not be political and should steer clear of anything bordering on politics. I think we can agree that pastors should not be overtly political in the pulpit. But today, pastors have become cowards. If any subject, no matter how much it encroaches on the church, should become a subject within politics, too many pastors will steer clear of it—even if the issue is, at its core, moral, but with political implications.

Most pastors attempt to end a sermon with an application to life. Every sermon should, in some way, affect your life. But too often pastors think life should not affect the sermon. It should. Pastors should not shy away from what, for example, man's creation in the image of God means for the Christian view of abortion. Pastors should not shy away from the fact that God created us as male and female—a truth that has unavoidable implications for marriage.

There are relevant discussions going on in families, communities, schools, and Sunday school classrooms about the wildfire raging across our culture. We are all aware of a great shift happening. But too many preachers are hiding behind not the two kingdoms doctrine but a corrupted version of it to avoid talking about anything controversial in our society, because they are afraid of the impact controversy might have on their church—as if it were actually *their* church and not God's church, which even the gates of Hell cannot stop.

Christians right now need moral clarity. They need to know what Christian love is and *is not*. They need to know that being liked by the world is not the goal of the church. Pastors need to stop being cowards, stop being obtuse, and engage their congregations by applying biblical wisdom to the issues of our present age. The world is at war with the things of God. Pastors must be willing to lead us into the fray, wielding the Word of God, which is "sharper than any double-edged sword" (Heb. 4:12). Pastor David McNeely, director of young families and adults at Perimeter Church near Atlanta, sums up the call upon every Christian shepherd: "It is my job as a pastor to faithfully preach and teach the whole counsel of God. It is not my job to protect people *from the Word*. It's actually my job to protect people *from the world*. . . . My job is to help politicians be the most Godly politicians they can be based on the Word."[6]

Dr. Russell Moore notes that the reality of ministering in the real world means you cannot run from cultural issues and remain faithful to God's call—no matter how much pastors may want to do so: "It's very easy at the beginning of a ministry to say, 'We're not going to engage on these social and political issues at all,' but then once you're actually leading a ministry you have to inform your people about how they are to think about whether or not they should participate in a same-sex wedding, or whether or not they ought to have that gender reassignment surgery, or whether or not they ought to be foaming at the mouth and bashing immigrants in their community. **Those are things that they have to know**" [emphasis added].[7]

It is the sacred duty of every pastor and priest to tell them.

PULLING OFF THE MASKS

A Baptist church in North Carolina recently announced they would no longer condemn homosexuality as sin and would ordain homosexuals and transgendered individuals. The church's new policy was put into place after a "six-month discernment process" in which church members discussed *their feelings*, what they thought Scripture taught, and "who they believed they were as Christians and Baptists."[8] Note the abandonment of transhistorical truth on which the Christian faith is grounded in favor of a discussion of what works for them within their own community. The pastor told Greenville Online that "a crucial step of the process was assuring church members no one would tell them their personal convictions were wrong."[9] And here I thought that was what churches were for—to tell us when our thoughts disagreed with God's thoughts. As it turns out, the pastor "personally believes the Bible has no family value system for the twenty-first century. 'What we believe about marriage and family is culturally driven, not biblically driven.'"[10]

That much was obvious. A quick search online reveals the members of this church to be far more formal in their worship style than most Baptists I know. There seems to be a pattern here in Protestant circles: the more liberal a church becomes, the more it invests in all the trappings of the appearance of religion. The more it compromises the truth, the more it seems to try to compensate with impressive liturgies, pompous ceremony, and clerical garb. The compromisers seem to want you to get a feeling of spirituality from the way they conduct the service—not from the words they use. It's as if they want to be judged by the color of their robes and not the content of their sermons.

The gay rights movement has spent a decade trying to reinterpret the New Testament. In spite of this example in a more liberal Baptist denomination, for the most part it has failed to convince churches that still hold to the authority of God's special revelation in Scripture.

And the only churches showing consistent growth in America are the ones that still hold to biblical inerrancy and to God's definition of marriage, not Anthony Kennedy's. All others are in decline. And rightly so. After all, why do we need a church that endorses destructive behavior—just to play dress-up on Sunday?

I am reminded of this truth from Orthodox priest Father Lawrence Farley:

> In every age, there are Christians who compromise with the standards of their age, and accept the world's values as their own. These people always call themselves "Christians" and denounce those who disagree with them as rigid and wrong. But the Christ whom they preach is not the real Christ. They in fact misrepresent Him, and preach a Christ made up by themselves, one who conforms more closely to their own secular age. **St. Paul, St. John, and St. Athanasius pulled the mask off them in their day, and denied them the label of "Christian."** It is time that we Orthodox follow in their footsteps now and do the same to those who offer a counterfeit faith and another Jesus.[11] [emphasis added]

It's time for pastors who believe the Word of God to start calling out church leaders who call evil good. They must start pulling off the masks of those who couch their rebellion against God in Christianeze. These compromising "Christians" have concocted another gospel, a false gospel that feels more compatible with the Spirit of the Age. The actual gospel is death to them because the actual gospel is death to sin. They have traded the gospel of eternal life for the gospel of the here and now. The real gospel would make them new, but the real gospel means there are things they *ought* to do—because Christ died and showed them grace. And those who think the Bible is neutral on homosexuality, for example, reject the *oughts* of faith. A gospel that does not call for repentance of sin—as God defines it in His Word—and belief in Christ as Lord is not the gospel of Christianity. It is something else entirely. And pastors should have the courage to make that distinction clear, even if it means days of suffering may lie ahead.

Christianity is, in this life, a religion of suffering. We have forgotten this truth in America. Put bluntly: if you do have a comfortable path through life with no fears at all of persecution, you probably are not a true Christian. The suffering may not be major. It may be an accumulation of small slights over time. It may be the loss of a friend or just the expulsion of your Christian group from your private school. But Christianity is a religion of suffering and persecution. Jesus was blunt: "Then Jesus told his disciples, 'If anyone would come after me, let him deny himself and take up his cross and follow me. For whoever would save his life will lose it, but whoever loses his life for my sake will find it. For what will it profit a man if he gains the whole world and forfeits his soul? Or what shall a man give in return for his soul?'" (Matt. 16:24–26).

Christ said this *before* His crucifixion, calling for others to set aside their self-interest in favor of the interests of eternity. He is essentially saying, "Take up your noose," "Take up the firing squad," or take up whatever manner of execution might come your way. The Disciples knew that the cross was the Romans' form of execution. Christ is telling them to pick it up. Be prepared to die to follow Christ.

If you follow Christ faithfully, the world is going to come after you. The world will label the sinner a *hypocrite*, though Christ labels the sinner *forgiven*. Pastors, do not let the fear of death control you. Do not let the desire to please the world override the desire to please Christ. You have a critical responsibility in these perilous times to speak the truth in love. See it not as a curse, but—as it truly is—a blessing: "Blessed are those who are persecuted for righteousness' sake, for theirs is the kingdom of heaven" (Matt. 5:10).

Let me leave you with this perspective from David McNeely, drawn from a reflection on John 21 and what it means to be called to follow Christ as a pastor in America today:

> We have enjoyed an unprecedented period of time in which the church has been able to flourish with very little opposition. So, **when we talk about persecution in America, we're talking about child's play here historically.** I don't know that we'll experience the same things they're experiencing in the Middle East, where Christian pastors are marched out into the streets, and their families' eyes are plucked out, or they're beheaded in front of them. I don't know that we'll go there in my lifetime, and hopefully never in America.
>
> That being said, the call remains. Jesus called Peter, and as he was looking back at John, Peter asked, "What about him?" **Jesus literally says, "If I want him to remain alive until I return what is that to you? You. Me. Follow."** My role as a pastor is to follow Jesus and remember the promise that he gave to his Disciples, "In this world you will have trouble." The way that we have defined trouble in America has been on various levels of minor to major inconvenience in life. The days ahead may include things that others would have experienced, such as Martin Luther King in the civil rights movement. It's entirely possible that there will be imprisonment for pastors. I don't see that coming quite yet, but the point is this: **Am I or am I not going to follow Jesus, who, as he walked the earth, experienced suffering, and persecution?** When Jesus says, "Follow me," we're following him into what John Piper says is an invitation to come and die, and it's usually a slow death over a period of time. So are we pastors going to follow Jesus or choose a fairly easy career? I haven't had to choose

that in the past. **But that day of decision is coming in America.**[12] [emphasis added]

That day is coming. It may be closer than we think. But the calling from Christ remains: *You. Me. Follow.*

PART II
THEN THEY MAKE
YOU CARE

CHAPTER 9

RAINBOW STICKERS AND SUPREME SILLINESS

*A system of government that makes the People subordinate
to a committee of nine unelected lawyers does not deserve to
be called a democracy.*

—ANTONIN SCALIA[1]

K im Davis is a Christian. She believes marriage is a sacred covenant between a man and a woman. She was elected to serve as the clerk of court in Rowan County, Kentucky. Part of her job description is to issue marriage licenses. When the U.S. Supreme Court redefined marriage in *Obergefell v. Hodges*, on June 26, 2015, Kim Davis refused to comply. On September 2, 2015, a federal judge found her in contempt of court and sent her to jail.[2] Not fined, not reprimanded, but jailed for her faith. Some are comparing her to Rosa Parks, Martin Luther King Jr., and others who've stood up for their beliefs and been carted off to jail as a result. But it didn't need to be this way.

By all accounts, Kim Davis is a relatively new convert to Christi-anity. Her faith seems sincere. Yet I think she weakened her case in a way that Christians must be careful not to do in these times of testing. Permit me to explain. In an attempt to avoid claims of discrimination, Davis stopped issuing marriage licenses altogether.[3] The laws of the Commonwealth of Kentucky require her to issue marriage licenses. When she was elected to office, she took an oath to issue marriage licenses for heterosexual couples. In other words, she stopped doing the job that voters had elected her to do. Had she continued to issue licenses to heterosexual couples, she could have made the claim that she was doing her job consistent with the laws of Kentucky. But when she put all marriage licenses on hold, she did what Christians should not do in the face of secular oppression—fail to do their duties to the extent possible before God.

In fact, by refusing to issue marriage licenses at all, Davis not only weakened her position, she did exactly what Anthony Kennedy and the other four Supreme Court justices did in *Obergefell v. Hodges* when they overturned the law to fit their own personal preferences—and engaged in nothing less than supreme silliness.

Several other clerks have also refused to issue licenses, but without the fanfare surrounding Kim Davis's case.[4] One has also refused to issue any marriage licenses at all, just as Davis has done. I don't agree with how Davis has gone about it. But I do relate to her desire to do the right thing regardless of what secular tyrants may say.

Regardless of her methods, Kim Davis didn't deserve to be thrown in jail. San Francisco mayor Gavin Newsom forced government clerks to issue marriage licenses for same-sex couples in violation of state law in California, and none of them was thrown in jail.[5] When the mayors of Los Angeles and New York refused to enforce immigration laws, declaring their cities to be "sanctuary cities," they were not incarcerated. When Barack Obama's administration refused to enforce the Defense of Marriage Act passed by Congress and signed into law by President Clinton,[6] no one carted him off to a cozy cell. There was no need for the imprisonment theatrics in Kim Davis's case—except to send a message to others that such behavior would not be tolerated. She could have been fined. No doubt donations would have poured in to support her.

At the time of this writing, the situation remains unresolved. Kentucky officials should make arrangements for government employees such as Davis to perform the duties they were elected or hired to do while still preserving their consciences. And Kim Davis should be open to working with them. As "aliens and strangers" in the world, Christians should not expect the secular culture around them to conform to their beliefs. But it is not unreasonable to expect a culture that prides itself on tolerance to figure out a way to protect consciences. Unless we have laws that protect the right of people of faith to object, there will be some elected offices in which Christians and people of conscience cannot serve—a sad commentary for a country founded on the principle of religious freedom.

THE DISASTER OF *OBERGEFELL*

The Supreme Court decision in the case of *Obergefell v. Hodges* was a significant cultural marker for our country. My friend Hunter Baker called it a divorce between the America built on Judeo-Christian beliefs and the postmodern America embracing a new secular religion.

I saw it coming. Actually, a lot of people did. But Anthony Kennedy and his four progressive allies on the court went further than I thought they would dare to go. I thought they would say that states can choose not to redefine marriage for themselves but, under the full faith and credit clause, they must recognize same-sex marriages from other states. That would have eventually gotten them where they wanted to go. Instead, they declared the right for anyone to marry anyone to be a fundamental right under both the due process and equal protection clauses of the Constitution—making the decision far more dangerous for other fundamental rights also protected by the Constitution. Because those rights precede this newly imagined right, it can be argued that the new right that the Supreme Court claims to have discovered in *Obergefell* overrules those older rights—such as freedom of religion—as something new and better—a replacement right, if you will. Under the equal protection clause, all people in protected classes are treated equally. So every race, creed, religion, ethnicity must be treated equally. And because they're all treated equally, there's a *greater good* aspect that you can't discriminate among these groups. What the court did in practice was to add "sexual orientation" to that list—*without defining sexual orientation.* The bottom line is that the ruling created protection under the law for a class of people based on *nothing more than what they say they feel*. Because sexual orientation may now be viewed as a part of the greater good of society, you can believe that homosexuality is a sin, but you cannot act on that belief in public life. That's how this new interpretation—an exercise in jurisprudential calisthenics—can trump the free exercise clause and take away our constitutional right to freedom of religion. As Chief Justice John Roberts warned, "Religious believers can take no comfort from the majority's opinion today."[7] And since we are all believers in something, no American, even those celebrating the ruling, will find much comfort in it in the years to come.

Essentially what the Supreme Court did was finalize a trend we've seen accelerating for the last forty years: the Constitution is no longer viewed as a legal document ordering governmental relations among the states, between the states and federal government, and between the people and the governments. It has now become an aspirational cultural document in which people can find new rights and liberties—and even meaning for their lives. The Constitution has been redefined as an organic document from which new rights can be derived. It has moved beyond being an instrument for organizing government to an instrument for organizing your life. In the *Oberge-fell* decision, the U.S. Supreme Court let its newly invented constitutional right to shape your own identity trump the free exercise of religion in America. Justice Kennedy has consistently advocated such postmodernist drivel for decades, going all the way back to *Planned Parenthood v. Casey*, in which he said, "At the heart of liberty is the right to define one's own concept of existence, of meaning, of the universe, and of the mystery of human life."[8] His majority opinion in *Obergefell*, which cites mostly his own rulings as legal precedent, reads more like love poetry than law. It could have just as easily been written by Walt Whitman, the American transcendentalist poet who penned the famously self-absorbed lines:

> I celebrate myself, and sing myself,
> And what I assume you shall assume....[9]

I concur with Justice Antonin Scalia's thoughts on the emotionally charged, self-absorbed ruling: "If, even as the price to be paid for a fifth vote, I ever joined an opinion for the Court that began: 'The Constitution promises liberty to all within its reach, a liberty that includes certain specific rights that allow persons, within a lawful realm, to define and express their identity,' **I would hide my head in a bag.** The Supreme Court of the United States has descended from the disciplined legal reasoning of John Marshall and Joseph Story to **the mystical aphorisms of the fortune cookie**"[emphasis added].[10]

In addition to being the host of a nationally syndicated radio program, Hugh Hewitt also teaches constitutional law at the Chapman University School of Law and has lectured on the subject for two decades. Although I am an attorney, I asked Hugh if he could translate the legal jargon of the *Obergefell* ruling into everyday language. Here's how he describes it:

> [I]t boils down to this: if the government is acting any-where, at any time, in any form, even if that government is a school board, even if that government is a coalition of high schools playing sports together, some of which are private, some of which are public—if the government is involved, if they're giving a college money, the government may not act toward people of different races differently. That's the Fourteenth Amendment. We passed the Four-teenth Amendment to provide privileges or immunities and due process and equal protection to all Americans. At the time, it was intended to remove the badges of slavery from African Americans, who'd just been emancipated by the Thirteenth Amendment.
>
> Over time the Fourteenth Amendment has become the vehicle for assuring that not only are certain classes of citizens protected from invidious discrimination, based upon their race, or their religious belief, or their gender, and not only those, but also certain fundamental rights—the right to travel, the right to marry, the right to procreate, the right not to procreate. These rights have been explained by the court as being anchored in the Fourteenth Amend-ment's commitment to due process and equal protection.
>
> Until very recently, it was never thought that sexual ori-entation was among the suspect classes, nor was the right to marry someone of the same sex among the fundamental rights. But in [*Obergefell*] it was decided that the latter is true, that the fundamental right of marriage must be extended to any two people in the United States, provided they are of age and within the standard laws against being too closely related.

> **And that is a new revelation.... The idea that the court found this new right is troubling because clearly it wasn't intended in the 1800s, when the Fourteenth Amendment was framed and ratified in the aftermath of the Civil War. But the court uses a living, breathing document, and, therefore, now a fundamental right is the right to marry someone of your same sex.[11] [emphasis added]**

I want to be careful to point out that the *Obergefell* ruling stops short, though just barely, of giving the gay mafia its entire wish list. Charles LiMandri, founder of the Conscience Defense Fund and longtime legal advocate for religious liberty, makes this important point:

> The gay lobby wanted the Supreme Court to come out and specifically state it is a protected class; it certainly moved in that direction. You even have Justice Kennedy, who wrote the majority decision, saying twice that homosexuality is immutable, citing the American Psychological Association's *amicus brief*, which, by the way, nowhere states it is immutable. They don't reach that conclusion. They go far toward it, but that holding has not been made yet. But that is the next step to end the debate.[12]

One very disturbing aspect of the *Obergefell* ruling is that five members of a Supreme Court that is highly unrepresentative of the country as a whole are telling a majority of people in a majority of states that they are wrong on something so basic to human existence as the definition of marriage. The court's decision short-circuited a conversation that was evolving in the direction of support for gay marriage. Polling after the decision suggests that now suddenly most Americans are *not* in favor of gay marriage.[13] So you can argue that the Supreme Court manufactured a right and set it back at the same time, meanwhile increasing animosity and division in the country by short-circuiting democracy. We have become an oligarchy more than a democracy. The whims of five unrepresentative people on the Supreme Court who can't be held accountable save for impeachment are now dictating the moral standards in America.

In his dissenting opinion, Justice Scalia made this blistering critique:

> Judges are selected precisely for their skill as lawyers; whether they reflect the policy views of a particular constituency is not (or should not be) relevant. Not surprisingly then, the Federal Judiciary is hardly a cross-section of America. Take, for example, this Court, which consists of only nine men and women, all of them successful lawyers who studied at Harvard or Yale Law School. Four of the nine are natives of New York City. **Eight of them grew up in east- and west-coast States. Only one hails from the vast expanse in-between.** Not a single Southwesterner or even, to tell the truth, a genuine Westerner (California does not count). **Not a single evangelical Christian (a group that comprises about one quarter of Americans), or even a Protestant of any denomination.** The strikingly unrepresentative character of the body voting on today's social upheaval would be irrelevant if they were functioning as judges, answering the legal question whether the American people had ever ratified a constitutional provision that was understood to proscribe the traditional definition of marriage. But of course the Justices in today's majority are not voting on that basis; they say they are not. And to allow the policy question of same-sex marriage to be considered and resolved by a select, patrician, highly unrepresentative

panel of nine is to violate a principle even more fundamental than no taxation without representation: **no social transformation without representation**.[14] [emphasis added]

The secular oligarchy, led by Apostle Kennedy, has received new and special revelation from the Spirit of the Age. It has recorded this message in the sacred text of progressives—a Supreme Court decision. Like Pharaoh in *The Ten Commandments*, the oligarchy has spoken and expects to be obeyed: "So let it be written. So let it be done."[15] Like Pharaoh and the Egyptian hosts, the oligarchs may be in for a rude awakening.

YOU DON'T NEED A RAINBOW STICKER ...

The Left has been quite successful at portraying gay marriage as a civil rights issue. But obviously it was not a civil rights issue when the Fourteenth Amendment was ratified—in 1868. It was not a civil rights issue even in the 1960s. It has only been portrayed as a civil rights issue in the past ten years. Even many conservatives who should know better have fallen for the argument that being black and being homosexual are somehow morally equivalent. It's a comparison I find to be offensive and grossly disrespectful to all the brave leaders who sacrificed so much to ensure racial equality. Nevertheless, the gay rights movement is intent on equating the struggle for black civil rights with their own quest to redefine marriage.

You don't need a rainbow sticker on your car to tell the world you are black. Or Asian. Or a woman. The struggles for civil rights and for equality between genders and races are inherently and objectively different from the gay rights movement, which seeks to define a legally protected class of people based solely on what they say they feel or, even worse, what they say they do in their bedrooms. It is the first time we have defined a protected class based on someone's self-proclaimed identity, not their objective identity. When you allow a subjective identity to define a protected class, legal standards begin to break down, because legal standards depend on objectivity.

Yet the gay agenda depends on equating the two struggles. Through mythology [insert your favorite historic person and he'll probably be declared gay], pseudoscience [you're born gay, but you pick your gender], and organized harassment of critics, the gay rights movement silences dissent to establish legitimacy in its quest for normalcy. The Stonewall riots are their Selma. Pay no attention to the absence of dogs in the street, poll taxes at the voting booth, and "heterosexual only" water fountains. That isn't stopping the Left from trying to use the cry of discrimination to pummel all who oppose its agenda into compliance.

We've been conditioned to think that all discrimination is bad. But that's simply not the case. You discriminate all the time. So do I. Essentially, every individual discriminates in some fashion. Gay rights activists refrain from eating at Chick-fil-A because the company funds traditional marriage organizations. Abortion rights activists boycott Domino's Pizza because its founder contributes to pro-life organizations. Obamacare advocates boycott Papa John's because of its owner's comments on Obamacare. Many evangelical Christian churches have stopped serving Starbucks on Sunday mornings because Starbucks actively contributes to both gay marriage and abortion rights organizations.

Religious organizations, like individuals, discriminate on the basis of their religion. Some do not have female pastors. Some require that teachers be single and celibate unless married. Some require that married couples be heterosexual. Only certain kinds of discrimination are wrong. The Supreme Court has previously held that race-based discrimination is pernicious and that there is a compelling governmental interest in prohibiting it that applies even to religious organizations. That seems reasonable to most of us. And it has an obvious basis in the Constitution. After all, the Fourteenth Amendment actually was written and ratified to outlaw discrimination against black Americans. If the government has a compelling interest in preventing a certain kind of discrimination, that interest will trump citizens' First Amendment rights to exercise their religion freely—as in the case of the Mormon Church and laws against polygamy, which the Supreme Court has upheld as constitutional. Incidentally, that's why gay rights activists say they only want religious freedom protection with "non-discrimination" provisions. What they are really saying is that they want to force *their own views* on churches and the religious.

What we see today with the attacks on our freedom of conscience, such as throwing Kim Davis in jail or harassing grandmothers and photographers into compliance, is very different from the civil rights–era *Heart of Atlanta Motel* case that dealt with discrimination against blacks in this country. There is no business I am aware of that has a "no gays allowed" policy. Rest assured, if there were, the media would be all over it. The question that has come into play within the last decade is a very different one—whether two people of the same sex can be married. For several thousand years, the answer has always been *no*. Gays had just as much right to marry as straight people. We all had the freedom to marry someone of the opposite sex. Equality has never been the issue.

The other issue is not whether a business can deny service to someone who's gay, but whether it can refuse to perform or provide goods and services for a wedding ceremony under this newly invented definition of marriage. It is not an argument about discrimination against a person or persons. It is a question of condoning one specific act. In just the same way that a black baker shouldn't say, *No whites allowed*, but he can say, *I'm not baking a cake for a KKK rally*, a Christian baker should be able to say, *I'm not baking a cake for a gay wedding ceremony* while being prohibited from saying, *No gays allowed.*

In this brave new world of supreme silliness and rainbow stickers, we must find a way to move forward together as a nation—without putting believers in jail. Hugh Hewitt is right when he says, "We're really into an uncharted area. A giant clash between tectonic plates is occurring between elite opinion and traditional opinion. It's stirring up mountains of disagreement that we have to figure out how to get up and down safely without destroying the country in the process."[16]

CHAPTER 10

WHAT DIFFERENCE DOES IT MAKE?

Marriage is the unexamined assumption of our time.
—ANDREW T. WALKER AND ERIC TEETSEL[1]

"What difference at this point does it make?"[2]
We've all heard that line from Hillary Clinton—someone I don't quote very often.

But I hear the same question a lot these days from Americans, especially millennials, about marriage. When it comes to the Supreme Court's redefining marriage as something other than between a man and a woman, they're asking, *What difference does it make? Why should I care who gets married to whom?*

It's a question that previous generations could never have imagined anyone asking. Marriage has been "the unexamined assumption of our time."[3] But given the Left's infatuation with progress and societal evolution, no assumptions can remain unquestioned.

It has always been this way is now sufficient grounds to overturn it—whatever *it* may happen to be.

Christian apologist G. K. Chesterton challenged the wisdom of such thinking, which automatically devalues the past as irrelevant:

> In the matter of reforming things, as distinct from deform-ing them, there is one plain and simple principle; a principle which will probably be called a paradox. There exists in such a case a certain institution or law; let us say, for the sake of simplicity, a fence or gate erected across a road. The more modern type of reformer goes gaily up to it and says, "I don't see the use of this; let us clear it away." To which the more intelligent type of reformer will do well to answer: "If you don't see the use of it, I certainly won't let you clear it away. Go away and think. Then, when you can come back and tell me that you do see the use of it, I may allow you to destroy it."[4]

So my first response to those who see no reason why we should not reimagine the social institution of marriage is to ask: Before you tear down the institution all of humanity built and affirmed for millennia, do you know why marriage exists in the first place? And if not, perhaps you should go away and find out—*before* you destroy it.

FIRST COMES LOVE, THEN COMES MARRIAGE ...

I don't pretend to be an expert on all the *-ologies* connected with marriage—biology, philosophy, sociology, theology. Many other experts have written entire volumes on these subjects, so I will not attempt an exhaustive defense, although I encourage everyone to read the books I reference here if you are serious about understanding marriage before dismantling it.

Why is it that every civilization, with or without any organized religion, has recognized the importance of marriage? Even the Greeks, who, in some instances, prioritized homosexual relationships over heterosexual ones, never dared meddle with the institution of marriage. It was as if they saw it as essential to the flourishing of society. Hugh Hewitt, explaining the value of marriage to a younger generation, often compares it to a load-bearing wall in a house:

> I use an analogy of a home. Whether or not they know it, there are weight-bearing walls in every house, walls that you cannot remove without endangering the structural viability of the house. I believe that **marriage is the weight-bearing wall of the West, because it produces healthy children.** The West has always, from Roman times, from Greek times, understood the family as being the weight-bearing wall of civilization. What we did in the last fifteen years, *vis-a-vis* marriage, is put a door in that weight-bearing wall.... **From a political theory basis and from a theological basis, both the philosophers and God, as I understand it in Revelation, have said, "Don't mess around with that weight-bearing wall. Bad things will happen."**[5] [emphasis added]

Robert P. George is the McCormick Professor of Jurisprudence at Princeton University and a visiting professor at Harvard Law School. In *Conscience and Its Enemies* he offers this introductory explanation of what marriage is and why it matters for everyone, not just people of faith:

> Marriage is an all-encompassing sharing of life. It involves, like other bonds, a union of hearts and minds—but also, and distinctively, **a bodily union made possible by the**

sexual-reproductive complementarity of man and woman. Hence it is ordered to the all-encompassing goods of procreation and family life, and it calls for **an all-encompassing commitment,** one that is pledged to **permanence and sexual exclusivity** and fidelity.... Marriage unites a husband and wife holistically, not merely in an emotional bond but also on the bodily plane in acts of conjugal love and in the children such love brings forth—for the whole of life....

These insights into the nature of marriage as a human good require no particular theology. They are, to be sure, consistent with Judeo-Christian faith, yet thinkers untouched by Jewish or Christian revelation—including Aristotle, Plato, Socrates, Musonius Rufus, Xenophanes, and Plutarch—also distinguished conjugal unions from all others, as do many nonbiblical faiths to this day. **Nor did animus against particular persons or categories of person produce this conclusion,** which arose in various cultures long before the modern concept of "sexual orientation."[6] [emphasis added]

Marriage has always been understood to be about two people becoming "one flesh" in a permanent and exclusive way, oriented around the purpose of procreation. Even in circumstances where reproduction was not possible (infertility or disability), the organizing purpose has been the same—to become one entity as only a man and woman can do. In *What Is Marriage? Man and Woman: A Defense,* George is joined by one of the leading advocates for marriage today, my friend Ryan T. Anderson, as well as Sherif Girgis. Their book is an intellectually robust defense of marriage. The coauthors describe the two choices we face:

The conjugal view of marriage has long informed the law— along with the literature, art, philosophy, religion, and

social practice—of our civilization. It is a vision of marriage as a bodily as well as an emotional and spiritual
bond, distinguished thus by its comprehensiveness, which
is, like all love, *effusive*: flowing out into the wide sharing
of family life and ahead to lifelong fidelity. In marriage, so
understood, the world rests its hope and finds ultimate
renewal.

A second, revisionist, view has informed the marriage
policy reforms of the last several decades. It is a vision of
marriage as, in essence, a moving emotional bond, one
distinguished by its intensity—a bond that needn't point
beyond the partners, in which fidelity is ultimately subject
to its own desires. In marriage, so understood, partners
seek emotional fulfillment, and remain as long as they find
it.[7]

These two views of marriage, the conjugal and revisionist,
emphasize different aspects of the institution. The former revolves
around reproduction of the species and providing a stable environment in which offspring can be reared; the latter centers on the
feelings one person has toward another at any given time. But
everyone who has ever experienced family knows that feelings make
for a flimsy foundation for healthy relationships. As the *What Is
Marriage?* authors note, "People really unite by sharing a [common]
good, but feelings are inherently private realities...we have no
direct control over them."[8] My parents' marriage did not survive
for fifty years because they always felt good about one another. No
marriage does. Unfortunately, we live in a society that has decided
that marriage should be all about personal feelings. Anthony Kennedy said as much in his majority opinion in *Obergefell*, essentially
claiming that people are entitled to whatever relationships make
them happy—and we should call those relationships *marriage*. But

happiness is the byproduct of a healthy marriage—the more you work on oneness in your marriage, the happier you become—not what makes a relationship a marriage in the first place.

At its most basic level, marriage is the making of a completed soul, which then produces more souls. To put it bluntly, you need both the male and female connection, not only anatomically—a biological fact necessary for reproduction—but metaphysically. Men and women are different. And marriage requires what each of them brings to the relationship. God, in Genesis, took a part of Adam to make Eve. Marriage joins man and woman together in completion. Dr. Brian Mattson sums up the reality: "We cannot eradicate the fundamental biological truth that man plus woman equals children."[9]

The authors of *What Is Marriage?* explain, "In coitus, and there alone, a man and woman's bodies participate by virtue of their sexual complementarity in a coordination that's the biological purpose of reproduction—a function that neither can perform alone."[10] It's not complicated, really. Once we get past the emotions distorting our view, we see that marriage requires an essential link to procreation. The authors conclude: "In short, marriage is ordered to family life because the act by which spouses make love also makes new life; one and the same act both seals a marriage and brings forth children. That is why marriage alone is the loving union of mind and body fulfilled by the procreation—and rearing—of whole new human beings. Relationships of two men, two women, or more than two, whatever their moral status, cannot be marriages because they lack this inherent link to procreation."[11]

It is no coincidence that the very first instruction given by God to Adam and Eve was to "be fruitful and multiply" (Gen. 1:28). Although their relationship was to be about so much more than sex, reproducing was the foremost reason God created them for one another as the first husband and wife. The ability to be part of the making of new life was essential to the first marriage and to all that would follow.

The simple truth is that when God says man should not be alone, he doesn't create another man. He takes Adam's rib and from it forms a woman. It would have been a whole lot simpler to just make another man, but there would have been no ability to reproduce. Game over.

So marriage revolves around reproductive sex. But still, why should we care? In *Same-Sex Marriage: A Thoughtful Approach to God's Design for Marriage*, John Stonestreet and Sean McDowell point out that "what happens in the bedroom doesn't stay in the bedroom." Sex has public consequences, and marriage ensures that men and women take responsibility for those consequences: "Marriage marks two people as sexual partners and makes them publically responsible for their sexual behavior. This is important because **sex, though (hopefully) done in private, has very public consequences.** Forced sex brings fear to an entire community. Procreative sex creates new life that must be cared for and integrated into the community. Promiscuous sex risks the mental and physical health of many in the community. Underage sex jeopardizes the potential of the community. Marital sex secures the future of the community" [emphasis added].[12]

Dr. Russell Moore makes a similar point: "Marriage isn't just a registering of *this is my special someone*. Marriage is about connecting the generations in the past, mother and father together, and connecting this union and this couple with generations that are to come...."[13] My friend Maggie Gallagher, the cofounder of the National Organization for Marriage, editor of ThePulse2016.com, and coauthor of *Debating Same-Sex Marriage*, cuts through the clutter to state succinctly, "Sex makes babies. Society needs babies. Babies deserve mothers and fathers." Gallagher makes the connection between marriage and what is best for children:

> Social institutions arise to solve problems that are social, not merely individual. If it's just *my* problem, either I solve it or I don't, and that makes my life better or worse. But

when you see something called *marriage* arising again and again in so many different societies, it's pointing to the deep human need. It's really the difference between organized human sexuality and disorganized human sexuality. And in our case, **our strong monogamous marriage system is deeply rooted in the idea that every child has a right to the protection and care of his mother and father; it's terrible when a child is subordinated to the sexual interests of adults,** and yet from abortion to gay marriage, that's really the society that we're creating. We're saying if someone has to suffer, let it be the child, not the adult. As a result, we're creating both more adult and child suffering because we're not pointing arrows toward the only home where sex and love can be compatible, which is this idea of **a marriage commitment oriented to the good of family.**[14] [emphasis added]

WHAT ABOUT THE CHILDREN?

We know from all the sociological evidence that children who have a two-parent heterosexual nuclear household do better in life long term. Even the progressive-friendly Child Trends admits it: "[R]esearch clearly demonstrates that family structure matters for children, and the family structure that helps children the most is a family headed by two biological parents in a low-conflict marriage.... [I]t is not simply the presence of two parents...but the presence of two biological parents that seems to support children's development."[15]

Children who grow up in a family with two biological parents are less likely to be impacted by arrests, drug addiction, and lack of academic advancement. Across all cultures and ethnicities, the two-parent nuclear household has historically been the best way to keep society perpetuating itself and stable at the same time. When dads are not present, for example, children suffer. Having a biological mother and father in the home produces vastly more stable, productive future members of society. No one disputed that fact until the last decade or so. And yet, as Brian Mattson points out, "All of these redefinitions [of marriage and gender] are taking place with *zero* consideration for children. These are all manifestations of adults expressing themselves and who they feel themselves to be. Justice Kennedy's reasoning in *Obergefell* was strictly about self-actualization. Anybody who knows anything about civil marriage knows that those marriage laws are there to protect children. [Yet] Justice Kennedy hardly mentioned children in his entire opinion."[16]

The New Family Structures Study (NFSS) is the first to make a direct comparison of heterosexual parents with homosexual parents using large, representative samples. Lead researcher Mark Regnerus published the first article based on the findings in the journal *Social Science Research* in June 2012. The study shows "rather clearly that children raised by gay or lesbian parents on average are at a significant disadvantage when compared to children raised by the intact family of their married, biological mother and father."[17] But to those who hate the truth, truth sounds like hate. The Left has viciously attacked Regnerus for daring to study the impact of redefining marriage.

The NFSS revealed much that progressives do not want to acknowledge:

> "The empirical claim that no notable differences exist must go," University of Texas sociology professor Mark Regnerus said in his study in Social Science Research.
>
> Using a "gold standard" data set of nearly 3,000 randomly selected American young adults, Mr. Regnerus looked at their lives on 40 measures of social, emotional and relationship outcomes.

He found that, when compared with adults raised in married, mother-father families, adults raised by lesbian mothers had negative outcomes in 24 of 40 categories, while adults raised by gay fathers had negative outcomes in 19 categories.[18]

The Family Research Council has summarized five key points from the NFSS:

1. **The "intact biological family" remains the normative setting for child-rearing in America today.** Although social reengineers are fond of dismissing the "traditional" nuclear family as an unrealistic relic of a bygone era, "58% of the 15,058 persons screened [for the study] report spending their entire youth—up until they turned 18 or left the house—with their biological mother and father."

2. **Children do better when raised by their own, married mother and father.** Even *without* the data on children whose parents had same-sex relationships, the NFSS would be a significant contributor to the already large body of evidence showing the superiority of the "intact biological family" over all other household structures.

3. **Children suffer when raised by homosexual parents—** not only in comparison to being reared by a married mother and father, but also in comparison to *all* other family structures. [That's not homophobic or hateful, just truthful. And speaking that truth shows compassion for children.]

4. **Homosexual relationships are intrinsically "unstable."** The fact that only two of over 200 children with a parent who had a same-sex relationship lived with that

parent and his or her partner from birth to age 18 shows how extraordinarily rare "stable gay relationships" really are.

5. **Public policy should continue to encourage the raising of children by a married mother and father,** while discouraging, attempting to reduce, and/or refusing to affirm or subsidize alternatives such as out-of-wedlock births, single parenthood, cohabitation, divorce, *or* "homosexual parenting."[19] [all emphasis in original]

A similar study, by Douglas Allen, published in the journal *Review of the Economics of the Household* (2013), was based on census data in Canada, where same-sex marriage has been legal since 2005. Drawing from a 20 percent sample of the census, Allen says three key findings stood out: "[C]hildren of married opposite-sex families have a high graduation rate compared to the others; children of lesbian families have a very low graduation rate compared to the others; and the other four types [common law, gay, single mother, single father] are similar to each other and lie in between the married/lesbian extremes."[20]

In general, same-sex couples often had higher-than-normal levels of education themselves, but their children performed quite poorly in school compared with others. Allen found that "girls living in gay households are only 15 percent as likely to graduate [from high school] compared to girls from opposite-sex married homes."[21]

The reality is this: kids do best when reared by their own moms and dads. For most of us, this is common sense—but not for the Left. "[W]e should disavow the notion that 'mommies can make good daddies,'" says David Popenoe, Rutgers University sociologist, "just as we should disavow the popular notion...that 'daddies can make good mommies....' The two sexes are different to the core, and each is necessary—culturally and biologically—for the optimal development of a human being."[22] If we want society to flourish, we would be wise to take a second look at the fence of marriage that progressives are bull-dozing. The democracy of the dead, as Chesterton describes the generations who have preceded us, recognized and protected marriage as being oriented around sexual reproduction for many reasons, not the least of which is the creation and rearing of healthy children for the future of civilization.

The well-being of yet-to-be-born children, however, has never been a high priority for the Left.

CHAPTER 11

ABOLISHING MARRIAGE

Fighting for gay marriage generally involves lying about what we are going to do with marriage when we get there.

—MASHA GESSEN[1]

A fter the Supreme Court ruled on *Obergefell*, social media was full of celebrations of #marriageequality—as if that were the issue at stake. For some, perhaps even most, gay advocates, the appearance of normal is what they wanted. But for many others, including those driving the sexual revolution movement on the Left, equality has nothing to do with it.

They do not want to be included in marriage. They want to destroy it—and all who dare oppose them. And they have begun by altering the definition of the word *marriage*. As I noted in the last chapter, marriage cannot be redefined to mean same-sex anything. Any union that is not "made possible by the sexual-reproductive complementarity of man and woman"[2] is not marriage.

By altering the definition of the word, they have not expanded it for use by others, but destroyed it—for the benefit of none. Robert P. George exposes the results of stripping marriage of its conjugal core: "In truth what they have done is abolish marriage as a legal category and replace it with something quite different—legally recognized sexual-romantic companionship or domestic *partnership*—to which the label *marriage* has been reassigned. So, strictly speaking, **we are talking not so much about a redefinition as an abolition of marriage**" [emphasis added].[3]

Respected theologian N. T. Wright gives a dire warning about the danger of redefining key words:

> **When anybody—pressure groups, governments, civilizations—suddenly change the meaning of key words, you really should watch out.** If you go to a German dictionary and just open at random, you may well see several German words which have a little square bracket saying "N.S.," meaning National Socialist or Nazi. The Nazis gave those words a certain meaning. In post-1917 Russia, there were whole categories of people who were called "former persons," because by the Communist diktat they had ceased to be relevant for the state, and once you call them former persons it was extremely easy to ship them off somewhere and have them killed.[4] [emphasis added]

Words have meaning. They serve as tags for ideas. And ideas have consequences. Many well-intentioned Americans, even many people of faith, have bought into the language of equality and compassion while marriage, the most basic building block of society, is being abolished before them. They refuse to believe that there may be another agenda for sexual progressives intent on forcing their religion upon the rest of us. Maggie Gallagher, cofounder of the National

Organization for Marriage, is one person who saw this coming decades ago: "I became aware very early that gay marriage was not just about having Tom and Steve have access to some nice benefits to let them live their lives. It was about creating and using the power of government to institutionalize a new moral norm, which is what marriage equality, as they now call it, means…. **The big lie is that we're just going to add some new people to the existing institution of marriage, and that will help them, and life will just go along the same**" [emphasis added].[5]

To understand the Left's agenda when it comes to marriage, we must face the reality that progressives see marriage between one man and one woman as an oppressive institution, standing in the way of the Gospel of Societal Evolution. They are championing the Spirit of the Age; they're the ones on the right side of history. Lest we forget, however, it was Soviet Communist premier Nikita Khrushchev who pounded his shoe upon the lectern at the United Nations, claiming, "Whether you like it or not, history is on our side and we will bury you."[6] We saw how well that turned out for him. It has been said that those who do not learn from the mistakes of the past are condemned to repeat them. But what if they don't think of them as mistakes?

If you want a sample of the truly mind-bending ideology behind the Left's push for equality, check this out: Masha Gessen is a prominent lesbian reporter whose work appears in such publications as the *New York Times*, the *Los Angeles Times*, and *U.S. News & World Report*. In other words, she is not a fringe voice. In an interview with ABC Radio, she spoke bluntly of the Left's agenda: "It's a no-brainer that [homosexuals] should have the right to marry, but I also think equally that it's a no-brainer that **the institution of marriage should not exist**…. [F]ighting for gay marriage generally involves lying about what we are going to do with marriage when we get there—because **we lie that the institution of marriage is not going to change, and that** is a lie.... The institution of marriage is going to change, and it should change. And again, I don't think it should exist" [emphasis added].[7]

Gessen is not alone. Far from it. Consider an article that appeared in *Slate* shortly after the *Obergefell* decision legalizing same-sex marriage. The topic was LGBT movement strategy going forward. Tamara Metz, associate professor at Reed College, argued that the next step is to "[a]bolish the legal category [of marriage]. Even as we savor the victory for civil equality this week, **we should start to push for disestablishing marriage**" [emphasis added].[8] In other words, if you like your marriage, you can keep your marriage—until it is abolished altogether.

What is to replace conjugal marriages between one man and one woman? Well, that may require some familial calisthenics that, to quote Hillary Clinton yet again, "would require the willful suspension of disbelief."[9] Masha Gessen gives us a glimpse of the brave new post-marriage world that lies ahead: "I have three kids who have five parents, more or less, and I don't see why they shouldn't have five parents legally.... I met my new partner, and she had just had a baby, and that baby's biological father is my brother, and my daughter's biological father is a man who lives in Russia, and my adopted son also considers him his father. So the five parents break down into two groups of three.... And really, I would like to live in a legal system that is capable of reflecting that reality, and **I don't think that's compatible with the institution of marriage**" [emphasis added].[10]

I'm pretty sure the closest thing to a legal system "capable of reflecting that reality" would be found in Toontown with Roger Rabbit and friends. Yet this is the belief system people on the Left want to impose upon us all, while crying that it is we who are imposing our faith upon them. The difference is that the conjugal view of marriage has been shown to work for over six thousand years of recorded civilization.

The madness burning like a wildfire across our culture will have appalling consequences. *Mere Orthodoxy* founder Matthew Lee Anderson warns that the need to make such blatant falsehoods about reality sound believable can only lead to one thing:

> Humans are fundamentally and inescapably truth-telling beings, and...falsehoods require an elaborate and complex support structure if they are to take hold and endure for a long period of time. A child might believe that Santa Claus is real and get on with the world just fine. But as they grow older, the kinds of backflips, self-deceptions, and tricks they would have to go through in order to maintain such a belief would be dazzling.
>
> Now, momentarily return to that peculiar and strange thought that same-sex sexual relationships, whatever other [perceived goods they] have, lack particular features which make heterosexual relationships morally unique. Given human sexuality's clear importance, and given humanity's truth-telling nature, what kind of artifice would need to be in place to support and sustain such a deception within a society over a long period of time? ... And once this structure is built, would it have the structural integrity to allow for meaningful and public dissent? Or would it be so fragile, because false, that it had to "stamp out" competing accounts of the world?...
>
> In other words...**same-sex marriage will lead to a soft-despotism *because it has to*.**[11] [boldface emphasis added]

As long as we have two-parent nuclear households in this crazy new society the Left wishes to construct, we have the *dangerous* potential for parents to instill their values in their children. And if those parents happen to be *deviant* Christians who believe that there is a God to whom they are accountable and who says there are things called *sins*, well then that God—myth that He is—must be made to care. The only way to stamp out this threat is to make parents vessels of the state through which the state, not the family, repopulates itself.

What we are witnessing with marriage is an attempt to shift societal order even beyond the worst decadence of Greco-Roman society. It is more and more obvious, based not only on how progressives are living their own lives, but also on how they expect others to live theirs, that they do indeed want to diminish or destroy the institution of marriage. They want to destabilize the family so that all must rely on a civil order that they control. I don't think they're ultimately going to be successful at it, but that won't stop them from trying to make us all homogeneous automatons indoctrinated in secular religious beliefs. By faith, they believe people are born gay. By faith, they believe that humans got marriage and child-rearing wrong for more than a thousand years. By faith, they believe that a society can remain healthy after biological parents no longer rear their own children.

Let me be frank: those proposing the abolition of marriage will eventually breed themselves out of existence. It's simple biology. Men can't have kids without women. Women can't have kids without men. Married couples will continue to reproduce *because they can.* The families that will thrive over time will be those in two-parent nuclear households. These families today tend to be disproportionately religious, and religious households also tend to procreate at a greater rate than most secular households. Therefore, over time we will have many more people indoctrinated under the traditional beliefs that the Left views as a threat to its desire to reorder society.

No wonder the Left is hostile to large families. Conservative and religious families are large; therefore, they are the evil ones with the largest carbon footprints. I don't think it's a coincidence that there has been a push to make cars smaller and smaller, thereby driving up the cost of having a large family. It's clear that the progressives have to undermine the family at its root. They have to be able to show that dads don't matter. They have to be able to show that moms and dads are interchangeable. Any evidence to the contrary must be declared flawed and bigoted. Their aim ultimately is to establish a society that is made in their own image of limited procreators—instead of all those bigoted Christian families running around.

Over time, we'll see government policy choices oriented around the good of single-parent homes rather than one dependent on families to sustain their own children. Because fewer people will have children to care for them as they age, public healthcare policy decisions will need to change. It is no coincidence that as the population of Europe has aged, with fewer children to care for the elderly, assisted-suicide rates have risen there. Because the family support system has broken down, people are just going ahead and ending their own lives rather than dying alone. The end result of the redefinition process is the creation of a culture of death.

But even in Europe it has been impossible for the government to stamp out the traditional family. Despite a major realignment in priorities in Europe, and deep hostility toward religion and the Christian families that still exist there, families continue to thrive. In Germany, where homeschooling is prohibited, you still have families indoctrinating their children in Christian values. Like life in the *Jurassic Park* film saga, truth always seems to find a way.[12]

Internationally renowned Christian speaker, thinker, and cultural apologist Ravi Zacharias warns of the dangers of tossing marriage aside:

> What is being forgotten in the process is there's a large center to the people across five thousand years of civilization. No matter which religious worldview you take—the

pantheistic worldview; the monotheistic worldviews; the spiritual worldviews that have come from the near East; and, of course, the zenith of all this, the Judeo-Christian worldview—[people agree] that sexuality is sacred. It is deemed sacred. **For a large volume of people, the monogamous, heterosexual union of marriage in the sacredness of commitment is the way it was intended to be.** The biblical view is an exaltation of what marriage is about. [If] you take that away and make that abnormal and make everything else normal, you have actually wiped out a whole lot of civilization's history and the sacredness of belief. To make all sexual choices purely a matter of freedom is to ultimately attack the sacred belief of millions of people. And it is more than just belief. You take the teachings of Jesus on marriage, you take the practice of the Hindu world or the Muslim world and so on, and whether we agree with all of the doctrines of these [religions] is really secondary; the most important thing is that they believe life at its core is sacred and that desacralization leads to what Chesterton said, that **the danger of disbelief in God is not that a person may end up believing in nothing; alas, it is much worse. A person may end up believing in *anything*.**[13]

That *anything* is what we are watching right now. Chesterton also said there's only one angle in which you can stand straight and many angles at which you can fall.[14] What will happen to the person who proposes this freedom to believe in any form? [What will happen] when polygamy becomes the norm, or any other kinds of choices become the norm, which they themselves are uncomfortable with? If you remove the fence, then there's nothing to stop any kind of belief. I think the dangers are huge for generations to come. Let me just give you a simple example. As we're talking I have just returned from one country overseas that I will leave unnamed. And my colleagues and I were startled in a nice hotel where we were staying to see the open carrying on of prostitution. This is a very, very fine place, a normal business-type hotel. Watching what was happening there in the lobby and outside was heartbreaking. As I was speaking to some political leadership the next day at a breakfast, I said, "These people are someone's daughters, someone's sons being marketed." While we were having dinner, we would see the same person being pedaled three or four times during an hour and a half. Is this really what we want in society? Is that where we are headed? What are the dangers that loom for the family, for homes?

At the core, people want fidelity. People want sacredness. People want some boundaries. **Where are we going to get those boundaries if we don't get it from the starting point of the sacredness of sexuality and marriage itself?**[15] [emphasis added]

Where indeed? The state did not create marriage, and it should not now try to redefine that which it did not create. Those of you who are Christians who support gay marriage will one day have the words of Leo Tolstoy burning in your ears: "Wrong doesn't cease to be wrong because the majority shares in it."[16] That's why Christians fight to defend marriage. It is not to force our faith on others, but to keep others from forcing what we believe to be morally wrong upon us.

CHAPTER 12

REDEFINING GENDER

The first effect of not believing in God is to believe in any-thing.

—G. K. CHESTERTON[1]

Marriage isn't the only thing being redefined these days. In the same week that the U.S. Supreme Court handed down its *Obergefell* ruling, a less noticed but equally important decision cleared the courts in New Jersey.

A Jewish Orthodox counseling agency, Jews Offering New Alternatives for Healing (JONAH), has offered resources and referrals to counselors for people with different types of sexual issues for the last fifteen years. JONAH has provided resources and materials that share its religious viewpoints on different behaviors. Its ministry has enabled hundreds to overcome same-sex attraction and other sexual temptations of all sorts. JONAH founder Arthur Goldberg

151

has invested thousands of hours in the organization as a labor of love, not charging anyone for the services received.

But in June 2015, a jury ruled the nonprofit agency to be guilty. The crime? Consumer fraud—claiming it could bring "healing" to men who wanted to overcome same-sex attraction. Four young men, former clients of JONAH, claimed that it had committed fraud by saying it could help men overcome same-sex attractions. With the help of the radically progressive Southern Poverty Law Center, the four men sued JONAH using New Jersey consumer-protection laws. JONAH's attorney, Freedom of Conscience Defense Fund president Charles LiMandri, has been a defender of religious liberty in numerous court cases over the past twelve years. According to LiMandri, New Jersey law made for a challenging defense: "The New Jersey Consumer Fraud Act is the most liberal in the country and is touted as such. You really don't have to show it was an intentional misrepresentation or even a negligent misrepresentation to subject one to liability. **Even if it's technically true but potentially misleading, it could subject one to liability. Even if the person who hears it doesn't believe it's true and doesn't rely on it, he can still sue under the act....**" [emphasis added].[2]

The essential issue at stake in the case was whether homosexuality is fixed and immutable. Because it is, according to the prosecution, claiming homosexuals can change is fraudulent. Since there is no scientific foundation for making the claim that homosexuality is fixed and immutable, LiMandri and JONAH thought they could defend themselves in spite of the liberal New Jersey laws. But that was before truth was barred from the courtroom. LiMandri explains: "The judge excluded all of our experts. We had six treatment experts in psychiatry, psychology, licensed professional counselors and the like. **The court ruled that none of them could testify on the threshold issue as to whether homosexuality is a disorder or abnormal because, from the court's point of view, that is a misstatement. [The judge said] he's** not going to let people testify to that.... So, that was the fatal blow. The other side had experts. We had no experts. We had these adverse rulings that pretty much directed a jury to find against my clients" [emphasis added].³

In a case that hinged on whether homosexuality was fixed, immutable, and normal, the judge would not permit anyone who challenged the secular dogma of the Spirit of the Age. LiMandri says, "We believe the lawsuit should have been dismissed because whether homosexuality is normal or abnormal or disordered or not really is an opinion...." But "the court found that [homosexual behavior] is basically normal and to say it's abnormal is a violation of the Consumer Fraud Act."

For daring to counsel people in a manner consistent with nearly every major world religion, JONAH was slapped with a $75,000 fine— a steep price for any nonprofit to pay. But the fine print of the judgment will raise the cost to a truly ruinous level. LiMandri explains that with court costs, JONAH will be liable for more than $3.5 million:

> [T]he real hammer here, besides the gross infringement of freedom of religion and freedom of speech, is that if you lose on the Consumer Fraud Act, you automatically have to pay the other side's attorneys' fees. The Southern Poverty Law Center had some fifteen attorneys working on the case, including attorneys from a big New York firm with over six hundred lawyers. They've already said **their attorneys' fees are going to be over $3.5 million!** ... [I]n terms of the type of punishment being levied against an organization for simply trying to help people live their lives in conformity with what the Bible teaches, **it really is the most onerous type of penalty that's come down in the history of this country** that we're aware of, based upon using the law as a weapon against those who don't share your ideological viewpoint....

[T]he judge actually made a statement when he was giving us the jury instructions that you can't even say [that homosexuality is disordered] if you're a rabbi in a synagogue, or by extension a pastor in his own church, unless you make it very clear you're only talking from a religious perspective. If you talk about it from a psychological perspective or **anything other than purely religious, that's a violation of the Consumer Fraud Act, even if you say it in church**. So, no one is safe under the thinking in this case. People need to know they're going to start using these consumer-fraud statutes all over the country to go after anybody who is willing to follow their religious beliefs and say homosexuality is abnormal.[4] [emphasis added]

The secular priests have spoken on the issue of same-sex attraction. They have declared it to be fixed and immutable. Homosexuals are born that way, and there is nothing they can—or should—do about it. (What ever happened to being pro-choice?) Any claims to the contrary have been ruled to be out of bounds—a ruling that will be enforced by costs in the millions of dollars. Of course, you don't have to agree with them, but you will be made to confine your opinions to your private faith box—even within the walls of your own church, synagogue, or mosque.

What I find most ironic is that we are told we cannot choose our sexual orientation—and yet we can redefine our gender as often as we want. Neither of these conflicting claims has any basis in reality. LiMandri notes the same thing:

The judge realized that even liberal professional organizations can't agree on what causes someone's sexuality. The American Psychiatric and Psychological Associations have both issued statements to the effect that many experts believe it's caused both by biological and environmental factors—so you've got the whole nature-versus-nurture thing. They said many experts think it's both. **If you don't know what causes it, it's kind of hard to really conclusively say it can't be changed; if it can be changed, it's not immutable.**

The plaintiffs were basically arguing it *is* immutable—once gay always gay—which is ironic, because [the Left] has no problem with saying people can go from straight to gay, or a man can change into a woman and a woman can change into a man despite their *immutable* chromosomes and their physical anatomy. But they would have people believe that no one can go from gay to straight...even though no professional organization holds that viewpoint. In essence, what was being said is that you can't change people. Maybe they can change on their own, but if you try, you're only going to end up hurting them—which is *ludicrous*.[5] [emphasis added]

In a state where Jimmy Hoffa and his mobster pals once ruled, the Jewish counselors at JONAH have been told by the gay mafia to take their faith for a long walk off a short pier—with $3.5 million in concrete footwear. At the time of this writing, their case is under appeal. If only they had counseled men with same-sex attraction to follow in the footsteps of a Photoshopped Olympic legend, they might have been spared the assault on their right to believe.

THE BRUCE JENNER FIASCO

I hope a lot of people are praying for Bruce Jenner, who won a gold medal in the men's decathlon at the 1976 Summer Olympics, and in April 2015 announced to Diane Sawyer on ABC that he would no longer be identifying as a man but rather as a woman named

Caitlyn. A little surgery later, Bruce appeared on the cover of *Vanity Fair* in an obviously touched-up photo. Hollywood and even the White House applauded Bruce when he decided to change his gender from *he* to *she*.[6] ESPN gave him the Arthur Ashe Courage Award ahead of other worthy candidates such as "Iraq War vet and double amputee Noah Galloway—a crossfit athlete, distance runner, and recent third-place finisher on 'Dancing With the Stars.'"[7] David French contrasts what he calls Jenner's "Hollywood courage" with Galloway's feats: "Noah Galloway, by contrast, sacrificed his body for his country—defending ESPN's right to make its pitiful cultural statements—then showed perseverance through pain that we can scarcely comprehend. But whatever. He has to marry Caitlyn Jenner for ESPN to care."[8]

Jenner now claims he was a woman all along. If so, journalist Patrick Howley is right—Jenner is the best female athlete *ever*: "The evidence is clear. Jenner is the only woman in Olympic history to finish a full decathlon, boldly breaking down barriers at the 1976 Montreal Games by defeating male athlete Guido Kratschmer of West Germany. In scoring a then-world record 8,616 points in the event, Caitlyn proved that one woman can set a new standard for ALL of the 31 different gender classifications."[9]

Washington Post opinion writer Jonathan Capehart says, "You don't have to like it. You don't even have to understand it. But you must respect [Bruce Jenner's] decision to come out as Caitlyn."[10]

No, Jonathan. Actually, we don't.

The Left applauded Bruce Jenner for trying to become something he is not and never can be. And it expected everyone else to applaud him, too. In fact, applauding Jenner is not enough. The applause must be *sufficient*. When ESPN presented Bruce Jenner with the Arthur Ashe Courage Award, cameras at the event caught former Green Bay Packers quarterback Brett Favre in the crowd. Favre clapped four times unenthusiastically, then rubbed his hands together. Left-wing activists went online to slam Favre for not being enthusiastic enough about Bruce Jenner getting a courage award.[11]

Bruce doesn't need applause. He needs therapy. When a sixty-five-year-old former Olympian tells you that he has decided after all these years that he is a she and that his new name is going to be one fashionable among seventeen-year-old girls, including his own son's girlfriend, your first reaction should not be to congratulate the man on finally finding his "authentic self,"[12] but to steer him toward professional help.

Look, I realize this is going to piss off those of you who already live in a perpetual state of pissed-offness, but if an alcoholic told you that his authentic self was to drink, you would not encourage that. If a person told you his authentic self was to be attracted to small boys, you would not encourage that. If a person told you that his authentic self was to mutilate his body, you would not encourage that. Or would you? As a matter of fact, that's exactly what our society is doing in Bruce Jenner's case. This is nuts...and, oh, by the way, Bruce Jenner still has his—for now.

An authentic self needs no surgery and hormone therapy. He is not a she. It is not bigoted to point that out. It is reality. We need to show Bruce Jenner compassion for his mental issues, not celebrate the nutty choices his issues are driving him to make. But we live in a society where up is down, bad is good, and normal is so passé. All must bow and pay homage to the Spirit of the Age. Bruce Jenner certainly has issues. But the bigger issue for us is that society itself has become mentally sick—celebrating an extreme form of mental illness that really deserves our compassion.

Vanity Fair does not care about Bruce Jenner. It cares about selling magazines. Its cover makes me wonder if the media would have rushed to support the mainstreaming of transgenderism before Photoshop. Probably not. ABC News does not care about Bruce Jenner. It cares about ratings.

And most of those applauding Bruce Jenner right now care about an agenda more than about a person. Here is a man who has serious issues. He needs help, and he needs prayer. He no more needs affirmation for what he is doing to himself than an alcoholic needs another drink. But our society is affirming his delusion because our society has gotten drunk off its own narcissism—keeping up with the Kardashians in new and exciting ways.

WHAT *CRAZY* LOOKS LIKE

A lady called in to my radio show last summer complaining that a local college campus had made many, if not all, of the bathrooms unisex. Most of the girls no longer felt comfortable going into the bathrooms anymore because of the boys. Several dozen other universities have done the same thing, replacing traditional male and female bathroom signs with ones that indicate all bathrooms are open to everyone. When Emerson College joined the list, David Kotter, executive director of the Council on Biblical Manhood and Womanhood, made a point very similar to Chesterton's in the epigraph to this chapter. "I am saddened, because the solution to feeling uncomfortable about 'having to choose a gender at the bathroom door' is not a change in the signs but a return to the biblical truth about God's design of men and women. This is not shocking, but what can be expected when we become unmoored from God's design."[13]

Cities such as Charlotte, North Carolina, have considered ordinances that would force local businesses to provide transgender people access to whatever restrooms they desire. The Charlotte ordinance was defeated by only one vote.[14] Some states have tried passing legal protection for those who prefer to find only men or women in their bathrooms. The Left calls such commonsense protections an assault, with headlines like this one from *Mother Jones*: "Get Ready for the Conservative Assault on Where Transgender Americans Pee."[15] There seems to be no concern for where the rest of us will pee, only the manufactured rights of less than 1 percent of the population who need help figuring out who they are.

But have no fear, Big Sis is on the job. Janet Napolitano, former head of the Department of Homeland Security under Obama, has her priorities in the right place. As the president of the University of California (UC) system, she has initiated changes to the schools' admission forms to include six gender options. According to Fox News, "Applicants can choose male, female, trans male/trans man, trans female/trans woman, gender queer/gender non-conforming and 'different identity' to describe their 'gender identity.'" In contrast, students will only have three choices for sexual orientation: "'heterosexual or straight,' 'gay or lesbian' or fill-in-the-blank."[16] You can't make this stuff up. (And trust me, I'm sure someone has already complained about there being only three options.) Napolitano says there is more work to be done: "I'm proud of the work we've done so far, but it doesn't stop there—we must continue to look at where we can improve so everyone at UC feels respected and supported."[17] Everyone, that is, except those who dare to call boys and girls what they are.

The University of New Mexico (UNM) has gone even further, allowing students to identify themselves by their "preferred name" based on their gender choice rather than their legal name. So John Smith, for example, can now officially call himself Janet or Julia Smith. UNM's LGBTQ Resource Center director, Alma Rosa Silva-Bañuelos, called for the university to "take some of those obstacles away from these students so that they can be their whole authentic selves.... A student should not be charged with academic dishonesty for not presenting the way their ID shows them." Sorry, but if you are using a name other than your own, you are being neither authentic nor honest. Silva-Bañuelos rationalizes the move in a particularly revealing way: "Suicide rates are very high for our [LGBTQ] community, so we want to make sure we're as preventative as possible."[18] Sadly, she is right. Suicide rates are very high among people who are confused about their gender, just as we would expect them to be for any people who are mentally ill or emotionally troubled. According to the American Foundation for Suicide Prevention, 41 percent of people who identify as transgender will try to kill themselves, compared to only 4.6 percent of the general population.[19]

Those numbers aren't just sad; they are tragic. Media stories imply that the reason for the high suicide rate is that these transgender persons are picked on and bullied. Alleged mistreatment is supposed to be driving them to attempt suicide. But what if the real problems are the mental health issues that are being celebrated instead of treated? We should be compassionate to people who have this problem, but genuine compassion means calling it what it is—a problem—not seeing it as a reason to build more bathrooms or create yet another protected class of people based on how they say they are feeling inside.

Transgenderism is not normal. And no one should be made to say it is. The celebration of this mental illness is part of an intentional undermining of society by people who want to label *normal* as *deviance* and *deviance* as *normal*. I realize the word *deviance* is a loaded term, but I mean no offense. We are talking about people who have decided that they are somehow "really" the opposite sex from the one they were born. There's no scientific evidence to support them. There's no biological evidence to support them. Really, how different is the transgender delusion from the beliefs of other mentally ill people—that they're Napoleon or an alien from another planet, or that the CIA is sending them radio messages through the fillings in their teeth? Yet they demand that we accept and even celebrate their counterfactual belief. And the truly crazy thing is that we do. Our media and our society at large are enabling the reality-denial. Although that may appear to be the compassionate thing to do, the high rate of suicides among transgender people suggests that something profoundly unhealthy is going on here. But if anyone points out that transgenderism might be a mental health issue, he's shouted down and called a bigot.

In September 2015 more than 150 students walked out of a high school in Missouri to protest a boy who called himself a girl wanting access to the girls' locker room. Even though there is no indication from news reports that he is anatomically different from any other boy on campus, he thinks he is a girl; therefore, he should be allowed everywhere the girls go. The boy responded to the protest as if reading from the progressive script: "I think a lot of it has to do with how [the students] were raised. A lot of the people at my school were raised to be very bigoted."[20]

Yeah, that must be it. Those evil parents teaching their kids radical things like how to tell the difference between a boy and a girl. Riiiight. *That* must be what's causing the problem. "There's a lot of ignorance," said the boy. "They are claiming that they're uncomfortable. I don't believe for a second that they are.... I think this is pure and simple bigotry."[21] Wait a minute, I thought we were now defining reality based on what each of us says we feel inside. And yet more than a hundred of this boy's fellow students are saying they feel uncomfortable with him going into the girls' locker room, and how does he reply? He doesn't believe them. Imagine that. They're claiming their sexual identity is being harmed, and what does he do? He resorts to name-calling. Who will make him care? Certainly not the school districts across the nation who lose their federal funding if they fail to cooperate with the madness.[22]

This boy needs help. And what are we doing to help? We're encouraging more and more kids to embrace gender confusion as a way of life. One child in Fairfax County schools was born a girl but then identified as a boy when she entered kindergarten. *Kindergarten.* I. Kid. You. Not. No child naturally reaches that conclusion by the age of five without some adult introducing the idea to her. But the encouragement is not surprising given the response of one proud mother, whose son gave what she calls a "mature" response to the girl who uses the boys' restroom at his school: "The way I learned about a transgender child in our school? My son explained it to me. One day, he matter-of-factly said: 'It just means that [the child] has a boy brain but was born into a girl body.' And they've all resumed playing Star Wars and Lego and pirates ever since."[23]

So a boy brain got put into a girl body on Darwin's genetic assembly line. Makes perfect sense except for one big problem—it's all completely and totally subjective. The same mother acknowledges as much: "Gender identity is not about sexuality. It is about **whether a person feels they are male or female**, despite the below-the-belt organs they were born with" [emphasis added].[24] You may be born with a penis, but that doesn't make you a boy, nor does the absence of one make you a girl. Not anymore. No wonder people who identify as transgender have such high suicide rates. According to progressives, they are screw-ups, freaks, and mistakes from birth rather than unique and valuable people designed by their Creator as either a male or female in His image.

Prior to the sexual revolution in the 1960s, the word *gender* was used when discussing grammar or as a euphemism by people who were uncomfortable using the word *sex*. But with the advent of the sexual revolution and then feminist theory in the 1970s, suddenly people believed that your gender and your sex could be different things. There is no scientific evidence for that belief. Progressives take it to be true on faith, based solely on what someone says he feels.

Dr. Paul McHugh, former chairman of psychiatry at Johns Hopkins and author of *Try to Remember: Psychiatry's Clash over Meaning, Memory, and Mind*, points out that gender reassignment surgery doesn't solve anything:

> [P]olicy makers and the media are doing no favors either to the public or the transgendered by treating their confusions

as a right in need of defending rather than as **a mental disorder that deserves understanding, treatment and prevention.** This intensely felt sense of being transgendered constitutes a mental disorder in two respects. The first is that the idea of sex misalignment is simply mistaken—it does not correspond with physical reality. The second is that it can lead to grim psychological outcomes.

The transgendered suffer a disorder of "assumption" like those in other disorders familiar to psychiatrists. With the transgendered, the disordered assumption is that the individual differs from what seems given in nature— namely one's maleness or femaleness.... Such ideas work like ruling passions in their subjects' minds and tend to be accompanied by a solipsistic argument.... For the transgendered, this argument holds that one's feeling of "gender" is a conscious, subjective sense that, being in one's mind, cannot be questioned by others. The individual often seeks not just society's tolerance of this "personal truth" but affirmation of it. Here rests the support for "transgender equality," the demands for government payment for medical and surgical treatments, and for access to all sex-based public roles and privileges.[25]

Thankfully, gender is one front on which the progressives are going to have a hard time winning in the long-term because nature itself reflects a male-female dynamic. It is very hard to find homosexuality outside of human beings, although leftist scientists certainly have tried. It is even harder to find non–gender normative animals out there. The drive to redefine gender seems to be confined to a minuscule segment of humanity. It also seems most popular among people who do not have children of their own because, as people have children, they discover that when they buy their boy a Barbie doll, he uses it as a gun. When they buy their girl a Tonka truck, she sleeps with it like a baby doll at night. Apparently God didn't check Facebook for gender categories before creating us male and female. It is not surprising that as the family has broken down, we have more and more people confused about who they are. But we shouldn't build new bathrooms to accommodate their troubled souls. We shouldn't create new labels to keep them from being offended by reality. We should tell them the truth, as lovingly as we can, even as we work as a society to create opportunities for them to—yes, I'll say it—heal.

A society that looks at a sixty-five-year-old male Olympic gold medalist and, with a straight face, declares *him* to be a *her*—and insists that this madness is to be the new normal—is itself delusional.

Such a society no longer distinguishes between *normal* and *crazy*.

CHAPTER 13

DISCRIMINATING
AGAINST TRUTH

*Plato is my friend—Aristotle is my friend—
but my greatest friend is truth.*

—ISAAC NEWTON[1]

Truth isn't what it used to be. It used to be that the university environment was all about the quest for *veritas*. But while the Latin word for truth still graces the mottos of some of the finest institutions of higher learning, truth itself is getting harder to find on college campuses across America—and even harder to express without being made to shut up. Being made to shut up soon leads to being made to care—in a place where you would think the free expression of ideas would be welcome.

Marquette is at least a nominally Catholic university.[2] It is a place where parents might reasonably expect their children's religious beliefs to be respected. But according to the *Atlantic*, one Marquette student discovered that progressive dogma supersedes Christian beliefs on issues of sexuality at his university.[3] The controversy began on October 28, 2014, when Cheryl Abbate, a graduate student in philosophy, asked students for examples of current events to which they could apply the philosophy of John Rawls. According to Abbate's own blog, "When one student rightly suggested that a ban on gay marriage would violate Rawls's Equal Liberty Principle, I wrote on the board, noted that this was the correct way to apply Rawls's principle to a ban on gay marriage and then moved on to more nuanced examples."[4] According to the *Atlantic*, there is evidence that Professor Abbate did not really "move on" quite so quickly. Abbate added that "if anyone did not agree that gay marriage was an example of something that fits the Rawls' Equal Liberty Principle, they should see her after class."[5]

One student in the class decided to pursue this issue with Abbate after class—and secretly recorded the exchange. According to published transcripts, the student said:

> I have to be completely honest with you; I don't agree with gay marriage. There have been studies that show that children that are brought up in gay households do a lot worse in life such as test scores, in school, and in the real world. So, when you completely dismiss an entire argument based off of your personal views, it sets a precedent for the classroom that "oh my God, this is so wrong; you can't agree with this; you're a horrible person if you agree with this." And that's what came off. And I have to say I am very personally offended by that....
>
> ... And I would stress for you in your professional career going forward, you're going to be teaching for many more years, that you watch how you approach those issues because when you set a precedent like that because you are the authority figure in the classroom, people truly do listen to you....

… It's wrong for the teacher of a class to completely discredit one person's opinion when they may have different opinions.

Graduate student Abbate replied:

Ok, there are some opinions that are not appropriate that are harmful, such as racist opinions, sexist opinions, and quite honestly, do you know if anyone in the class is homosexual? …

… And, don't you think that that would be offensive to them if you were to raise your hand and challenge this?

When the student replied, "If I choose to challenge this, it's my right as an American citizen," Abbate responded, "You can have whatever opinions you want, but I can tell you right now, in this class homophobic comments, racist comments, and sexist comments will not be tolerated. If you don't like that, you are more than free to drop this class."[6]

It's clear from this account that at Marquette the classroom is not a safe space to discuss the truth about same-sex unions. Such conversations can only be held in secret, it would seem, so as not to offend others.

Marquette professor John McAdams blogged about this interaction, offering this perspective:

[T]his student is rather outspoken and assertive about his beliefs. That puts him among a small minority of Marquette students. How many students, especially in politically correct departments like Philosophy, simply stifle their disagreement, or worse yet get indoctrinated into the views of the instructor, since those are the only ideas allowed, and no alternative views are aired? Like the rest of academia, Marquette is less and less a real university. And when gay marriage cannot be discussed, certainly not a Catholic university.[7]

When Marquette dean Richard C. Holz heard about the situation, he did what any compassionate bully would do—he fired Professor McAdams. In fact, he stripped the sixty-nine-year-old professor of tenure—which is supposed to protect professors' free speech rights.[8] It's not just the students who must be silenced by the Left. Even the professors must be made to care.

On college campuses across America, it has now become clear that *veritas* has left the building.

THREE TALES OF TOLERANCE

Story Number One: Emily Brooker. It was Emily Brooker's passion for helping people that led her to apply to the College of Social Work at Missouri State University the summer after her senior year of high school. The trouble began early on. In one of Emily's very first social work classes, Emily's professor assigned students to same-sex pairs and asked them to do a social experiment and write a paper about it. Brooker says of the assignment, "We were asked to just hold hands with the person, or if we felt comfortable, to display other homosexual behavior." A self-described naïve freshman caught off her guard, Emily decided along with her class partner, a fellow Christian, that they would fake the assignment instead of compromising their beliefs. They invented a story, wrote the papers, and turned them in. But Emily vowed that she would never again be forced to do a school assignment that violated her conscience.

As her years at Missouri State continued, Emily found that the conflicts between conscience and school requirements were frequent and that she was not the only student facing the problem. According to Emily, many other students felt forced to say or do things they didn't agree with.

In her senior year, Emily took a policy class required to secure her social work degree. The course centered on an advocacy project. Her professor dictated that the issue for which the students would advocate was same-sex adoption and foster care. At the time, there was a bill to support homosexual adoption going through the Missouri legislature. The assignment required students to send a letter to the legislature in support of the bill. The professor "brought a draft of the letter advocating homosexual foster homes and adoption to the class. He expected the students to use this draft, effectively dictating the students' position on the controversial subject."[9]

Emily could not in good conscience advocate for an issue that she believed violated her religious convictions. So she went to her professor, who was very passionate about the bill being passed. "I immediately asked him if I could do another topic that I was passionate about, or just try to find some kind of middle ground. Could I write my letter to the Missouri legislature with my points of view?"[10] His answer was *no*. She would be made to care. Unsure how the assignment would turn out, she continued with the rest of the class: "I completed the research for the assignment.... I even drafted a letter for the Missouri legislature, but I refused to put my signature on it and send it in, because I felt that doing that was a violation of my beliefs. I'm willing to learn about different people and different populations, but I'm not willing to put my name on something that I don't support.... I knew that [after graduating] I would probably go work for the state of Missouri, in foster care work, and I didn't want to be in the place of having a law that I would have to follow that would place children in a homosexual family."[11]

Emily didn't want to be in a position where she'd have to support, by law, something that her religious beliefs tell her is wrong. She wasn't advocating the opposite, pushing an anti-gay agenda, or harassing homosexuals. She just didn't want to put her name on something that went against her beliefs. But Emily's professor labeled her a troublemaker and refused a private meeting with her. So Emily attempted to meet with the social work department head. But before that meeting even happened, Emily was notified that there had been a grievance filed against her, the highest level of grievance that could be filed against a student at the university. Emily was ordered to appear before an ethics committee for a hearing.

Emily asked to have her parents present, but her request was denied; she was told that her faculty advisor would be her advocate. She asked to record the proceedings, but that request was also denied, and she was allowed only pen and paper with which to record what happened at the hearing. Emily was interrogated about her beliefs for more than two hours. "Basically, they said I would need to leave my beliefs at the door, because at this point I was violating our social work code of ethics by continuing in this course as a Christian," Emily says of the grueling experience. "There was definitely a point [when] I broke down and just cried in the room, because I felt like I wasn't being listened to."

After the ethics hearing was finally over, the department required Emily to write a paper on, as she describes it, "how I would lessen the gap between my personal beliefs and my professional obligations." Emily wrote the paper. Throughout the remainder of her college career, she had to go to extra meetings with faculty, some of which were spent being forced to learn more about the homosexual population.

Feeling like a second-class student, Emily finally earned her diploma and promptly sued the school. With the help of her attorney at the Alliance Defending Freedom, Emily took her case to the president of the university and the matter was settled out of court in just six weeks. To his credit, the president of Missouri State University publicly acknowledged that Emily's claims were largely correct and called in consultants from other universities' departments of social work to investigate Emily's accusations. The consultants found so much unethical conduct throughout the department that they issued a scathing report and recommended that the department be dissolved completely.[12] As a result, four tenured professors were moved to different departments and four untenured professors were fired.

Emily has continued with a successful career in social work, where her compassion and kindness, driven by her Christian beliefs and love of Jesus, have equipped her to serve all her clients well. Her story has a happy ending, but unfortunately the problems she encountered are common—and not every story turns out well.[13]

Story Number Two: Jennifer Keeton. Jennifer, whom we met briefly in chapter 1, is another woman who had a passion for counseling. She chose to pursue a master's in education at Augusta State University, hardly a liberal bastion—or so she thought. Halfway through her second year there, Jennifer received an unexpected phone call from a professor, saying that she would be required to meet with a panel of professors to discuss her participation in the program. With no clue as to what they might want, Jennifer attended the meeting, only to discover that the professors were questioning her competency as a counselor because of her religious beliefs. "They basically wanted to talk to me about information that I'd written about in my papers, or statements I'd made in class, or even private conversations that I had with students outside of class," Jennifer recalls.

She was understandably taken aback at this intrusion into her personal life.

From her early days in the program, Jennifer had heard the faculty tell students that the classes and the counseling community were a safe place for students to express their beliefs. "The whole idea of counseling is going a little bit deeper, and exploring what you believe and why you believe it, and discovering your identity in life, your purpose in life," Jennifer said. "We were told at the very beginning to come in with our set of values and beliefs and it's ok...we're a melting pot of those things." Apparently what was not welcome in that melting pot was Jennifer's Christian belief that engaging in homosexual behavior is a sin. Jennifer was never unwilling to counsel people who are homosexual or transgender, or who had questions about their gender. She was preparing to do just that.

But the school told her they feared her views wouldn't permit her to counsel people in the way they deemed appropriate. To fix what they perceived to be a problem, they presented Jennifer with a remediation plan that would determine whether she could continue studying to be a counselor. "[The remediation plan] stated a couple different things that I needed to do, or events that I needed to attend...but the fine print was that **I needed to write papers that basically stated that I'd changed my views**" [emphasis added], Jennifer said. She wasn't just being forced to complete their "diversity sensitivity training," she was being required to prove she had changed her religious beliefs.

Jen refused to complete their "remediation plan." She was booted from the program. She filed a lawsuit to protect her freedom to believe and exercise her faith—and lost. She never finished her degree, although she has put her counseling experience to work in both public and private schools she has worked for.[14]

Story Number Three: Ruth Malhotra. These stories of secular oppression on college campuses are not new, but they are growing. Back in 2006, two students at the Georgia Institute of Technology (commonly called Georgia Tech) filed a pivotal lawsuit against the school in a case that brought national attention to the administration's thuggish tactics. Ruth Malhotra, a conservative Christian and president of the College Republicans, and Orit Sklar, the president of the Jewish Student Union, had endured violation after violation of their First Amendment rights to their free speech and freedom of religion.

They were being told not what they could and could not say but how they should think.

Ruth's parents were immigrants from India, and her father was a marketing research professor in Georgia Tech's business program. Ruth grew up admiring the school's traditions and reputation. "I was really excited about going to a school that I respected and loved, and I knew it would be a very diverse environment with many different backgrounds and worldviews and academic opportunities," she said. Ruth declared international affairs and public policy as her majors and quickly became involved in student organizations. Though she never called herself an activist, Ruth joined organizations that reflected her strong personal convictions, particularly the sanctity of life, traditional marriage, and the Christian faith. She tried to live a life consistent with what she believed: "I always saw my faith as something that guided and that should guide every decision. My Christianity and belief in Scripture should be kind of the lens through which I see everything else, and so it was certainly my Christian convictions that led to my passion for life and to protect the definition of marriage, and even...things [like] personal responsibility and integrity."[15]

Ruth saw professors protesting the ROTC on Veterans Day, priests teaching that Jesus and his disciples were gay, and numerous sexually graphic promotions for one thing and another. She didn't take any of it as a personal offense. "I don't think we [Christians] should have a victim mentality whenever we see something we don't agree with," Ruth said.[16]

But then she began to experience Georgia Tech's double standard.

In Ruth's sophomore year, she was called into the office of the dean of the liberal arts college. According to Ruth, the dean said, "Ruth, you're asking too many questions, and you're here to listen and learn." When Ruth said she felt that some of the professors were practicing indoctrination rather than education, the dean responded with a statement that shocked her: "Ruth, students have been indoctrinated for the first eighteen years of their lives by their parents and by their churches, and we only have four years to undo the damage."[17]

The censorship spread beyond the classroom to the campus organizations and activities of which Ruth was a part. Students in those organizations were increasingly accused of violating the university's tolerance policy, a speech code that prohibited any speech considered intolerant or offensive. The only judges of what was intolerant were the school administrators themselves. In one instance, one of Ruth's student organizations planned to do an outreach to promote and explain their belief in traditional marriage. They purchased a wedding cake and handed out cake and pamphlets to students. Georgia Tech put a stop to this activity, claiming it was offensive.

"The things we were trying to do were very, I thought, basic in terms of just [saying], 'Hey, this is what we believe,'" Ruth recalls. "We knew that people out there agreed with us. We just wanted the right to speak like everyone else."[18]

In Ruth's senior year, the dean of student involvement called her into his office and said that the College Republicans organization, of which Ruth was president, was in trouble for, in essence, marketing themselves well. They had a display comparing what conservative women offered to feminism with what liberals offered to feminism. Because they "made their side look better," they were to be punished.

During Coming Out Week, an LGBT initiative sponsored by Georgia Tech, the College Republicans simply declined to participate. "We were not trying to shut anyone else down; we never said we wanted Coming Out Week canceled, or we wanted the Gay Pride Alliance to be kicked off campus," Ruth said. "In fact, we treated everyone with dignity and respect...but we said we cannot endorse or support, or in any way sign on to advocate for a worldview or belief system or behavior that is against our convictions. And that was unacceptable to the administration." The dean of students charged Ruth with being intolerant, telling her that high rates of suicide among gay students were because of people like her. You read that right. For remaining silent and doing absolutely nothing, Ruth was accused of being a killer.

The College Republicans were soon restricted to a tiny, obscure area of campus—called a Free Speech Zone—where they were permitted to hold their events and speak without fear of reprisal. But even these unconstitutional restrictions were not enough for Georgia Tech. Eventually, the president of the school called Ruth in and told her she had to change her views or she was no longer a good fit for the school. At the time, Ruth was only months away from earning her degree with the highest honors the institute had to offer. Yet she was being told she was not a good fit for the school—solely because of her beliefs.

At that point, Ruth took a stand for her freedom of conscience. She joined with Orit Sklar and the Alliance Defending Freedom to sue the school. "We did not want to do that. It was not something we ever set out to do. But when the president [of Georgia Tech] is telling you to change your beliefs or else, you don't really have any other options."

Ruth's life on campus went from bad to worse as the news media spun her story. The *Los Angeles Times* ran a piece with the headline "Christian Student Sues for the Right to Be Intolerant." Ruth began to receive hate mail, including rape and death threats. There was even a student organization, CLAM (Conservatives and Liberals Against Malhotra), formed for the sole purpose of hating and opposing her. This organization used racial slurs, doing despicable things such as handing out Twinkies while saying Ruth was yellow on the outside and white on the inside. To Ruth's knowledge, the school administration never accused CLAM of being intolerant. Despite the threats of physical violence, the school made no effort to protect Ruth. Outside law enforcement escorted her in public for the last two months of her senior year, even accompanying her to graduation.

Three years later, their case was resolved. Ruth and Orit won on each of the four separate policies they challenged. Among other changes, the speech code was repealed and Georgia Tech was subject to judicial oversight to make sure it was left behind for good. A policy called SAFE Space was also challenged. This LGBT initiative had been run through the offices of the dean of students and the dean of diversity. It employed a "scale of tolerance," which rated how tolerant different religions were, with Buddhists deemed most accepting and Southern Baptists the least. "These are taxpayer-funded administrators. It's not their role to tell me that it's better to be Buddhist than to be Baptist," Ruth said. "They're the ones that cry about separation of church and state all the time, but here you had a state school telling you what church you should go to." The judge ripped the policy to shreds, saying the SAFE Space policy violated the Constitution's establishment of religion clause. He added that it was "very puzzling to the court that...what they say is the promotion of tolerance actually amounts to intolerance on the part of the institute." Exactly what Ruth was saying all along.

Thousands of students are now experiencing greater freedoms because of her courageous stand. Ruth sums up her perspective now as she looks back on the testing of her faith: "We are called to be witnesses for Christ, not prosecutors for Him. I'm not trying to shove [my faith] down anyone's throat. I'm not trying to impose it, even when it comes to my view of human flourishing, whether it's life and marriage, or personal responsibility and fiscal discipline. I think the ideas stand for themselves; I just want the opportunity to present them and let people make their decisions."[19]

Ideas that cannot stand on their own—which includes all of progressive ideology—must be propped up by force. However, to borrow a popular phrase from the Wall Street bailouts of 2009, the Left is too big to fail. The precious belief system of progressives must be protected—at all costs.

And that's the simple truth.

CHAPTER 14

YOU HAVE
THE RIGHT TO
REMAIN SILENT

First they came for the Socialists, and I did not speak out because I was not a Socialist. Then they came for the Trade Unionists, and I did not speak out because I was not a Trade Unionist. Then they came for the Jews, and I did not speak out because I was not a Jew. Then they came for me, and there was no one left to speak for me.

—MARTIN NIEMÖLLER[1]

The famous quotation above came from a German pastor who lived through the Nazi rise to power in the 1930s. Perhaps after hearing stories of oppression by radical secularists, you're thankful you're not a florist, baker, photographer, pharmacist, college student, pizza parlor owner, adoption agency, or any of the other professions that have been attacked for holding to the beliefs on which Western civilization was formed. But you have to admit, the list of *safe* occupations is getting smaller by the day. The sideline is gone. Everyone is fair game. Everyone—including you—will be made to care.

Mat Staver has updated Niemöller to better fit our current context: "First they came for the adoption ministry, but I did not speak out because I did not do adoptions. Then they came for the wedding photographer, but I did not speak out because I did not photograph weddings. Then they came for the baker, but I did not speak out because I was not a baker. Then they came for the florist, but I said nothing because I was not a florist. Then they came for me, and there was no one left to speak for me."[2]

Wherever we are in this process as a culture, there can be no mistaking that the Left has the momentum. Unless the progressives begin to encounter resistance, they will continue to steamroll our freedom of conscience until words like *religious liberty* go the way of the dinosaurs and our grandchildren speak of them in the same way— neat things that once roamed the earth but now survive only as fossilized remnants. When that dark day comes, it will take more than computer animation to revive them.

Edmund Burke is said to have warned, "When bad men combine, the good must associate."[3] Now those who believe are being told to shut up, sit down, and wait until it is your turn to be made to care. Each of us has a choice to make—to exercise our right to remain silent or to act on our sacred duty to speak up. Your time of testing is coming. For Aaron and Melissa Klein, the owners of Sweet Cakes by Melissa, mentioned in chapter 1, that time has already arrived.

BOUND AND GAGGED IN OREGON

Melissa Klein caught the baking bug when she made her son's first-birthday cake. With directions from a book she picked up at a craft store, Melissa created a double-layer work of art complete with an airplane and car-shaped cookies that brought landscapes of blue and green frosting to life. Everyone loved it. That's when this mother of five children first discovered her ability to bring joy to others through her baking creations.

Melissa honed her talents and partnered with her husband, Aaron, to launch a family business—Sweet Cakes by Melissa. As devout

Christians, Aaron and Melissa saw God's hand blessing their work from the outset when they secured the ideal location for half the asking price. Before the shop opened, the Kleins invited their pastor and church friends to the building to dedicate the business to the Lord.

Sweet Cakes by Melissa soon took off, garnering a following of repeat customers and a network of wedding venues that would refer customers to their shop for their tasty wedding cakes. One such repeat customer was a younger woman who, along with her same-sex partner, wanted to purchase a cake for her mother's wedding ceremony. As Melissa describes it, she and the three women had a lot of fun picking out the perfect cake for the occasion. Melissa says she noticed how the two younger women acted toward each other but didn't treat them differently from any other customers. In fact, the women were so impressed with the service and the cake that the younger woman came back a few months later to order a cake for her own wedding ceremony.

The date was January 17, 2013. When Aaron asked the young woman for the names of the bride and groom, she giggled and said there would actually be two brides. Same-sex marriages were not legal in Oregon at the time. Aaron's response was simple and apologetic: "I'm sorry, but we don't do cakes for same-sex weddings." He explained that the Kleins' consciences would not allow them to participate in events that contradicted their faith and beliefs. According to Aaron, the young lady was visibly disappointed but the interaction was neither hostile nor mean-spirited. But as is often the case in these situations, what appeared to be the end of the matter was only the beginning.

Days later, the Kleins were notified that a complaint had been filed against them using that dreaded word—*discrimination*. The complaint alleged that the Kleins had violated the women's civil rights by declining to participate in their wedding ceremony. In spite of the fact that the two women had found plenty of other bakers from whom they could purchase a wedding cake, and in spite of the fact that gay marriage was not even legal in Oregon at the time, they claimed to have suffered a myriad of physical and emotional damages from the Kleins' refusal to bake their cake, including but not limited to the following: "acute loss of confidence," "doubt," "excessive sleep," "felt mentally raped, dirty and shameful," "high blood pressure," "impaired digestion," "loss of appetite," "migraine headaches," "pale and sick at home after work," "resumption of smoking habit," "shock," "stunned," "surprise," "uncertainty," "weight gain," and "worry." Not surprisingly, none of these alleged conditions was substantiated by a medical doctor or psychiatrist.[4]

The complaint made its way to the Oregon Bureau of Labor and Industries where the Oregon labor commissioner, Brad Avakian, seemed only too willing to make the Kleins care. Far from being an unbiased arbiter of the law, Avakian had advocated for LGBT rights as a state senator, and he would later celebrate on social media when the Supreme Court legalized same-sex marriage in June 2015. Reporters have since documented ongoing meetings with gay rights advocacy groups throughout Avakian's handling of the complaint.[5] Even more troubling were his public comments made about the complaint prior to the beginning of any investigation. They sound as if they were lifted from a speech by Stalin or Mao, not a theoretically neutral mediator in a land where "liberty and justice for all" is supposed to be a cultural norm. Avakian told the *Oregonian* that his goal "is never to shut down a business. The goal is to rehabilitate." *Rehabilitate.* What kind of people need *rehabilitation*? Criminals or unfortunate souls with mental or physical illnesses. Apparently that is how Avakian perceived the Kleins because of their refusal to bow to the Spirit of the Age.

While the Kleins waited for the ruling, they lost most of their wedding referral business. Anyone who partnered with Sweet Cakes by Melissa was harassed and threatened by allies of the gay mafia until they dropped the shop from their list. Without the income from wedding cakes, which had made up 70 percent of their revenue, they had to close the shop. Aaron got another job, and Melissa did some baking out of her house as she was able. The business the Kleins had dreamed of passing on to their children was gone.

Both Aaron and Melissa have explained many times that they had no issue with the lesbian women themselves and that they have never refused to serve anyone based on sexual orientation. Aaron explains that they're not acting out of hate: "I'd rather have people understand that I'm a loving, caring person and that I would love for them to enjoy the freedom that Christ has given me." But they do object to being made to participate in an event that celebrates something their faith describes as sinful. Melissa points out that a baker has the mindset of an artist—every cake is a canvas that bears her signature. She simply cannot put her heart and soul into designing cakes for a purpose she believes to be wrong.

But the State of Oregon no longer tolerates such deeply held beliefs.

In April 2015, the Oregon Bureau of Labor ruled that the Kleins had discriminated unlawfully against the couple based on their sexual orientation. The case went to an administrative judge to decide the Kleins' punishment for refusing to bow to the secular gods. Judge Alan McCullough, appointed by Avakian, recommended that they pay the lesbian couple a total of $135,000 in damages. McCullough did, however, have the sense to throw out another argument that the women's lawyers had made about what they called the business's advertising. The prosecution claimed that when the Kleins talked about their beliefs publicly, they were advertising that their shop would discriminate in the future—in violation of Oregon's laws. Judge McCullough declined to rule that the Kleins' statements about marriage indicated future action on their part. But when the ruling returned to Commissioner Avakian for approval, he overruled the judge and reinstated the bogus advertising-discrimination claim.

So not only would the Kleins be bound by the oppressive six-figure fine, they would be gagged to keep them from telling their story to anyone. The admittedly nebulous ruling apparently prohibited them from speaking about their religious beliefs about marriage and sexuality in the context of their business. According to their attorney Anna Harmon, "Their previous statements about their faith and their intention to remain true to their faith had led to the gag order, so we could only reasonably infer that the same kinds of comments would violate the order." But the Kleins refused to be silenced. They have continued to speak out in multiple interviews (including one for this book) and on their Facebook page. Aaron explains why they will not be silent: "I will not be told to be quiet by a man who has no authority to tell me to be quiet. Our freedoms in this country are given by God, that's what the Preamble to the Constitution says: we have the rights to life, liberty, and the pursuit of happiness, and no government official can tell us to not do that. He does not have the legal authority to tell me to be quiet. And so, guess what, Mr. Avakian, I won't be quiet."

The Kleins have refused to be silenced by this unconstitutional gag order issued by yet another compassionate bully of the Left. But he's not the only one trying to silence them. After a campaign to help pay the Kleins' fine raised more than $100,000, GoFundMe abruptly shut down the account, saying that it prohibited "campaigns in defense of formal charges of heinous crimes including violent, hateful or sexual acts." Shortly afterward, GoFundMe announced they had changed their rule to cover even *claims* of actions they deemed to be hateful. Apparently, the GoFundMe demigods have the right to deny service because they disagree with the Kleins' beliefs, but Aaron and Melissa have no such freedom when it comes to exercising their faith. (GoFundMe took similar action to shut down fund-raising in support of the Washington florist Barronelle Stutzman. Another site, ContinueToGive.com, has since stepped up to facilitate fund-raising for Sweet Cakes by Melissa.)

As is often the case, the progressive agenda is backfiring, as the Kleins have indeed been made an example—not of effective *rehabilitation* but of how far the Left will go to silence those who disagree—and of how Christians will nevertheless stay faithful. Their case is on appeal now and may ultimately end up before the U.S. Supreme Court. But as Aaron says, there are greater forces at work here:

> I don't believe God's Word has changed any. This is about freedom, not just for us, but for every American. We really need to be vigilant and try to fight for freedom. If the government can tell us we have to think and feel a certain way, they can tell a homosexual to think and feel a certain way.... We can see in the Bible what the Apostles did. We can see that they were not always successful in winning the battles, but they were faithful to Christ and that's what we're called to do.... We've been really lax in doing that in this country. We need to start standing for God's truth. We need to be salt and light in society and it's time to start doing that in a real, tangible way. If that means that you have to stand in the gap with your business, your personal belongings, then so be it. It all belongs to God anyway.

Melissa urges other Christian business owners not to be afraid, but to "stand on God's Word, because when you do that, it's truly amazing what God does in your life.... He won't forsake you. He will constantly be there with you. We have to remember that all these things here, they're material, even our business—it doesn't go with us. And we should be willing to give even that up for the Lord. Christ gave His life for us, so that we could live. The least we can do is we can give Him our business."[6]

The secular elite on the Left are only too happy to stand in the place of the Almighty and take it.

SHUT UP. SIT DOWN. WAIT YOUR TURN.

The CEO of Starbucks invites shareholders to sell their shares if they disagree with his revisionist views of marriage and is applauded for his courageous stand,[7] while a young couple making wedding cakes in Oregon is put through hell for living out basic Christian beliefs? You betcha. Welcome to the new America as defined by progressives. There is no more room for dissent in this new land of the compliant and home of the cowardly. After the *Obergefell* ruling by the Supreme Court, one newspaper went so far as to announce a ban on other viewpoints:

> On Friday, the United States crossed a similar threshold [as the 1967 decision in *Loving v. Virginia*, which found state bans on interracial marriage to be unconstitutional], continuing a long road to acceptance of same-sex unions.
>
> And this news organization now crosses another threshold.
>
> As a result of Friday's ruling, PennLive/The Patriot-News will very strictly limit op-Eds and letters to the editor in opposition to same-sex marriage.
>
> **These unions are now the law of the land. And we will not publish such letters and op-Eds any more than we would publish those that are racist, sexist or anti-Semitic.**
>
> We will, however, for a limited time, accept letters and op-Eds on the high court's decision and its legal merits.
>
> The march of progress is often slow, but it is always steady.

On Friday, the United States took another step toward
the ideal of equality envisioned by its founders. And we
are all more free as a result.[8] [emphasis added]

I don't recall any of America's founders citing same-sex marriage
as their ultimate end in securing "the blessings of liberty to ourselves
and our posterity." But facts matter little to bullies who know their
arguments cannot win if left to stand on their own. There is no shortage of similar examples where the Left is using bullying to force its
beliefs onto those who refuse to be silent:

- Twin brothers **David and Jason Benham** had their
  HGTV show pulled from production after being
  labeled as "anti-gay, anti-choice extremists" for leading
  a prayer rally. According to the Benhams, HGTV officials knew of their involvement in the rally, but it only
  became an issue after vocal gay rights advocates pressured the channel's decision makers.[9]
- **Mozilla cofounder Brendan Eich** resigned after only
  nine days on the job as CEO after a firestorm erupted
  over his support of marriage and Proposition 8, a constitutional amendment passed by the majority of Cali-
  fornians (more than seven million) to protect conjugal
  marriage.[10]
- In a case at Vanderbilt University that I mentioned
  briefly in chapter 1, the university required religious
  organizations to let people who do not share their
  religious beliefs serve in leadership in the organizations—effectively ending the groups' ability to function
  in a manner consistent with their beliefs. As **Tish Harrison Warren,** who headed up a chapter of **InterVarsity**
  at the time, and others pleaded their case to university

officials, they found that "top officials seemed blind to their assumptions, insisting all religious groups were welcome while gutting our ability to preserve defining beliefs and practices."[11] Fourteen religious organizations no longer exist on the Vanderbilt campus.

- The Denver city council delayed approval of a **Chick-fil-A** restaurant in the Denver airport, citing concerns about discrimination based on the company's history of "funding opposition" to an assortment of LGBT causes that the city officials deem important. They discriminated against Chick-fil-A in spite of there being no evidence of any discriminatory practices and despite the well-settled legal precedent that denying a private business a permit because of its free speech is a clear First Amendment violation.[12]

- When **a female Planet Fitness customer** found a man in the women's locker room, she wanted to know why. The answer was that Planet Fitness has a "No Judgment" policy, which lets people choose locker rooms based on "their sincere, self-reported gender identity." After she insisted that people with "male parts don't need to be in the women's locker room," her membership was terminated because the "manner in which this member expressed her concerns" was deemed "inappropriate and disruptive to other members."[13]

- A **female theology teacher at a Catholic school** in New Jersey was suspended for posting opposition to same-sex marriage on her Facebook page. According to NewJersey.com, her posts suggested "sexual orientation was a matter of choice and not an inborn trait, dismissing as 'bologna' the idea that gays are entitled to 14th Amendment protections. In the same post, she also said gay activists want to cause the 'extinction of Western civilization.'"[14] Somehow I don't think I would make it past homeroom if I taught at that school. The school first forced her to deactivate her Facebook page before suspending her without pay. In spite of her attorney being told she would never under any circumstances be permitted to return to the school, officials later relented and restored her to her role in the classroom. A letter sent to parents stated, "It is the School's position that a Catholic school teacher must always communicate the faith in a way that is positive and never hurtful."[15] I wonder if they would have let a young rabbi from Nazareth address the student body after reports of His table turning in the temple had come to light.

- **Four Christian firefighters in San Diego** were ordered to participate in the city's gay pride parade against their will. They were on the job and in uniform but instructed to stay in the truck and not respond even if an emergency were to occur. After originally being told they would not be required to participate in the parade, they were told otherwise once they showed up for work that day. During the parade, they were subjected to taunting, public nudity, and obscenity. The firefighters sued, citing sexual harassment, and won in a jury trial. They then prevailed on appeal.[16]

And the list goes on and on. Maggie Gallagher, cofounder of the National Organization for Marriage, explains why so many others are choosing silence instead:

I know there's a pervasive fear that if you're known to oppose gay marriage, your children's livelihood, your ability to earn a living, is going to be put in jeopardy in a wide variety of ways, some of them formal from government and some of them [from] being blackballed by powerful cultural elites. There's a woman I know who e-mailed me because she was going on the Internet, writing things opposing gay marriage. She was an ex-lesbian, so she felt that she was really under the gun. They really hated her, and what happened is they tracked her down, stripped her of her anonymity (which she was not an expert in maintaining), and posted her home address on the Internet. They found out where she worked and went to her boss and said that they were going to picket—she worked fifteen hours a week cutting hair in Pennsylvania. The owner of the salon was told that they would picket and protest unless she fired this worker. And the owner negotiated an agreement where the woman agreed not to say anything anymore and she would be allowed to keep this job for fifteen hours a week.

The capacity to organize, to live communally, to be out publicly advocating for and trying to live your lives by basic Christian principles—which are shared by other religions as well—is in jeopardy in a brand-new and very serious way. There are two questions: (1) Will they succeed in making us ashamed of our own faith? (2) Will we start to self-censor and submit to this new second-class citizenship?

If they can get us to do it to ourselves, they won't have to apply stronger, legal, moral and cultural pressures.[17] [emphasis added]

Fear is a powerful weapon. But for those who believe the truth claims of Christian Scripture, "he who is in you is greater than he who is in the world" (1 John 4:4). Ed Morrissey of *Hot Air* says the only way to lose this fight is to be quiet: "What we're talking about here with progressives is really a small percentage of people who are just really vocal, and they're trying to push the debate in a certain way that shuts everybody else out. But honestly, the democratization of the [debate] through Internet channels may have boosted them, but it boosts everybody else, too. The only way you lose that fight is if everybody else leaves the [town] square."[18]

So speak up while you still can. Don't stand by, waiting for someone else to do it or keep quiet for fear of what names you may be called. Rick Warren explains why real love requires us to tell the truth: "Our culture has accepted two huge lies. The first is that if you disagree with someone's lifestyle, you must fear or hate them. The second is that to love someone means you agree with everything they believe or do. Both are nonsense. You don't have to compromise convictions to be compassionate."[19]

Understand also that, in the end, being nice won't always make a difference. In spite of the many good deeds he did and the healing miracles he performed, Jesus still ended up nailed to a cross. In the words of Alfred in *The Dark Knight*, "Some men just want to watch the world burn."[20] To paraphrase another character from the same film, what we are seeing today is what happens when a movement that thinks it is an unstoppable force of history meets a people who believe truth is an immovable object that transcends history.[21]

You will be made to care. You will not be given the option of silence or the sidelines. The sidelines are gone. Everyone is fair game now—even mild-mannered wedding cake designers with five kids. As Barronelle Stutzman, the grandmother florist, said, "If we don't start standing up for our Constitution and for our rights, our beliefs, there's going to be nothing to stand up for."

If you choose to be silent now as they come for your neighbor's conscience, I wonder: Who will be left to speak up for your freedom to believe when it's your turn to be made to care?

PART III
HOW TO WIN
THE WAR

CHAPTER 15

THE RESURGENT COMMUNITY

We have all of us—the whole church and the whole community—been thrown into the Tempter's sieve, and he is shaking and the wind is blowing, and it must now become manifest whether we are wheat or chaff! Verily, a time of sifting has come upon us....

—MARTIN NIEMÖLLER[1]

Call it postmodernism, secularism, or just crazyism—whatever you call it, it's raging through our culture like a wildfire. Right now we're in a time of sifting and testing of our culture that will reveal what we really believe to be true. The pace at which the transformation is taking place is breathtaking. Just ten years ago, same-sex marriage was unthinkable. Today we're talking about taking tax-exempt status from churches because they don't approve it? And what's next? Let's have polygamy, throuples, group marriage, or any other combination you can dream up—all of these have already been called for since the disaster of *Obergefell*, and not from fringe groups but from mainstream media sources.[2] This is where we're headed.

For many of us, it feels as if society has lost its mind in an adolescent effort to try something new and bold. Anything for progress! But wildfires eventually burn themselves out because nature—or nature's God—always catches up. It won't be next week; it won't be next year. In fact, it's probably going to get worse for people of faith in America before it can get better. But it will get better. God always wins. That's why He tells us to trust Him. That's why Scripture reveals that the righteous shall live by faith. My coauthor, Bill Blankschaen, defines faith as "doing what you believe to be true, often in spite of what you see, sense, or feel." Now more than ever, Christians and all people of faith will need to do just that—live what we believe to be true based on the revealed Word of God, *especially* in the face of the constant media barrage telling us that we are the bigoted extremists for refusing to convert to the secular religion.

If you are a Christian or a political conservative who recognizes the importance of religion to human flourishing, you have plenty of reason to feel down these days. You're tired of electing leaders who stab you in the back once in office. You rose up to resist the tyranny of the Obama administration with the Tea Party, only to have Republican leaders fail to fight. You watched Obamacare fundamentally transform our healthcare system and force government deeper into each of our lives. You watched spending skyrocket to unimaginable levels. And now you have seen marriage dismissed nonchalantly by some guy named Tony who passes off love poetry as law while lounging around D.C. in a black robe. You never imagined you would see attacks on freedom of conscience in America as we are seeing now. I think many of us are ready to throw up our hands, dust off our feet, and be done with it all. And maybe some of us do need to step back, catch our breath, and try to make sense of it all before we rush back into the fray.

America has withstood threats to freedom before, but they have usually come from without, not within. We are now engaged in a fight for the heart and soul of our culture. But it is more than that. It is a war between good and evil, between freedom and tyranny. We have two options—go with the flow and bow to the Spirit of the Age, or stand up and refuse to be shut up. We can accept our newly assigned status of second-class citizens (as Christians are treated in many countries throughout the world) or insist that all people of all faiths are created equal. We can speak up for the religious liberties of all, even those with whom we disagree, or we can wait until they come for us. The one thing we cannot do is quit. Quite the opposite.

We need a *resurgence*.

WHAT WE NEED NOW

I founded my new site The Resurgent (TheResurgent.com) because I believe we are not really a country divided between red states and blue states anymore. That was a dichotomy that existed once, but less so now. At present, too many politicians in Washington, regardless of party, show contempt for people of faith. And some allegedly faith-based organizations are more interested in being team players with political parties than advocating for the positions on which they raise funds.

So instead of the red-versus-blue paradigm, I see us—the resistance to the suddenly dominant Spirit of the Age—as a group of conservatives and faith-filled people united against the forces of the Left. Sensing what is at stake in the conflict, many of us have found our voices and are willing to be bold, to become a resurgent people of free ideas, faith, and family. We are willing more and more to engage not just in politics, but also in culture itself. There is a resurgence under way of people committed to our nation's first principles. The Resurgent site exists to help foster those ideas, empower those people, and cultivate the community that will be vital to the resurgence already under way.

Several years ago my wife was given six months to live. Thankfully, she was misdiagnosed and is still very much alive. But during her stay in the hospital, before we knew she would still be with us, we had the conversation you can only have when you think death is imminent. My wife told me she viewed my life as that of a catapult—putting good people and ideas into the arena. Through RedState and now through radio and TheResurgent.com, I feel called, more than ever, to find good people with good ideas who share a common worldview and to put them forward for consideration.

Now is not the time for checking out. Now is the time to surge forward together with renewed vigor. A crisis such as we face today reveals the character of a nation. I, for one, believe our best days could be ahead if we are willing to engage with unwavering belief.

A lot of good people trumpet the wisdom of America's founders—and we should. A lot of people champion the Constitution—and they're right to do so. While we should never neglect our heritage no matter how much it is vilified by the Left, we must be careful not to focus so much on the past that we fail to articulate the blessings of freedom to new generations. Thus while we should never concede our exceptional past as a nation, we cannot coast on the patriotism and faith of yesteryear. We must reclaim our freedoms and engage afresh, with a faith that cannot be shaken.

The resurgence we need is one that honors and respects our blessed past while boldly surging forward to a brighter tomorrow. It's a movement committed to living out what we believe regardless of the opposition we may encounter. We can't wait for someone else to step up and lead; this resurgence will have to be led by people like you and me who choose to lead from where we are. We're not expecting an easy road ahead. The Apostle Paul tells us that "we do not wrestle against flesh and blood, but against the rulers, against the authorities, against the cosmic powers over this present darkness, against the spiritual forces of evil in the heavenly places" (Eph. 6:12). Russell Moore warns of the temptation to buy into a false narrative:

> [T]here's a temptation for Christians to buy into the narrative of our opponents that what is happening around us is just an upward progress toward some sort of progressive utopia and that Christians are on the wrong side of history. Sometimes Christians can buy into that narrative and become very gloomy or they become very angry—and that is a theology of losers. That's not a theology of Christians.
>
> Yes, we're on the wrong side of history. We started on the wrong side of history. The "right" side of history was Rome as the eternal city, and a Roman cross is the wrong side of history. The French Revolution was the "right" side of history. We were on the wrong side of that. Scientific materialism was the "right" side of history. We were on the wrong side of that. State socialism was the right side of history. We were on the wrong side of that. And so, we've always been on the wrong side of history.
>
> **The question is not who's on the right side of history, but who's at the right hand of the Father?** If Christians have confidence that Jesus Christ is alive, then that means that we're not going to be a hand-wringing, gloomy people. We're going to recognize that the Kingdom of God has always been a minority view in every single culture, and that the Kingdom of God brings with it its own power to change minds and change hearts and move itself along by the power of the Spirit.
>
> **I think Christians need to be the most confident people in American society, not the least confident people.**[3] [emphasis added]

The Left has momentum. We know that. Our secular overlords control key cultural institutions in politics, media, education, the judiciary, business, and even some mainline denominations that still try to pass themselves off as being Christian.

They want you to feel like you're on the wrong side of history, because then you will be more likely to bow to their beliefs. They want you to think there's no one else out there who believes as you do. They want people of faith to feel like freaks. They want Christians to feel as if they don't belong in culture anymore. They want children to conclude their Christian parents are a bunch of homophobic weirdos.

If you are going to be made to care, you must first be made to feel alone. You must be made to conclude that resistance is futile, as if everyone else agrees with popular culture, the gay activists' agenda, and the secular dogmas of the Left. They will try to convince you to silence yourself—they have to, because their worldview will not hold up under scrutiny.

Most important, the Left works to ostracize you because they know you are a relational being. You want friendships; you want to be accepted by others. We all do. So they want to convince us that silence is the price of companionship and acceptance by others. It is not true. You are not alone. In the face of these attacks on our freedom to believe, we must be intentional about cultivating the one thing that will matter most through the times of testing ahead—*community*.

WE NEED COMMUNITY

To survive the wildfire and position ourselves to be part of the resurgence, we must surround ourselves with like-minded believers in order to ensure the Left does not succeed in isolating us and making us feel alone. Jesus Himself wrestled with the temptation to feel alone. He found His comfort in the truth that He was not—He was always in community with the Father (John 16:32). Likewise, we must remind ourselves of our connection with other people of faith if we are to thrive.

JONAH attorney Charles LiMandri rightly notes, "We need to be smart like the other side and do it from a position of strength so they're not picking us off one at a time.... Christians converted the Roman Empire because these pagans looked at the Christians to see how they love each other...."[4]

The early church came together in unprecedented bonds of community both out of love for one another and out of necessity, as persecution soon scattered them throughout the world. "May they be one" (John 17:21) was the prayer of Jesus in the Garden of Gethsemane. And ever since, the Evil One has sought to separate us from the fold to repeat his question from Eden: "Did God actually say...?" (Gen. 3:1). Pastor Steve Smothermon describes the tactics of the Serpent who threatens our faith:

> If the devil can get us in the wilderness, he will devour us, but if we stay in the sheepfold, the flock, we're protected by a shepherd, and the great and chief shepherd is the Lord Jesus Christ. Then he has under-shepherds, which are people like myself and you, and others who are strong believers, and other pastors, and what we call lay leaders, and deacons, and elders—however your church functions. There's protection in that flock. But when you get outside on your own, man, that's when you're going to get devoured; you're going to get deceived; you're going to be discouraged. We need each other. We need relationships.[5]

If we know we need the fellowship of other believers, why do we seem to be so cloistered in our own homes? I don't know about you, but one of the greatest barriers keeping my family from connecting with other believers is a very practical concern—a clean house. It sounds crazy when we think about it in the context of facing persecution for our faith, but the first thing people have to be willing to do to cultivate community is to stop worrying about how their home looks. I'm not saying you shouldn't do what you can to keep it clean, but don't let a little mess keep you from inviting fellow believers into your home to build authentic relationships. In my experience, so many of us go to work all day and think we can't have people over because the house is a wreck. In places where there's a strong sense of community, people just don't care that your house doesn't look like a sitcom set. They prioritize the interaction with fellow believers over having a spotless home. Inviting people into your home—even over a store-bought meal—is one of the most essential steps to fostering faith-building community. Once we realize that no one is going to hate us for not having a spotless house, we'll be far more likely to invite others in and develop a community of friends who share our faith.

People with children seem especially prone to isolating themselves because they tend to be so focused on their kids' schedules. They try to compete with other families, it seems, to see who can be more involved in athletics or academic competitions. As a result, we're so busy that the last thing we want when we go home is to have visitors. We may have a mantel full of plastic trophies, but no one comes over to break bread and fellowship around our deeply held beliefs. Consequently, we don't show our kids how to build relationships with people in our home.

It may not be easy for a lot of us. We've become so insulated from meaningful interaction with our neighbors. Eye-to-eye contact is now eye-to-iPhone contact. Don't get me wrong. I'm a fan of technology. Yet when we think of notable memories in life, we often recall a smell or a sense of touch that gives them depth. As a result of limiting our personal interactions to the digital world, we have fewer and fewer of those multisensory experiences. A lot of us spend time building a digital community around the world, but that digital community can't come into our homes without an Internet connection. We've reordered our lives to build communities of common interest with those who are far away, but we struggle to relate to people who live next door or sit next to us in church. We relate to our friends on the basis of fantasy football, politics, or a hobby. But it is our faith that needs the most support. We were not made to follow Christ alone. We were made to be part of a body, a member of a community of disciples defined by belief and made visible by shared geography.

In a day and age when it feels as if the whole world wants to tell us we're wrong, we need a community of believers around us to remind us not only that we are right, but also that there are plenty of other people who agree with us. And our children need to see that to be true. I suggest starting by building a community of believers with whom you break bread on a regular basis, and later inviting others who don't share your faith to join you. It's not going to work out well for you if you start by inviting a bunch of random strangers into your house. There's got to be a common foundation of shared beliefs, but that common foundation should allow you to branch out into areas of un-commonality and to try to understand differences.

The key is making sure you're surrounded with people who *share* your worldview, since it seems there are more and more pressures on you to *abandon* your worldview. You've got to put yourself in a situation where you feel comfortable being yourself, believing all that you believe, including the values that you've been raised with, so that when the world comes and tells you you're wrong and you're alone in your beliefs, you can say, "No, actually, I have this great group of friends who believe the same thing." Just as God assured the despondent prophet Elijah that the Lord had "seven thousand...who have not bowed the knee" to a false god (1 Kings 19:18), so we need to be continually reminded of the basic but powerful truth that we are not alone.

Ravi Zacharias explains why community is so vital to us all, but especially to Christians:

> For the Christian worldview, there are three starting points: *identity*—who we are. If you go back to the laws of logic, the first law of logic is a law of identity. If A, then not non-A. And then there is *intimacy*—how do we find the purity of one intimate relationship, which we all long for? The third is the outworking of *community*. We all seek for *identity*, *intimacy*, and *community*.
>
> From the Christian point of view, that *community* moves in the direction of worship. Yes, it's not a perfect community. Yes, we have fallibilities, and we have weaknesses. Sometimes hypocrisies are revealed, but just because we have our failings and our shortcomings does not mean we should remove the direction in which we want to walk. And **that is the whole point of the New Testament, a community of worship**. The book of Acts is really what happened when believers had that belief in common. You have to have certain shared identities, certain shared meanings of the past. Cultural revolutions become realities when those shared meanings of the past are lost. Community is vital.[6] [emphasis added]

Ironically, those in the LGBT lifestyle often do a better job at building community than Christians, according to Rosaria Butterfield, a former lesbian who is now a Christian:

> "The LGBT community is a real community," she said. When she was a lesbian "everyone's home in our community was open every night...an open home with a meal and

friendship was what stood between you and suicide, or you and boredom, or you and alcohol."

By contrast, she added, "often the Christian community looks very bounded and guarded, very rule driven, very inaccessible.... Quite frankly, from my perspective, it has often seemed that Christians have just grown comfortable having a starvation diet of community. It's hard for starving people to have a meal. It just is."

Butterfield also cited 1 Corinthians 10:13, which says that when you are tempted God will "make a way to escape" (KJV).

"What if my home is a way of escape, but I'm too busy being concerned that there's cat hair on the couch? Right? Who cares? People are going to die of loneliness faster," she said.[7]

If our faith is to survive—let alone thrive—in the times of testing that lie ahead, we need to surround ourselves with a community of fellow believers. Over the next four chapters, I invite you to join me as we drill a little deeper into what it means to be *resurgent* as a member of the evangelical Christian community, although many of the lessons and applications will benefit all people of faith.

CHAPTER 16

THE RESURGENT BELIEVER

Anyone who really believes in God must set God, and the truth of God, above all other considerations.

—FATHER JOHN COURTNEY MURRAY[1]

One of my favorite podcasts is *The History of Rome* by Mike Duncan. The eighty-seventh episode explains why Romans viewed Christians as such weird anomalies in society. The Romans thought of Christians as a form of Jew, but the Jews made sacrifices for the emperor. The Jews would make sacrifices to Yahweh on behalf of Marcus Aurelius, Diocletian, or other emperors. But the Christians flat out refused; they could not do it and remain faithful to their beliefs. Their unwillingness to compromise contributed to the Romans' decision to persecute the Christians for their beliefs.

In addition to being thought of as just plain weird, Christianity was not the religion of the elite in society. It embraced the radical philosophy that all people are equal before God as sinners in need of grace. Consequently, it threatened to upend the social order and the spirit of the age. For example, Christianity embraced a values system that encouraged turning the other cheek in the midst of a litigious Roman culture that retaliated for every perceived slight. It wasn't only that Christians were revolutionary with respect to the Roman way of life; they were thought to be aliens, so different that Romans struggled to understand them. They became *other*. And that—to a degree—is what practicing Christians are becoming here in America—*other*.[2]

This is precisely why the resurgence must start with the individual believer. Each of us is going to have to choose—believe in Christ's teachings or the world's teachings, but either way you will be made to care. Jesus himself said it: "No man can serve two masters...." (Matt. 6:24). For far too long, Christians in America have been able to coast in peace on the faith fumes of yesterday's believers. But a peaceful people is seldom a religious people. And coasting can only take you one direction—downhill. It has been said, "Never let a good crisis go to waste."[3] We tend to change direction in life for one of two reasons. Either a crisis forces us to make a move, or our own vision for a better life pulls us in a new direction. Christians in America have largely lost our internal drive to grow our faith—because we haven't had to. Because everything still looked okay on the outside, we thought we could afford to drift. We were wrong. The culture that we live in will no longer permit Christians to remain invisible, and that's not necessarily a bad thing for the Kingdom of Heaven, even though it may be briefly painful for believers in America.

Believers need to remember that our faith and loyalty to God are distinct from our love for our country. Not always incompatible, but different. And Christians may soon need to choose between the two as they are accused of being freaks and *enemies of the state*, of upending the social order of the secular elite. There's going to have to be a resurgence in orthodox belief and boldness among believers so we can say we are Christians first and Americans second. The Judeo-Christian foundation we once shared with most people in our culture is no longer there. Russell Moore correctly notes that we can no longer make the assumption that people share what we believe: "There was a time when Christians could assume that most people in American culture agreed with us on values, if not on gospel. Even the way that some Christians engaged [culture] was to say, 'This is not the *real* America. These are just some elites in Hollywood or somewhere else.' Well, looking around now, those issues that were once wedge issues for the Right are now wedge issues for the Left in almost every category—on marriage, on sexuality, on marijuana, on drug use, on all of those sorts of things."[4]

Yes, the winds of change are blowing, and the changes do not necessarily favor the comfort of individual believers. Like countless Christians who've gone before us, we might wish we could avoid the war on our freedom to believe, but that choice is not ours to make. As Gandalf noted in *The Lord of the Rings*, we do not get to choose the battles of our time:

> "I wish it need not have happened in my time," said Frodo.
> "So do I," said Gandalf, "and so do all who live to see such times. But that is not for them to decide. All we have to decide is what to do with the time that is given us."[5]

It is not for us to choose the challenges to our faith, only how we will respond to them. Our faith compels us to action, if it is faith at all. As Dietrich Bonhoeffer once said, "Mere waiting and looking on is not Christian behavior. Christians are called to compassion and to action."[6]

In addition, we cannot have authentic community among believers if we do not know who truly believes and who is simply going through the motions. One blessing of persecution is that it tends to winnow out the poseurs from the true believers. If we are faithful, we will find that we are not alone.

But in our actions and our struggles, it often seems that the Christ followers—a term I use to separate those who actually follow Christ from those who call themselves Christians by habit and nothing else—are dealt setback after setback. Truth be told, our frustration gets the best of us on occasion. We sometimes want to sit it out, to go into seclusion and meditation. The writer of Psalm 73 lamented the fact that those who feared God appeared to struggle, while those who rejected God appeared to prosper. Nothing has changed. The secular crowd that routinely attacks evangelicals and people of faith—in other words, the folks who want to take God out of the national conversation or, at minimum, turn Him into something He is not—always seem to do pretty well in this life.

Asaph wrote, "I envied the arrogant when I saw the prosperity of the wicked. They have no struggles; their bodies are healthy and strong. They are free from the burdens common to man.... Therefore, pride is their necklace; they clothe themselves with violence." Asaph was pretty put out. But he returned to the truth when he entered the house of the Lord. When he reconnected in fellowship with other believers to worship God, he began to reacquire the right perspective. He realized, "God is good...to those who are pure in heart." Of those wicked who were prospering, he wrote, "Surely you [God] place them on slippery ground; you cast them down to ruin. How suddenly are they destroyed, completely swept away by terrors!" (Ps. 73).

That's a mystery of this life. The wicked do often prosper for this season of existence. But victory ultimately belongs to those who know God in a real way based on the truth He has revealed. Victory comes, though we know not when. We must be happy warriors until the end. For those of you who struggle with what is going on today, who see retreat and capitulation, and who feel like our society holds dear those things you hold as blasphemous—be cheerful. Be happy. God isn't surprised by any of it. His promises remain, unhindered by man's feeble protests. Victory is already yours. Take heart. Have courage. And prepare yourself to fight on.

Shortly after the *Obergefell* ruling, pastor and bestselling author Kevin DeYoung made a comment to the effect that we should consider ourselves blessed to live in a time when being a Christian actually gets to mean something. When I asked him to expand on his thoughts, he shared this perspective:

> Paul told Timothy that anyone who desires to live a godly life in Christ Jesus *will* be persecuted. And that's been a verse that for most Christians in this country has been maybe something that prompts us to pray for brothers and sisters around the world, but what does it actually mean for us? It seems to me Jesus has a pretty broad view of [persecution] in the Sermon on the Mount. He talks about people reviling you, people calling you names, people hating you. Certainly it can be much more serious than that, but the disciples were told to count it all joy when people reviled them. In Acts they counted it a privilege when they could suffer for the name of Christ. So while we don't want to be saying, *Look at us, we're martyrs*, [we want] to be able to say, *I follow Christ. I believe and affirm the truth that Christian churches have always believed.* To pay some sort of cost for that is going to be inconvenient. It's going to be painful; but it's also a privilege because it means that we take up our cross and follow Christ. That's what He told us to do, because that's what He did.[7]

As Christians facing the cultural pressures of our time, we really have only two options before us: *surrender* or *resurgence*. You can choose how to respond to the war on your freedom to believe. "If it is evil in your eyes to serve the LORD, choose this day whom you will serve.... But as for me and my house, we will serve the Lord" (Josh. 24:15).

I choose to be a resurgent. And I invite you to join me.

THREE STEPS FOR EVERY
RESURGENT BELIEVER

So what can you do as a Christian to be part of a resurgent community of believers? Let's keep it simple. There are three main things you can do to prepare yourself and your faith to thrive in the days ahead. You have to know what you believe, you have to live it, and you have to be able to express it.

Number One: Know What You Believe

• *Get clear about what you believe.* If you've been coasting, stop. When the time of testing reaches your front door or place of business, it will be too late to study up on your beliefs. You will be made to choose eventually, so it's best to get intentional now. Figure out *what* you believe and *why* before you face a crisis. Decide what is principle and what is opinion. Which hill are you prepared to die on? If Jesus is Lord, then there are nonnegotiable beliefs. Do you know what they are and where you will choose to take your stand?

• *Reconnect with the past.* Christians are not immune to the anti-tradition movement that has captivated the Left. Evangelical Christians in particular have often disconnected from historical Christianity. There is a myth being peddled now by people who aren't Christians that many of the doctrines of faith are open for debate, even though the church has taken great pains over two thousand years to reach agreement on them. They're not really issues anymore. But Christians who don't know better, who've never studied the creeds of the church and gleaned insights from "the great cloud of witnesses" who've gone before, don't know that to be true. In some Christian circles, the Left is trying to refight arguments settled at church councils more than 1,500 years ago. Study up on the tenets of your faith, and get to know its history as well.

• *Discover how your faith applies to cultural issues.* In our sincere attempts to preserve the gospel and live holy lives, we've lost the ability to think deeply about how our faith integrates with culture. Instead of trying to do as John Calvin suggested and "think God's thoughts after Him,"[8] we make it up as we go. We put our own faith in a box and restrict what we believe to the sphere of the church instead of "liberating Christianity from its cultural captivity."[9] We should be seeing everything through the lens of a biblical worldview instead of accepting a blended viewpoint that makes it difficult for us to respond to the secularist claims. We need to seek out the writings of Christians who've challenged us to think deeply about our faith and get to work studying to show ourselves approved unto God (2 Tim. 2:15).

Number Two: Live What You Believe

• *Don't just call yourself a follower of Christ; do what He has called you to do.* Love your neighbor as yourself. Examine your life and purge sinful influences from it. Root out hypocrisy in your own life and get real about living with a faith that moves you to move mountains. Unfortunately, churches don't always do a great job anymore of teaching the fundamental practices of the Christian faith. To learn the essentials of following Christ, I recommend my coauthor Bill Blankschaen's book *A Story Worth Telling: Your Field Guide to Living an Authentic Life.*[10]

• *Put first things first.* For too many of us, our faith is an add-on, something we squeeze in when we can. But if your faith is to stand strong, you must reprioritize your life to reflect what you say you believe. Simplify. Focus on what matters most. Resist the tyranny of the *next*—chasing every new gadget, comfort, or societal craze. New is not necessarily better. Progress is not always positive. As the Scottish caretaker of the Bond estate said in *Skyfall*, "Sometimes the old ways are the best ways."[11]

• *Surround yourself with people who will call you out for hypocrisy.* Because we believe human nature is fallen, don't assume you know where you might be compromising with the secular Spirit of the Age. Cultivate the community I mentioned in the previous chapter—not only for strength and comfort, but also for accountability. For that to work, you will need to create a margin in your schedule where authentic connection can take place. You will need to invest time in caring for others in your circle of influence to foster authentic community.

Number Three: Express What You Believe

• *Speak with humble boldness.* Don't seek out a fight, but don't run from one when God permits it to come. You have to be willing to be the one to say, *I don't agree with that*, instead of presuming that someone else will speak up. You must be willing to speak out in the public sphere—to say you disagree with something at your children's schools, to vote and engage political discourse, or to encourage your pastor to be bold on moral issues with political implications. In private, also, you must be willing to humbly yet unapologetically disagree with your friends. Most people just go along to get along. They don't want controversy. They don't want to be disliked. But being willing to say you disagree with something has power in an age where dissent takes courage. Kevin DeYoung says that we as individual believers have an opportunity in the midst of this cultural shift: "The great opportunity we have is people understanding and seeing now that to be a Christian in our culture is going to have to mean a willingness to be different. And that's really what being a Christian should always have been like. [It's an opportunity] to be true *not* to our fallen selves, but who we are in Christ."[12]

- *Speak the truth in love*. The Apostle Paul tells us in his letter to the Ephesians that speaking the truth in love is how the body of Christ is built up (Eph. 4:15). This simple yet often neglected command is at the very core of the gospel. Yet we usually choose either to be silent or to rant in a way that makes us sound hateful. Theologian Brian Mattson thinks fear is what drives us to take a harsher tone in our cultural struggles: "God is not surprised by any of this. He has purposes for this. There's no reason to get fearful. One of the problems that Christians have is that when we become fearful, our speech sounds indistinguishable from hate.... The way not to sound like you're hateful is not to be fearful. We should be happy warriors. We should advocate for what we believe, cheerfully, lovingly, but firmly at the same time."[13]

According to Nancy Pearcey, we need to develop a mission mindset that interacts with unbelievers in words they can understand:

> Too often we've thought of missionaries as people who went to other countries [because] America was still essentially Christian, the consensus was Christian....
>
> I'd suggest that we are ambassadors for Christ; we're missionaries.... Our job is to learn the language of the people we're trying to speak with. Too often we just slide into using Christian jargon and then wondering why people shut us down. Well, it's our responsibility to learn their language; it's not their responsibility to learn ours. We're called by God to be the missionary. And so, learning the thought forms and the language of the people around us and that we're trying to reach is vital.[14]

- *Confront your fears*. Make no mistake. Expressing what you believe to be true will require courage. But remember the words of Christ: "Do not fear those who kill the body but cannot kill the soul.

Rather fear him who can destroy both soul and body in hell." The gay rights activists who yell "bigot" at those who disagree with them are the jihadists of America's cultural ghetto. They will incite injury, financial or otherwise, to those who disagree with them. They want victory and know the only way to get it is to destroy, ruin, and shut up any who get in their way. But they are on the losing side of the One who created history. Christians should take heart. The faith that is flourishing even today in Communist China will survive this present turmoil. And as Pastor David McNeely reminds us, the short-term outcome isn't really our concern to begin with:

> My hope cannot lie in an outcome. My hope for the Christian life cannot lie in God providing an escape for me from persecution. My hope cannot lie in any outcome, however desirable that would be. My hope has to lie in a person. To be prepared for what's coming in the future, the only way I know to do that is to go back to the fundamentals of the faith.... It is about a walk with God. So the best way I can prepare for future persecution, however small or however large, is—I pray. I talk to God. I read His Word. I go to church. I get plugged into my local congregation so that I can have the support of others where it's not just me pursuing God, it's *we* who are pursuing God together. Then I trust God as I become active in sharing my faith. I'm willing to say, "Here's an alternative. Here's a God of the universe who actually demands and deserves your worship." I trust Him that the gospel message has power, that I need not be ashamed of it.[15]

McNeely's words allude to a verse that has been close to my heart throughout my career. It is one every believer should know: "I am not ashamed of the gospel, for it is the power of God for salvation to everyone who believes, to the Jew first and also to the Greek." The gospel is the good news the world needs. It brings freedom for captive souls, hearts, and minds. It has produced the greatest flourishing the world has ever known. It will continue to so do for all eternity, no matter what the forces of darkness may do to try to silence it.

I am a follower of Jesus Christ. And I am not ashamed.

What will you do?

CHAPTER 17

THE RESURGENT FAMILY

*The foundation of national morality must be laid
in private families.*

—JOHN ADAMS[1]

W hen it comes to the sorry state of families in America,
we need a resurgence because—candidly—we are on the
road to hell. Let's face it: the *Obergefell* decision came
after decades of disrespecting marriage. You would be hard pressed
to name three popular sitcoms in the last twenty years that showed a
stable family environment centered around the marriage of one man
to one woman, but there is no shortage of dysfunctional examples
that come to mind. The truth is that we Christians and conservatives
alike need to take responsibility for our role in the decline of marriage
and the family.

But the situation is not as bleak as many people of faith believe.
For *The Good News about Marriage*, Shaunti Feldhahn dug into the

data and discovered that being actively engaged in religion makes a difference in marriage:

> The widespread belief that "the rate of divorce is the same in the church" is actually an urban legend based on a significant misunderstanding of the Barna Group research. Barna was studying only belief systems—finding the divorce rate was the same among people who hold to Christian, Muslim, or atheist belief systems, for example. But Barna specifically excluded worship attendance from the analysis. So I partnered with Barna and we re-ran the same data set, but with worship attendance factored in, and among those who were in church in the last 7 days, the divorce rate was 27 percent lower compared to those who were not.[2]

According to Feldhahn, reports of the death of marriage have been exaggerated. The actual divorce rate has never gotten close to 50 percent, most marriages are happy, and most remarriages succeed. The percentage of women still married to their first spouse is 71 percent.[3] In spite of these facts, the perception remains that we have devalued marriage to the point where the next generation fails to see why it is worth saving at all. And there is a valid case to be made there. Divorce has hit the church hard, even if not at the same rate as the rest of culture. Divorce degraded marriage long before the Supreme Court abolished it. Andrew T. Walker explains how our lax attitude toward divorce set up our culture for the disaster of *Obergefell*:

> To understand *Obergefell* from June 2015, you have to actually understand the subtle redefinition that occurred in marriage prior to that, starting back in the 1960s and

1970s with the introduction of no-fault divorce. And I hate to say this, because Ronald Reagan was actually the first person to introduce no-fault divorce into our laws, and I am a huge Reagan fan. But he definitely got this wrong, in my opinion. Essentially, no-fault divorce introduced this understanding into the law that no one has to be at fault in order for a marriage to be dissolved. Nowadays, a contract between a barista and a consumer at Starbucks has more contractual binding than the marriage between a man and a woman.... So, essentially we have this understanding that marriage is not permanent that gets seeded into the culture, starting in the 1970s.[4]

If we are to experience a resurgence of healthy families in our culture, it must begin with each of us committing to make our own marriage a healthy example for others to follow. We must be intentional about it, because the dominant forces of our culture are actively seeking to tear down the nuclear family organized around conjugal marriage. The best way to defend marriage in our culture is not to elect the right leaders or swap out Supreme Court justices, but to improve your own marriage and make it something worth protecting in the first place. The wildfire that is burning in our culture—and will continue to burn through it in the years ahead—will leave extensive damage to families and children in its wake. Your marriage, your family, must offer a healthy alternative to the dysfunction. It is incumbent upon Christians and all people of faith to give the world something to talk about.

Christians and other people of faith can do at least three main things toward the resurgence of healthy families that our culture so desperately needs: build a faithful marriage, rear faithful children, and create a faithful family culture.

THREE STEPS FOR
THE RESURGENT FAMILY

Number One: Build a Faithful Marriage

• *Keep your marriage vows.* Here's novel concept: take responsibility for your own marriage. Instead of just complaining about how the Left is abolishing marriage, focus first on making your marriage what it should be. To paraphrase the words of Jesus, remove the beam in your own eye and then you will see clearly to help others who are struggling to understand the value of the institution. It starts with living a life of integrity, staying fully committed to your spouse, and resisting the temptation to drift apart—including ensuring pornography has no place in your life.

• *Take divorce off the table.* If you truly believe that marriage is between one man and one woman for life, live it out. Don't say that is what marriage should be *for everyone else* and then toss it under the bus when the going gets tough in your own life. Know the difference between the fantasy portrayed in the media and the reality that marriage is hard work. Maggie Gallagher describes where our focus should be in marriage:

> The evil that is done through divorce on a daily basis—we see it but we don't really think about the extraordinary evil that people do every day by suppressing their awareness of how bad [the impact of divorce] is going to be. The alternative is not your romantic ideal, but the ordinary marriage where a man and a woman get up every day and say, *This is the person God has given me to love. How do I love them? How do I love them better? How do I build the family where love is visible and real and can be relied on and not buffeted around by the winds of desire that our culture teaches us is important?*[5]

• *Become one.* Being committed to the idea of oneness in your marriage means that you become one complete person, not two separate individuals living two separate lives. Of my numerous younger friends who have been divorced, I don't know one who had a shared checking account with his or her spouse. They all kept their individual checking accounts, and so it was really easy to walk away when life got tough, because their finances—and their lives—were never truly comingled. The idea of marital oneness in the Bible suggests an actual complete person, and one human being should have one checking account. One human being should have one set of friends. So often today, people want to get married but keep a separate single identity. Marriage doesn't work that way. The problem is only growing worse among millennials, who, because of their cynical views of marriage, are more frequently choosing cohabitation prior to marriage. That only sets them up for greater marital failure because they are used to living as if their relationship is on a trial basis.

Number Two: Rear Faithful and Focused Children

• *Make more babies.* I am not prescribing a one-size-fits-all number of children each family should have, because each family situation is unique. But do the math. Secularism self-destructs. It is not kid friendly and thus not a viable strategy for cultural sustainability—hence the progressives' enthusiasm for immigration while they support the killing of millions of unborn children. If you need further convincing on this point, Mark Steyn's book *America Alone* gives demographic data to demonstrate the connection between having babies and sustaining our freedom. The truth is that most couples don't want the hard work of rearing children. But as Andrew T. Walker and Eric Teetsel put it, it is in this mundane task that the real impact is made: "The task of parenting in marriage is extremely mundane in the sense that everyone does it, but it is in that mundaneness where real impact is made over time. We cannot necessarily be looking for incredible change day-by-day, but as week-by-week, month-by-month in obedience to that call that God has placed on us to be husbands and fathers where the change gets made."[6]

• *Invest time and resources into building relationships with your children, especially when they are young.* Tell them you love them—often. Show them you love them—often. Demonstrate for them how to live out your faith. Values are caught more than they are taught, so model your faith in front of your kids. Read the Bible and pray with and for them.

• *Teach your children well.* Make learning about your faith part of your family culture. Teach them the faith as a Way of Life, just as your secular counterparts do. Remember the call of Scripture to teach your children to walk *coram deo*—before the face of God—at all times: "You shall love the Lord your God with all your heart and with all your soul and with all your might. And these words that I command you today shall be on your heart. You shall teach them diligently to your children, and shall talk of them when you sit in your house, and when you walk by the way, and when you lie down, and when you rise. You shall bind them as a sign on your hand, and they shall be as frontlets between your eyes. You shall write them on the doorposts of your house and on your gates" (Deut. 6:6).

And don't restrict your teaching to private spirituality, thereby reinforcing the secularist's call to keep faith in a box. Teach your children to think critically, encouraging them to apply their faith to the culture even as you guard them from undue influence by it. For one of the unpopular things that resurgent families have to do is turn off popular culture. I'm not calling us to return to the 1950s or some bygone era, but to actually unplug from media and influences that shove the secular religion down your throats. Turn the page. Change the channel. Better yet, shut off media entirely at times and simply enjoy one another's company over a board game or a walk in the woods. When you do engage popular culture, view it with a critical eye. For example, when you watch movies with your children, push pause on occasion and ask, *What do you think of what you just saw? Does the Bible address this issue? Where is God on this issue and why?* Talk *with* them, not *at* them. Teach them to think biblically and apply their faith as they live in but not of the world.

Number Three: Create a Faithful Family Culture

• *Slow down.* As a society, we are living fast lives. Our schedules are all jammed, including the kids'. Paul Virilio rightly says, "The more speed increases, the faster freedom decreases."[7] We all face competitive pressures to keep up with the Joneses. We're all subject to that unshakeable feeling that if we don't do something, it's not going to get done. We operate in our daily existence as if it all depends on us and not on the Almighty God. The Bible does call on us to "work out your own salvation," but adds "for it is God who works in you" (Phil. 2:12–13). All too often, we crowd Him out of the schedule. We drown Him out of the conversation and are not still enough to know that He is there and He is not silent. We get our kids too focused on sports, academics, or getting a scholarship to pay for college. We hustle them here and there. We don't slow down enough to enjoy each other's company. Christian households have got to reassess just how much we want to look like the rest of the world. If your family looks just like the rest of the world, your family is probably going to fail. But the more we take the time to help our kids embrace faith and see that it's not something abnormal or deviant or weird, the better off they will be in the long-term. Far too many Christian parents are focused on getting their kids into a good college instead of getting their kids through life as believers.

• *Treat your children like children.* Television often portrays kids as smaller, more intelligent versions of adults; they are not. You are the adult. Act accordingly. Set boundaries for your family. Protect your kids from harmful influences. Love them enough to tell them *no*. Be willing to be an authority figure, unpopular if necessary.

• *Foster family unity.* Fragmentized families happen naturally in our individualistic culture. If your family is going to be different, here are seven simple things you can do to foster greater unity:

- Eat together.
- Play together.
- Worship together.
- Learn together.
- Serve together.
- Pray together.
- Read together.

Slow down. Smile more. Watch less. Pray harder. Live generously. Borrow less. Give more. Forgive often. And keep moving forward.

A WORD TO FATHERS

When God sent a flood as judgment for the sin of a corrupt culture, it wasn't only Noah who got a ride in the ark. His children were kept safe because of their father's faithfulness. God told Noah, "I will establish my covenant with you, and you shall come into the ark, you, your sons, your wife, and your sons' wives with you" (Gen. 6:18). He later commands, "Go into the ark, you and all your household, for I have seen that you are righteous before me in this generation" (Gen. 7:1). The word *you* is singular. God did not find Noah's wife to be righteous. He did not find Noah's sons to be righteous. He did not find Noah's daughters-in-law to be righteous. God found only Noah, the father, to be righteous. "Noah was a righteous man, blameless in his generation. Noah walked with God" (Gen. 6:9). But because God found Noah to be righteous, his wife and children were blessed.

There is a critical lesson in that truth for fathers today. We face a crisis of fatherhood in the new America of absentee dads. The cultural shifts in marriage and gender mean that children with strong fathers in their lives will have a tremendous advantage. Incredibly, some critics have actually suggested that we may need to abolish the family to level the playing field for children who do not have a mother and father together at home.[8] It's not a coincidence that as secularism has risen in the country, so has the voice that says fathers don't really matter. But in reality mothers and fathers are not interchangeable. The only social science that has suggested otherwise has been politically motivated.

I myself am often guilty of neglecting my children by focusing so much on earning a living to provide a roof over their heads that I don't invest time with them at home. Fathers have to play a key role in their children's lives. They have to play a disciplinarian role in their kids' lives. They are not to be their friends, but their fathers, giving moral instruction and shaping the character of their children, a role that reflects our Heavenly Father's guidance of us all. Where moms tend to offer temperance and compassion, dads supply firmness and conviction. Our society is full of kids who don't have convictions about the way they should go in life because they don't have a father willing to guide them.

Today we have a millennial generation that is more temperate and compassionate partly because so many of them have been reared by their mothers. They lack the unique qualities that fathers bring to the family equation. When you don't have a father playing the father's role, you have the mother playing both roles, and something critical gets lost in translation. I am not saying that to discourage the single mother doing the best she can; I am calling out fathers who have failed to remain faithful to their families and have compromised their children's future in the process.

As a Christian apologist, Ravi Zacharias has wrestled with the breakdown of the family for many decades as he has traveled the world applying the Christian faith to life. When I asked for his thoughts on the role of fathers and the health of families, here is how he replied:

> I was in a country [recently] in their leading city. They have Father's Day on a different day of the year than we do here in America. I was sitting with the leadership—civic leadership, law enforcement leadership—and the chief law enforcement officer was to my right at lunch. He said to me, "I have 20,000 law enforcement people working under me. I've concluded that our society's problems boil down to a very simple reality with which we live. There are no fathers in the households, no fathers to model what it means to be strong and gentlemanly and courteous at the same time. Not far from where you and I are sitting is a part of this city where Father's Day is the loneliest day of the year, because **90 percent of [the children in] that community do not know who their father is.**" It was a stunning statement that he made.
>
> This is the reality of the distinctiveness in the way God has fashioned [men], to show both physical strength and gentleness and law-abiding proclivities. To show how to treat people weaker than you with respect and dignity, and [to make] no distinction of any inequality of worth and value. To show that your muscle power is not used to throttle people, but to show where real strength and character lies in raising a family. **The collapse of the home may be the most significant death of our time.** And a lot of this depends upon how the fathers have lived their lives for decades working on strength, endurance, and all that goes along with the muscle building and so on. We've shown that athletic prowess is still big in our sporting fields, that

there is big money in it. That strength is not to be used to abuse people, but that strength can be shown in respecting and caring for people who don't have the same power as you do. This happens whether it's power in office, or power in physicality. I think it's gone into the home and to children.

One Middle Eastern leader of a royal family said that the greatest need of our time is the modeling of leadership and the examples we need to set to the young. If the young do not see that modeling of leadership, he said, there's only destruction that lies ahead. The loss of the father figure in the home is one of the key elements in what's happening in the lawlessness in society today. The home is the microcosm. As you move out into the branches of society and culture, [the problem] emerges from the microcosm of the home. The home is under serious threat today, and if law enforcement officers are telling us that is where they see the problem, we'd better listen to them carefully.[9] [emphasis added]

CHAPTER 18

THE RESURGENT CHURCH

*Flight into the invisible is a denial of the call. A community
of Jesus which seeks to hide itself has ceased to follow him.*

—DIETRICH BONHOEFFER[1]

J esus said the gates of hell would not prevail against His church. And
yet the Christian church seems to be losing everywhere we look in
America today. In an earlier chapter, I decried the mistakes of pastors
and priests and how they've contributed to that decline. I didn't point out
their shortcomings because I believe the church to be without hope. Quite
the opposite. I agree with Pastor David McNeely, who thinks the cultural
crisis we face, the time of testing that lies before us, offers the Christian
church the opportunity to recalibrate and experience a *resurgence*:

> I think this is a tremendous opportunity. I really do. I believe
> that the cultural church is shrinking. I believe that the true
> church that only God knows is growing. The darkness is

getting darker, and darker, and darker in America. But that light is shining brighter, and brighter, and brighter now through the church. As the salt of the earth, as the light of the world, we have a real opportunity to stand in the midst of culture and to say, "We function differently."

Think how powerful that message was when the people in Charleston were saying, "I forgive you. I forgive you," while the man who killed their family members and friends was inside the court. They're gathering outside and singing songs like "Amazing Grace." The secular media is covering it and then they're asking the question, "Can you believe this?" What they did shone so brightly. Where did they get that from? It wasn't something that was mustered up from within. They got it from a man who hung on a cross and looked down and said, "Father, forgive them, for they don't know what they're doing." When we live as Christians, when Christ is empowering us, when He is living His life through us, [there is] the potential now for them to see the true unique, distinct difference between the world and the church. As the church gets more purified I think we can become even more evangelistic and more impactful.[2]

The days ahead will not be easy ones for pastors, priests, and believers alike. But I do believe there are at least three main things pastors and church leaders can do to prepare: preach the gospel, teach the truth, and prepare for persecution.

THREE STEPS FOR THE RESURGENT CHURCH

Number One: Preach the Gospel
• *Unite grace and truth.* The seeker-friendly movement that has dominated the megachurches in Protestantism for the last few decades

(and to which the Catholic Church has not been completely immune) has left the church full of grace but often lacking truth. Yet Jesus Himself embodied both (John 1:14). The Christian church should welcome all people, but we should stop being so concerned about making the gospel seeker friendly or palatable to unbelievers and start ensuring that our churches are truth friendly. For it is the truth that our culture desperately needs; it is the one thing that can truly set them free. Ravi Zacharias, who has observed the church for decades in his ministry, says it needs both a heart full of grace and a mind full of truth:

> What I noticed happening in the '60s and '70s when the popularization of the message was taking place was how much the integrity of the Christian faith was being compromised in order to reach the masses. **Not only was the *message* being diluted, the *method* was becoming highly suspect. The commercialization of the gospel *lost* the gospel in the process.**
>
> And then the competition began—how do we keep our young? How do we hold on to the young people who are supporting other programs and not really taking their responsibility in the church? The methodology within the church changed without meeting something deeper. What was deeper was that the young person was being challenged in his faith in the public arena and in the academic arena, and there was no response from within the church to the questions of the mind that ultimately connected to the heart.... [I]n the church we forgot the mind; we forgot the thinking; and the heart sort of ran away with everything.
>
> **So to the church I say this: if we do not find the connection between the head and the heart, we will either become so cerebrally driven that the heart is lost or so**

emotionally driven that the head is lost. The church has to find the balance, and for that our very training has to be changed. A community needs the fellow [believer] in their time of need and in their time of grief and in their time of sorrow, but they also need to face the questions of our time. If that balance is not there with each passing generation, belief will be viewed as nothing more than just a myth and an escape rather than the real world from which everything else is interpreted.[3] [emphasis added]

• *Define love biblically.* After the Supreme Court's *Obergefell* decision, social media lit up with #LoveWins. Yet according to Scripture, God is both love and truth. Love is not a feeling. The Apostle Paul takes love out of the realm of ever-changing emotions in Romans 13:10 when he states this simple but profound truth: "Love is the fulfilling of the law [of God]" (Rom. 13:10). Love is not esoteric or subjective. Love is not simply being polite to someone. Love is not avoiding controversy. Love is not letting people do whatever they want to do and assuring them that everything will be just fine between them and their Creator. Pastor Kevin DeYoung points out that common understanding of love in our culture—acceptance without judgment—doesn't actually work in real life:

> Nobody actually lives out that kind of love or wants that kind of love except in an abstraction. Our culture's definition of love is unconditional affirmation. *You don't love me if you don't affirm all of my choices.* But consistency tells us that's just not true. Parents should understand that. If your kid wants to play with toasters in the bathtub, love is not to affirm that decision. When he's in the middle of the street and a car is coming, you scream loudly for him to get out. That is love.

At the same time that our culture has this mixed up definition of love, we're living in one of the most judgmental times in American history…. [T]here are judgments about the foods you eat, judgments about the cars you drive, your carbon footprint, your recycling, how you parent your kids, and how you feed your infants. Just look at what the debates are on Facebook, and you realize this is an extremely judgmental culture, which is not at all interested in affirming everyone and everything no matter what they do. [In today's culture] love is unconditional affirmation for those who think and act like I do.[4]

Love, as defined by God, is treating others the way He has revealed they should be treated. Love means being truthful with your neighbor about the consequences of sin. Love means speaking the truth even when you know it will probably not be well received. Whenever we separate truth from love, #LoveLoses. And the truth is that though the government may recognize marriage between same-sex couples, God does not. Pastors and all Christians have an obligation to continue engaging culture on what marriage is and why the heterosexual nuclear household is important as a bedrock for stable and flourishing societies. Churches and Christians must not shy from biblical truths just because the sound and fury of popular culture screams against us. It always has. It always will. The truth remains. And it always will.

Having said that, we must remember that biblical love requires us to care even for those with whom we disagree. Ravi Zacharias offers this caution for Christians:

It is important that this community [of believers] knows how to love those with whom we disagree. Loving does not mean affirming behaviorally. Loving just means not pejoratively viewing the person in an extension of affection and relationship. If there is dissent in my family, I never stop loving my son or my daughter. I still extend that love and that warmth of affection, even if the behavior is not in keeping with what I would affirm. This is the unique aspect of the Christian faith: we can disagree without losing the affection and the love that we can still extend to people.[5]

The worst thing a church can do is to let a sinner believe he or she is not a sinner, let someone believe a sin is not a sin, or that you don't have to repent. You're not being honest with that person, and that in itself is a sin.

Of course the church should not, it cannot close its doors to people who struggle with any one kind of sin, because then the temptation is to close the door to people who deal with other sins.

But the opposite mistake is much more common. For example, a lot of churches have decided to become "creedal churches," meaning they're not going to take a stand on anything that's not in the church creed. Well, when the creeds were being formulated in the first five hundred years of the church, no one was contemplating redefining marriage. There was simply no controversy about it. So marriage is not in the creeds, but it certainly is in the Bible. We need scriptural churches—not creedal churches. After all, the reason creeds were created in the first place is because there were issues about which there were no creeds.

• *Deal with sin.* It is well past time we revive the word used most often by the Apostles and Jesus Himself when calling people to a better life: *repent.* But before you preach repentance to your congregation, start by examining your own life. Too many pastors avoid certain topics like sexual sin because they are secretly struggling in that area or have fallen in the past. And other pastors avoid talking about sin altogether for fear attendance will decline. They avoid topics like God's definition of marriage and the biblical teaching on divorce for fear of offending some in the pews or in leadership positions at the church. It was Dietrich Bonhoeffer's good friend Eberhard Bethge who said, "The sin of respectable people reveals itself in flight from responsibility."[6] Churches have to get more serious about marriage—and sexual sin of all sorts, not only those deemed most abhorrent. Pastors have to figure out how to recalibrate the lines between forgiveness and not accepting divorce within the church, even if that means that they have members who decide to go elsewhere. When you have deacons or elders in your church community who are divorced, you might need to rethink their role in order to show your commitment to marriage.

Number Two: Teach the Truth

• *Give children the answers.* It used to be common among Christians to systematically teach the truths of the faith to their children. Catechism lessons (with questions and answers about the basic truths of Christianity for children to learn) were used for centuries by believers to ensure that their children understood what the Bible taught, what the church believed, and why. But we've lost our focus on teaching truth to children in the church these days. Some of that shift is due to the rise of secular schooling. Some of that change is due to pastors neglecting the need to guide children to understand the doctrines of the faith. Structured training has been replaced by media-rich fun designed to appeal to the casual visitor. Consequently, our kids don't know what to believe because they have never been told. Nancy Pearcey says that not having the answers is why most Christian young people leave the faith:

> In *Finding Truth* I mention a couple of studies on why young people are leaving the faith.... The researchers themselves were surprised because they expected it to be

due to emotional wounding, broken relationships, and things like that. But it wasn't; the top reason given was that they had unanswered doubts and questions.... The researchers summarized by saying that young people are leaving church becase of "intellectual skepticism." Youth pastors are especially prone to this. They often say, *You just need more relationships*, or they try to engineer more emotional experiences.... When you talk about the importance of worldview, this is the main reason we're losing our kids.[7]

Jesus said, "Let the little children come to me and do not hinder them, for to such belongs the kingdom of heaven" (Matt. 19:14). And He gave this warning: Whoever causes one of these little ones who believe in me to sin, it would be better for him to have a great millstone fastened around his neck and to be drowned in the depth of the sea" (Matt. 18:6). I wonder how much harm pastors and church leaders have done to Christ's "little ones" by failing to teach them the truth.

• *Speak out on cultural issues.* It's time for pastors to be bold, to go big or go home. The resurgent church should be unafraid to address the big cultural issues that their parishioners are already talking about around the dinner table and the water cooler throughout the week. Equip them with a biblical understanding of relevant issues so they can be the ambassadors they are called to be. Although I don't think the pastor's job is to preach on the news headlines, he should address the ebbs and flows of culture. In their letters, Paul and Peter spent a great deal of time explaining how Christians should live in a culture with vastly different beliefs from their own. Pastors today need to do what the Apostles did then—preach on the reality of the times. A pastor doesn't have to talk politics, but he does have to talk culture. He can't detach himself so much from the society around him that he can't relate to his flock. Andrew T. Walker reminds us that pastors have a civic responsibility they cannot avoid: "Pastors need to first and foremost realize that **by virtue of being a pastor you have a public office that is a morality-shaping institution.** So, I would say to the average pastor of a church in a town, it is impossible for you not to be shaping morality in one direction or another. It is a question of whether or not you are going to be shaping your congregants for a life in the public square positively or negatively" [emphasis added].[8]

How you shape your parishioners' morality will depend on the unique needs of your congregation and local community. The pastor in America today, confronted by the collapse of marriage and the family, the hostility of secular government, and threats to tax-exempt status for churches, should preach a different sermon from the pastor in Nigeria, where Muslim terrorists might burst through the church door at any moment and kill them all. Even though people halfway around the world may hear the sermon in a podcast, the pastor's primary obligation is to apply the timeless truths of Scripture to his local congregation.

Pastors need to equip us spiritually to deal with the world, because ultimately there is a fight that's happening around us in the unseen realm, and I don't think we can understand what's going on in this world unless we also have some level of a spiritual worldview to discern how what we can see is only a part of the ultimate battle. I don't need a pastor telling me how to vote, but I do need a pastor encouraging me to follow my conscience in political matters, especially when I start to doubt it. There's been a dangerous overcorrection in a lot of churches, particularly Southern Baptist churches, in overreaction against the Moral Majority and Christian Coalition fights of the '80s and '90s. Pastors don't need to be training up an army of political activists, but they certainly need to be training up an army of spiritual activists—and so much of the spiritual warfare in our culture goes on at the ballot box. Too many pastors have tried avoiding anything that sounded political for far too long. But now there is nowhere to run—even pastors are being made to care.

Russell Moore points out that pastors and church leaders have work to do on two levels:

> One of those levels is helping people as citizens to work for religious liberty and religious freedom, not just for ourselves, but for everyone. That is an inheritance that has been given in this country that we have the responsibility to steward. **We need to talk to people about why freedom of conscience matters.** And it doesn't just matter because *we've got the most votes* and so *we've got our rights.* No, we need to be standing up for that mosque down the street and say the gospel doesn't mean we give the state the power to zone that mosque out of existence. The gospel means that the state doesn't have any business with what goes on in people's centers of worship. That [defense] doesn't mean we think that Christians and Muslims are morally or eternally equivalent. It means that we have the right to argue with one another about the gospel without the state coming in and using the sword to punish either one of us.
>
> We articulate that, and then, at the same time, we create people who are willing to prize their deepest held religious convictions above the penalty of threat—people who can't be bullied. What I often tell churches is I have two jobs. **One job is to keep you out of jail. The other job is to make you willing to go to jail, because there's one thing worse than going to jail for your faith, and that's having a faith that's too safe for jail.**[9] [emphasis added]

• *Address sexual issues.* The church has gotten better about talking about sexual issues in recent decades, although being comfortable with them and addressing them biblically are not always the same thing. The cultural wildfire burning today is sexually charged, however, so the church must prepare to minister both to the victims injured in the blaze and to believers standing firmly against heightened temptations. Pastors must recognize that their congregants are already dealing with these sexual issues. They need to think about how best to help a growing number of people who wrestle with same-sex attraction. They need to prepare to answer questions they've never encountered before, such as how best to minister to a person who has been "divorced" from a "marriage" the church never recognized as legitimate in the first place. And they need to preach that Christ redeemed all of creation, including sex, from sin's dark curse. I like the creative approach of one church in Pennsylvania that rented a billboard with the message, "I Love Sex—God" to promote a sermon series on the subject. "What we want to do is let people know that the Bible is relevant to everyday life," says Dan Nichols, pastor of that church. "When it comes to sexuality…God is the inventor, author and creator of it."[10]

Number Three: Prepare for Persecution

• *Expect suffering.* The Scriptures promise it: "All who desire to live a godly life in Christ Jesus will be persecuted, while evil people and impostors will go on from bad to worse, deceiving and being deceived" (2 Tim. 3:12–13). Disciples of Jesus Christ should expect no less than the treatment the world gave to our Savior. Kevin DeYoung reminds us not to be naïve about what may be coming:

> The legitimization of same-sex marriage will mean the delegitimization of those who dare to disagree. The sexual revolution has been no great respecter of civil and religious liberties. Sadly, we may discover that there is nothing quite so intolerant as tolerance. Does this mean the church should expect doom and gloom? That depends. For conservative

Christians, the ascendancy of same-sex marriage will likely mean marginalization, name calling, or worse. But that's to be expected. Jesus promises no better than He Himself received (John 15:18–25). **The church is sometimes the most vibrant, the most articulate, and the most holy when the world presses down on her the hardest.**[11] [emphasis added]

• *Realize a winsome voice will not be enough.* I am not saying pastors and church leaders should rant, rave, and be rude. Jesus told us we are blessed when we are reviled for His name's sake, not because we're jerks. But understand that no matter how nice you appear, no matter how tolerant you sound, darkness hates the light. As you seek to live out the truth in love, evil will not surrender gracefully. DeYoung says some Christians, especially millennials, are in for a surprise:

There's a whole bunch of people who still hold to a biblical view of sexuality, but they figure that if we just lay down our arms, this cultural war will go away. They are right that it may, but the terms are unconditional surrender. This [conflict] is not one that Christians can just get out of by out-niceing people. That's what a lot of folks and a lot of churches think. We can just keep smiling, keep being as nice as possible, keep our heads down, don't speak out of turn, and that we'll be okay. The Louie Giglio incident at Obama's inauguration is just proof that that's not going to happen. Here's a [pastor] who did everything right from a social justice standpoint, yet sometime in his distant past he said something about traditional marriage and that's enough to put him on the forbidden list. I don't think people have their eyes open to what's coming. It's going to be more than just [unfriending] on Facebook. It's going to be much more consequential.[12]

• *Empower those on the front line.* In keeping with my emphasis on building an authentic community, I think pastors should work to ensure that their churches actively help facilitate a resurgent community to support believers and their families. Churches should be a safe haven, a rock and refuge where believers can recharge, rejuvenate, and get equipped to do battle on the front lines of culture. The pastor doesn't have to be the one testifying before Congress, but he needs to make sure that the member of the congregation who is testifying before Congress is prayed for, strengthened, and sustained when all the hate arrives from the Left. The church should be equipping and encouraging those on the front line. In order to do that, the pastor must first be morally centered and focused on the issues that matter to today's believers. A church that is ignorant of the cultural trends is a church that's either going to be knocked over by them or going to fall for them. Church leaders need moral clarity and the willingness to take a stand and take the lead. Truth be told, some pastors need to get out of the pulpit entirely because they don't really believe what they are preaching. It's really hard to ask Christians to go into the culture and save souls when the pastor's not willing to do that himself. Leadership doesn't work that way. Churches don't need to conduct voter drives, but they need to have the backs of the Christians who are doing them.

If there is one thing pastors, priests, and church leaders will need a lot of in the years ahead, it is *courage.* I am certain many of us would happily choose invisibility rather than embracing the opportunity to purify and reengage as the resurgent church. But when tempted to falter, remember the words of Dietrich Bonhoeffer: "It is by seeing the cross and the community beneath it that men come to believe in God."[13]

May He increase even as we decrease.

CHAPTER 19

THE RESURGENT CITIZEN

Whatever makes men good Christians makes men good citizens.

—DANIEL WEBSTER[1]

I
t is no coincidence that I address political action directly only in this final chapter. The resurgence required to defend our freedom to believe must begin from the ground up, not the top down. For far too long, Christians in America have looked to Washington and put their trust not "in the name of the Lord our God," but in horses, chariots, and Justice Antonin Scalia. That needs to change if we are going to be good and faithful stewards of the gospel. That being said, focusing on building local community, growing individual faith, and strengthening the institutions of family and the church does *not* mean that we run from political involvement. God instituted and ordained human government. He gave ample guidance to those in authority. As Christian citizens of a democratic republic, we have a responsibility to

engage in the political process and influence it for good to the extent we are able.

Nevertheless, we cannot lose our eternal perspective. We often think we are fighting short-term battles within election cycles when, in fact, there is a much longer conflict under way. The political fight is about protections not only for you now but for your children and grandchildren and generations to come. We need to apply that long-term perspective when engaging in political battles—otherwise we can become burned out quickly. I think that is what happened to a lot of conservatives and Christians who got worked up following Obama's election. They expected results immediately, and when they didn't get them they checked out and shut down because they simply were not able to sustain that level of angst for long.

If you're not naturally a political person, you're not going to want to fight every fight. You're going to get worn out. You have a life to live that requires your attention.

But there are some fights you can't sit out. The cultural shifts in our nation in the past few years prove that some fights cannot be avoided—you will be made to care. You will be forced to pick a side. You will be forced to engage. You will not be allowed to sit on the sidelines and say, "I'm not a political person. I'm a private citizen; leave me alone." The tolerant Left will not tolerate that. You're either going to engage on the side of protecting religious liberty and freedom of conscience or you are going to lose it. Believe me, I realize some of you really do not like politics. I totally understand why people find politics to be *icky*, but the political process is how we decide these issues in our country—or at least it should be. If you're not going to be involved in the process of deciding the issues, someone else will decide them for you.

CHRISTIAN OR AMERICAN?

In order to defend our freedom to believe and be a force for good in the face of rising evil, Christians are going to have to stop worshiping

America as much as they do. I love this country. It is the best nation ever to exist in the history of the world. This country was founded on beliefs and principles that were profoundly influenced by Christianity. Many of America's founders were Christians or supportive of the Christian faith. Early American culture was built around a shared Judeo-Christian ethos. But America is not a Christian nation. Christians need to get clear on the distinction between our loyalty to the Kingdom of Heaven and our loyalty to the USA. A lot of Christians had an idealized vision of America that didn't permit them to see the present radical cultural changes that were coming. In previous decades, some Christian leaders seemed to speak of America and Christianity as so intertwined as to be indistinguishable. But more and more believers are realizing that the great divorce has taken place. Now is the time for us to recognize that we are—and always have been—Christians first and Americans second.

Russell Moore pushes back against the notion that we are now in a "post-Christian" era:

> I'm really disturbed when I hear Christians talking about post-Christian America, because that puts the frame of reference in the past, as though there was a time when America was Christian. America is not post-Christian. America is, at best, *pre-Christian*. If we're defining Christianity simply in a nominal sense of how do we behave together, then America was Christian in some ways in the past. But that's not how the Bible defines Christianity in terms of the gospel. That's one berth short of reconciliation [to God]. Our frame of reference ought not to be, "Oh, we need to get back to the 1770s," or "We need to get back to the 1950s or the 1980s." We need to recognize that we've always lived in a fallen universe. We've always lived in a fallen culture. We've always been out of step with the culture, and now we see it in ways that we should have

seen it all along. That's why the New Testament is consistently telling us, *You're strangers and exiles; you're a royal priesthood; you're a different people, a particular people who have been called out of darkness and into light. Don't conform your mind to the pattern of this age.* Now we have the opportunity to do that because the issues are so clear around us.

That means we ought not to be panicked. We ought to instead embrace that, when it comes to patriotism and to America, it's a good thing to be patriotic. Patriotism, of course, comes from the root word for *father.* When we love our country and have gratitude for our country, we're honoring father and mother as the Commandments instruct us to do. But we do that in the same way we honor father and mother—we don't make father and mother ultimate.

The same Scripture that says, "Honor your father and mother," says, "If anyone comes to me and does not hate his own father and mother...and even his own life he cannot be my disciple" (Luke 14:26). **We love and we honor our family, but if we make our family ultimate, we've become idolaters. We love and we honor our country, its leaders, and its history, but if we make that ultimate, then we become idolaters.** In our system of government, that sense of kingdom priority makes us better Americans because the American experiment from the very beginning has said the state is not ultimate, that the state is dependent upon citizens who have moral intuitions and virtues that are formed from something other than the state. And that's what happens when Christians say, "We're glad to be Americans, but we're not Americans first." It enables us to be better Americans and better patriots.[2] [emphasis added]

Hugh Hewitt agrees that Christians should not view America as uniquely Christian, in spite of the fact that America does play a special role in defending our religious freedoms:

> I've never, ever believed that America is uniquely Christian or called to a unique role.... At the same time, **America is the defender of the West, and the West is about religious freedom**. We invented it; the United States did. We exported it. It's taken root in some places and has been tried in others. It is critical to the Enlightenment. It is critical to the Constitution. Lynne Cheney's book on James Madison makes it obvious that an animating force for Jefferson, Madison, and Hamilton was to keep the church out of politics and keep politics out of the church in a formal way, but *not* in an informal way. They understood, and Washington and others wrote explicitly on the need for character in citizens, and they counted on the church to be the source of that character.[3] [emphasis added]

Os Guinness makes a similar and compelling case for America's unique role as a defender of religious freedom, even though our government remains separate from any established religion. In *A Free People's Suicide*, Guinness describes what he calls the golden triangle of freedom—freedom requires virtue; virtue requires faith; faith requires freedom:

> The golden triangle of freedom must be stated with great care. For a start, the word *requires* in "freedom requires virtue, which requires faith" does not mean a legal or constitutional requirement. The First Amendment flatly and finally prohibits the federal government from requiring faith in any established way. But a proper and positive

understanding of disestablishment leads directly to the heart of the framers' audacity; **the American republic simultaneously rests on ultimate beliefs—for otherwise Americans have no right to the rights by which they thrive—yet rejects any official, orthodox formulation of what those beliefs should be.** The republic will always remain an undecided experiment that stands or falls by the dynamism of its entirely voluntary, non-established faiths.[4] [emphasis added]

Guinness makes the case that, as the faith of Americans has eroded, so has our virtue and character. As our character has eroded, so has our defense of freedom. And as our freedom has eroded, so has our ability to practice our faith. He adds, "Only virtue can supply the self-restraint that is an indispensable requirement for liberty. Unrestrained freedom undermines freedom, but any other form of restraint on freedom [other than virtue] eventually becomes a contradiction of freedom."[5] So while we must get our priorities right as Christians living in this world as "aliens and strangers," we also have a moral duty to preserve the freedom that permits faith to flourish and results in virtuous character that will, in turn, vigorously defend our freedom to believe.

LIVE-AND-LET-LIVE LEGISLATION

When the state of Indiana passed legislation to protect religious freedom in 2015, corporate America, which tends to worship a green god of its own, threatened to pull out of economic activity in Indiana. And the media ginned up a hypothetical case of discrimination. A reporter asked the owners of Memories Pizza, a family restaurant that does not even cater weddings, whether they would cater a same-sex wedding. When the owners said that to do so would violate their conscience, the media firestorm erupted—inspiring fake orders and death threats that forced Memories Pizza temporarily out of business. Governor Pence and the legislature quickly caved to the bullies on the Left and modified the legislation, and people of faith in Indiana found their religious liberties more at risk than ever. And we still did not have one case of actual discrimination to illustrate the rabid fears of discrimination against gay people.

Apple has been guilty of discrimination against Christians in its own business practices—banning from its App Store (read: *discriminating against*) the Manhattan Declaration app supporting conjugal marriage.[6] But Apple will not do business in Indiana as long as the state was insisting that the free exercise clause of the First Amendment remain on the same legal footing in the courts as the free speech clause of the First Amendment. And yet Apple CEO Tim Cook and his leftist friends in corporate America are happy to do business in countries that jail gays and stone them to death.

In 1993 President Bill Clinton, Chuck Schumer, Daniel Patrick Moynihan (all Democrats), and a nearly unanimous bipartisan Congress passed the Religious Freedom Restoration Act, legislation introduced by none other than liberal stalwart Ted Kennedy. What triggered the act was a ruling by the Supreme Court in a case where an individual was punished for using a psychotropic drug during a religious sect's ceremony.[7] He sued, saying that under the First Amendment he should have freedom to do so because his religion required the use of the drug for a ceremony. The Supreme Court essentially said that you can believe anything you want, but that doesn't mean that you can apply it in life. What both the Democrats and the Republicans in Congress agreed on was that the government should not restrict religious liberty—any more than our freedoms of speech and assembly—without a "compelling governmental interest." The basic argument was that the free exercise clause of the First Amendment should be given equal weight to the free speech, the free press, and the free assembly clauses. Simple enough. In short, RFRA places the burden of proof on the government. It requires the government to demonstrate a "compelling governmental interest" before burdening or restricting anyone's religious beliefs and the practice of those beliefs. Historically, the compelling governmental interests could be the life of a person, protection of property, national security interests, and race or national origin. For example, in the Hobby Lobby case (2014), the Supreme Court applied the RFRA standard and found that the government could in fact provide access to abortifacient drugs without impeding the religious beliefs of the business owners—so there was no "compelling government interest" in forcing the business owners to violate their consciences.

Unfortunately, court rulings after the legislation was passed revealed that while RFRA provided protection at the federal level, it did not extend to individual states (see *City of Boerne v. Flores*, 1997). Consequently, thirty-one states moved to protect the freedom of conscience and religious beliefs and practices in some way. Twenty states[8] have passed legislation that essentially just copied the federal legislation passed by a bipartisan Congress and signed into law by President Clinton. The overwhelming majority simply adopted the federal standard and mandated that the state government must have a compelling governmental interest to interfere in the free exercise of religion. If the government of a state can achieve its purpose without burdening someone's religion, the state should do so.

Indiana was simply the latest to do so. Arkansas did the same at about the same time. And yet while all hell broke loose in Indiana, one of the reddest of red states politically, little to nothing happened in Arkansas. Here in Georgia, cowardly Republicans who made a deal with the devil known as the Chamber of Commerce abandoned similar legislation. Republicans who controlled both houses of the Georgia legislature chose to abandon the protection of religious freedom in exchange for Democratic support of a massive tax increase disguised as a transportation bill. They decided they would rather serve Mammon. They have the thirty pieces of silver to prove it. One thing I have learned from the RFRA battles is that big business is deeply opposed to cultural conservatives. It is not necessarily reflective of the interests of customers, but of the interests of advocacy groups that harass the businesses. For example, in Arkansas, Walmart, whose average shopper is socially conservative, opposed RFRA but supported Obamacare.

RFRA is commonsense legislation if ever there were any. But opponents use a lot of distortion and outright lies to scare people. For example, they falsely claimed RFRA could be used to protect child and spousal abuse. And then they said they would be willing to accept the legislation if there were a blanket prohibition on "discrimination." The problem with a blanket "discrimination" prohibition like that is that the religious could be compelled to provide goods and services for gay weddings whenever a gay couple cried "discrimination." If "protected classes" now includes categories of sexual orientation, the very laws designed to protect religious freedom can be used to hammer the faithful into compliance under the guise of protecting society from the evil of discrimination. By including such a vague discrimination provision, Indiana and other states defeated the core purposes of RFRA. We're now seeing progressive activists going to cities in conservative states and expanding the definition of protected classes at the local level so they can use RFRA against believers and force them to care. When Pence and Indiana Republicans went back and included a discrimination prohibition in RFRA, they essentially gutted it, leaving churches and believers in the state in a worse position than they were before. It was a complete cave-in in Indiana, brought about by outrage orchestrated by gay-marriage-friendly businesses and the media.

In a speech delivered at Hillsdale College's Kirby Center, shortly after the events in Indiana, David French, a writer at *National Review* and long-time defender of religious freedom, summed up the lessons learned:

> From the grassroots to the intellectual elite, conservatives are girding themselves for a long war, and a long war it will be. Four truths are emerging: First, the battle is not between gay rights and religious liberty—although religious liberty is certainly at stake—but between the sexual revolution and Christianity itself.... Second, not a single orthodox denomination is making or even contemplating such changes. This means that tens of millions of Americans will remain—indefinitely—opposed to the continued expansion of the sexual revolution. Third, rather than going quietly, cultural conservatism is showing increasing strength at the grassroots—opposing leftist campaigns at the ground level, bypassing politics to support those most embattled by radical hate campaigns. And fourth, the conservative grassroots and conservative public intellectuals are united...there is no wavering among America's most influential conservative writers and thinkers. In short, if the cultural left is hoping to dominate the culture—and feels strong in its coastal bastions—it is overreaching, extending beyond the limits of its power. It is exposing itself to embarrassing cultural defeats and succeeding mainly in hardening conservative resolve. In the fight over religious freedom, the left will not prevail.[9]

What we are finding out from the controversy over legislation to protect religious freedom is this: *you will be made to care.* There will be no middle ground. Many people would like to find middle ground. Many churches would like to find middle ground. But there will be none, because homosexuals and their culture war warriors on the Left are unwilling to have a middle ground. They are intentionally removing it. Maggie Gallagher says, "There's increasing evidence that for...the Left elite, including the gay Left elite, [discrimination] is a tool they want to use to suppress people and views they find offensive and evil. So there's no desire to find a live-and-let-live solution yet in America among the Left."[10] Blanket discrimination provisions inserted into Religious Freedom Restoration Acts allow discrimination cases to go forward against religious individuals and organizations even if the discrimination claim does not reach the standard of a compelling government interest, such as the government interest in stopping discrimination based on race and national origin.

As we've seen throughout this book, we need live-and-let-live legislation to protect religious liberty. For-profit businesses can't discriminate based on race, gender, or sexual orientation, but they do reserve the right not to provide goods and services for events or engage in acts that offend the conscience of the business owner.

People should be free to live and work according to their faith without fear of being punished by government. That freedom of conscience is a basic human right that deserves protection under the law. Live-and-let-live legislation like RFRA simply ensures that religious liberty gets a fair hearing in court and protects *every* person's freedom from government intrusion, regardless of party, religion, race, orientation, or any other aspect of someone's identity. RFRA ultimately says that all of the First Amendment should be treated the same. It's a matter of being able to live your life based on the tenets of your faith. Andrew T. Walker of the Southern Baptist Church's Ethics & Religious Liberty Commission lays out the basic assumption that should undergird any religious liberty legislation:

No one—no institution, no person, no business or non-profit—should be penalized or targeted by the government for holding to the belief that a marriage is the union of a man and a woman. That is a rational, reasonable belief to hold. It has been a belief recognized through all of human history. It is not right for the government to treat those who disagree with this new revisionist understanding of marriage with hostility.

The role of legislation in all of this is to (A) recognize that there are goodwill debates on both sides of the aisle and holding to the traditionalist view of marriage is not irrational; and (B) put into law provisions that state that the government cannot penalize any institution, business, nonprofit, or for-profit from holding to that belief.[11]

WHAT WE DO NOW

In addition to supporting live-and-let-live legislation and leaders who demonstrate the courage to stand for your freedom of conscience, there is really something much more basic to Christianity that each of us should do as citizens—love our neighbors.

I don't mean love them in some sort of philosophical or esoteric way, but really and truly connect with the people in the community in which you live and do good to and for them. We derive our word *politics* from the Greek root of *polis*, the word they used to describe the city-state where people gathered to form a community. Not to engage in politics is to withdraw from engaging in the public business of the community, a community composed of immortal souls whose eternal destinies you help shape each day. C. S. Lewis famously reminded of this privilege and responsibility in his essay "The Weight of Glory":

It is a serious thing to live in a society of possible gods and goddesses, to remember that the dullest most uninteresting person you can talk to may one day be a creature which, if you saw it now, you would be strongly tempted to worship, or else a horror and a corruption such as you now meet, if at all, only in a nightmare. All day long we are, in some degree, helping each other to one or the other of these destinations. It is in the light of these overwhelming possibilities, **it is with the awe and the circumspection proper to them, that we should conduct all of our dealings with one another, all friendships, all loves, all play, all politics. There are no ordinary people. You have never talked to a mere mortal.** Nations, cultures, arts, civilizations—these are mortal, and their life is to ours as the life of a gnat. But it is immortals whom we joke with, work with, marry, snub, and exploit—immortal horrors or everlasting splendors.[12] [emphasis added]

Our duties as a citizen of heaven and of America coincide in a very real and concrete way as we serve our neighbors in our local community. The politics that most affects us is the politics closest to our door. Consequently, each of us should seek out opportunities to plug in to the civic community in which we live. Whether you run for school board, serve on the local parks and recreation committee, or become a person who helps keep your neighborhood informed, you've got to be engaged in your local community to show love to your neighbor. If each of us takes care of our local community, that care and concern will percolate up to the state and national levels. Only do what only you can do. Don't list all the ways you can't help in politics. Start with what you *can* do, right where you live, to help the people around you. Find a problem and solve it. "Mere waiting and looking on is not Christian behavior," Dietrich Bonhoeffer wrote from a prison cell. "Christians are called to compassion *and* to action."[13] The truth is that there is no one better suited to serve the community in which you live than the person who lives in that community—you.

You may not relish the thought of engaging in the political process, even at a local level. It can be hard work. You may not always like it. But as Os Guinness reminds us, "Freedom is not the permission to do what we like but the power to do what we should."[14] As long as we have the freedom to believe, we have the duty to act—not merely because the Constitution says so, but because the Lord has called us to do so.

YOU ARE NOT ALONE

As the cultural wildfire of leftist insanity has swept through America, the media have insisted that every American must be made to care. When a professional athlete comes out as gay, we must all applaud.

In 2013, National Basketball Association (NBA) player Jason Collins announced he was gay.[1] His career had been on a downward glide since 2012. But when he announced his sexual orientation, the national media heralded him as a hero. *Time* magazine listed him as one of the "100 Most Influential People in the World."[2]

The National Football League (NFL) got its turn, with Michael Sam in 2014. Once he declared himself to be gay, the media dared the NFL to decline Sam's bid to go pro in spite of the fact that he had been cut by the St. Louis Rams after training camp. The Dallas Cowboys gave Sam a chance on their practice squad, but he ended up playing a season in the Canadian Football League. He continues to maintain that if he had not declared he was gay he would still be in the NFL.[3] He finally left the Montreal Alouettes with mental health concerns.[4]

When Sam initially announced he was gay and intended to head to the NFL, the sports press insisted on getting other athletes on record. Peyton Manning, widely regarded as one of the nicest men in the NFL, announced that nobody cared: "You're drafted a football player. That's all we care about in the locker room.... What you do outside in your personal life is up to you."[5] But that wasn't good enough. Gay rights activists attacked Manning for not being sufficiently happy that there was now a gay NFL player. The gay press wrote, "But on the other hand, this 'nobody cares' attitude may swing the pendulum a little too far in the other direction. It erases Michael Sam's queerness, and is only a few steps away from 'we don't mind having gay people around, as long as they don't talk about it.'"[6]

Here in the twenty-first century, it is not enough to be okay with the Left's agenda. You must celebrate and approve. You must care about it sufficiently or suffer the consequences.

People of faith must be willing to forgive or fall into the same trap. Consider the actor Mark Wahlberg. He served time in jail for assault as a teenager. He became a rapper and underwear model, then transitioned into acting, where, in one role, he played a porn star. But Wahlberg has grown in his faith over time. When Pope Francis visited Philadelphia, in 2015, Wahlberg hosted a concert in the city for the pontiff. Some critical Christians attacked Wahlberg for playing any role, given his checkered past.[7] While Christians should not forget history or ignore the reality of the cultural wildfire around us, we should be willing to forgive generously and show more charity to others than is shown to us. Some might say that such love will only ensure our defeat. I think it actually shows we have already won.

We have won. Christ conquered death and reigns supreme. He will return to judge the living and the dead. We should live out our lives knowing that the victory is assured. That does not mean it will be easy in the here and now. In the previous nineteen chapters, I have chronicled stories of Christians feeling the yoke of the state for daring to be Christians. It is not going to be easy, but we should not give up. We should not grow angry or weary, for this will be a long race with eternal consequences. The late Reverend Jerry Falwell lamented that Christians often lose in politics and go home. And sometimes we win in politics and go home—we rest on our laurels after short-term victories, instead of persevering for the long haul. But we must remember that this world is not our true home. We are just passing through. That reality means we cannot give up and go home to our present physical addresses. We must continue to engage in the town square, in our community, and with our families. We must not give up after short-term losses, nor must we wash our hands of the fight after short-term victories.

Stephen, the first martyr of the Christian faith, spoke truth in the town square and was killed for it. But before going into the town square, Stephen spent time in prayer and in breaking bread with the Apostles. He heard eyewitnesses of the Christ tell stories of what God had done and was continuing to do. He drew strength from the community of believers that he served. The people whose stories I have told in this book have drawn strength from their faith communities who pray for and continue to support them. You and I must commit to a resurgence of spirit, family, and community. I invite you to join the resurgence at www.TheResurgent.com.

My coauthor, Bill Blankschaen, and I hope you have been made aware not only of the war on our freedom to believe—you will be made to care—but also of a path forward. The truth is that we live in an era in which the president of the United States has warned Christians and all people of faith that we will be forced to get in line with the sexual revolution and the Spirit of the Age: "We affirm that we cherish our religious freedom and are profoundly respectful of religious traditions, **but** we also have to say clearly that our religious freedom doesn't grant us the freedom to deny our fellow Americans their constitutional rights" [emphasis added].[8]

This from the man who only days earlier had had the audacity to tell Pope Francis that "we stand with you in defense of religious freedom and interfaith dialogue, knowing that people everywhere must be able to live out their faith free from fear and free from intimidation."[9] Instead of being discouraged by such rank hypocrisy, let us rise to meet the darkness with the light of truth and a ready smile—as happy warriors.

Most important, remember that the world wants you to feel isolated.

But you are not alone. And never will be.

Never forget it.

ACKNOWLEDGMENTS

ERICK:

I have dreaded writing a second book. Between time and family and other endeavors, the thought horrified me. But my friend Brian Mattson introduced me to Bill Blankschaen, who it turns out is a natural. This book would not have happened without Bill working with me, and I am forever grateful to Brian for the introduction and to Bill for his willingness to work with me.

I must also thank my wife and family for their encouragement, Matt K. Lewis for his demand that either I write a book with this title or he would, my friends at RedState, the Alliance Defending Freedom, the Heritage Foundation, and the Ethics and Religious Liberty Commission. Their insight and willingness to help and pray was heartening. Finally, I have to thank Reformed Theological Seminary for both helping me advance my education in theology and grounding me more and more in Scripture.

There have been so many others who have encouraged me, pushed me, and badgered me to finally write a book around the phrase "You will be made to care." Thanks to you all.

BILL:

Thanks to my wife, Faith, whose patience, love, and unwavering support make life possible and the impossible probable. Special thanks to my children—all six of them—for sharing me with this worthy project.

Thank you to Erick Erickson for his authentic faith, his commitment to being a happy warrior for truth, and his unwavering defense of liberty. It is a privilege to consider him a friend, and it has been a delight to collaborate with him on this book. And thanks to his family for sharing him, as well.

Thanks to members of my creative team who helped with researching, editing, and giving candid feedback: Jenifer Truitt, Courtney Coiro, Hanna Hafner, and Glenn Leinbach.

Thanks to my agent, D. J. Snell, and to Harry Crocker at Regnery Publishing for believing in the project. To the entire Regnery team, especially to editor Elizabeth Kantor, sincere gratitude for all your efforts.

Thank you to all who shared their stories to me firsthand— Chief Kelvin Cochran, Barronelle Stutzman, Aaron and Melissa Klein, Kevin Stormans, Ruth Malhotra, Jennifer Keeton, and Emily Landis. May your courage and faith inspire others to stand as you have stood. Thank you to all who gave input, including Hugh Hewitt, Ravi Zacharias, Kevin DeYoung, Nancy Pearcey, Andrew T. Walker, Russell Moore, Brian Mattson, Ed Morrissey, P. Andrew

Sandlin, Maggie Gallagher, Charles LiMandri, Ryan T. Anderson, Steve Smothermon, David McNeely, and McKay Caston. If I have forgotten any, know that it is due to my own poor memory and not a lack of appreciation for your contribution.

Special thanks to the Alliance Defending Freedom (ADF) for their vigorous defense of liberty, especially to Greg Scott, Kristen Waggoner, David Cortman, and all the many affiliated attorneys, such as Anna Harmon, who stand for freedom each and every day in America.

And to those who must remain unnamed whose support made this project possible, a special thanks for your legacy of generosity.

NOTES

CHAPTER 1
THE AUDACITY TO BELIEVE

1. "Remarks by the First Lady at the African Methodist Episcopal Church Conference," transcript, WhiteHouse.gov, June 28, 2012, https://www.whitehouse.gov/the-press-office/2012/06/28/remarks-first-lady-african-methodist-episcopal-church-conference.

2. Kelvin Cochran, personal interview by Bill Blankschaen, Atlanta, GA, July 1, 2015.

3. "Secretary Napolitano Applauds President Obama's Intent to Nominate Kelvin Cochran as U.S. Fire Administrator," press release, U.S. Department of Homeland Security, July 7, 2009, http://www.dhs.gov/

news/2009/07/07/president-obama-nominate-kelvin-cochran-us-fire-administrator.

4. "Mayor Kasim Reed State of the City Address," transcript, City of Atlanta, January 7, 2014, http://www.atlantaga.gov/index.aspx?page=1114.

5. Cochran, personal interview by Bill Blankschaen.

6. "Atlanta Fire Rescue Department Announces Upgrade in City's ISO Rating to Class 1," press release, City of Atlanta, September 16, 2010, http://atlantaga.gov/index.aspx?page=672&recordid=3015.

7. "Atlanta Fire Rescue Department Retains Accreditation," press release, City of Atlanta, August 14, 2014, http://atlantaga.gov/index.aspx?page=672&recordid=2982.

8. Cochran, personal interview by Bill Blankschaen.

9. Kasim Reed, Facebook post, November 24, 2014, https://www.facebook.com/kasimreed/posts/10152925936289669.

10. Katie Leslie, "Fire Chief Suspended over Book Controversy," *Atlanta Journal-Constitution*, November 24, 2014, http://www.myajc.com/news/news/fire-chief-suspended-without-pay-over-anti-gay-com/njFNt/?icmp.

11. Leslie, "Reed's Office Releases Internal Report into Fire Chief's Management," *Atlanta Journal-Constitution*, January 9, 2015, http://www.ajc.com/news/news/reeds-office-releases-internal-report-into-fire-ch/njkQG/.

12. Cochran, personal interview by Bill Blankschaen.

13. Ryan T. Anderson and Leslie Ford, "Protecting Religious Liberty in the State Marriage Debate," Heritage Foundation *Backgrounder* no. 2891, April 10, 2014, http://www.heritage.org/research/reports/2014/04/protecting-religious-liberty-in-the-state-marriage-debate/.

14. Ibid.

15. Maggie Gallagher, "Banned in Boston," *Weekly Standard* 11, no. 33 (May 15, 2006), http://www.weeklystandard.com/Content/Public/Articles/000/000/012/191kgwgh.asp.

16. Anderson and Ford, "Protecting Religious Liberty in the State Marriage Debate"; and Aaron and Melissa Klein, personal interview by Bill Blankschaen, Atlanta, GA, August 13, 2015.

17. Anderson and Ford, "Protecting Religious Liberty in the State Marriage Debate."

18. State of Washington v. Arlene's Flowers, and Barronelle Stutzman, State of Washington Benton County Superior Court, filed April 9, 2013, available online at ADFMedia.org, http://www.adfmedia.org/files/ArlenesFlowersAGcomplaint.pdf.

19. Barronelle Stutzman, phone interview by Bill Blankschaen, August 17, 2015.

20. Brief of Amici Curiae, Same-Sex Attracted Men and Their Wives in Support of Respondents and Affirmance, Obergefell v. Hodges, http://sblog.s3.amazonaws.com/wp-content/uploads/2015/04/14-556bsacSame-SexAttractedMenandTheirWives.pdf.

21. Charles LiMandri, phone interview by Bill Blankschaen, August 18, 2015.

22. Anderson and Ford, "Protecting Religious Liberty in the State Marriage Debate."

23. Grant Rodgers, "Grimes' Gortz Haus to Stop All Weddings in Wake of Discrimination Complaint," *Des Moines Register*, January 28, 2015, http://www.desmoinesregister.com/story/news/investigations/2015/01/28/gortz-haus-owners-decide-stop-weddings/22492677/.

24. "Judge Rules in Favor of Same-Sex Couple in Discrimination Case," American Civil Liberties Union of New Jersey, January 13, 2010, https://www.aclu-nj.org/news/2012/01/13/judge-rules-in-favor-of-same-sex-couple-in-discrimination-case/.

25. Jennifer Sinco Kelleher, "Hawaii's Aloha Bed & Breakfast Discriminated against Lesbian Couple By Denying Room: Court," April 16, 2013, http://www.huffingtonpost.com/2013/04/16/hawaii-bed-and-breakfast-lesbian_n_3092203.html.

26. Curtis M. Wong, "The '7 Careers Christians May No Longer Hold' because of Gay Advocates: American Family Association's Tim Wildmon," *Huffington Post*, April 24, 2014, http://www.huffingtonpost. com/2014/04/24/christian-careers-gay-rights-_n_5206014.html.

27. "Augusta State Univ. to Counseling Student: Change Your Beliefs or Get Out," press release, Alliance Defending Freedom, December 19, 2011, http://www.adfmedia.org/News/PRDetail/4384.

28. Kevin Rector, "Gallaudet Diversity Official's Discrimination Lawsuit against School Dismissed," *Baltimore Sun*, April 24, 2014, http://www. baltimoresun.com/features/gay-in-maryland/gay-matters/bs-gm-gallaudet-diversity-lawsuit-dismissed-20140423-story.html.

29. Tish Harrison Warren, "The Wrong Kind of Christian," Christianity Today, August 27, 2014, http://www.christianitytoday.com/ct/2014/september/wrong-kind-of-christian-vanderbilt-university.html.

30. "US Supreme Court Win Supports Wash. Pharmacist Case," press release, Alliance Defending Freedom, August 1, 2014, http://www.adfmedia.org/News/PRDetail/9239.

31. "A Poor Supreme Court Ruling on Hastings," *Los Angeles Times*, June 30, 2010, http://articles.latimes.com/2010/jun/30/opinion/la-ed-hastings-20100630.

32. Illinois Religious Freedom Protection and Civil Union Act, Illinois Compiled Statutes, 750 ILCS 75/.

33. Evangelical Child and Family Agency, *2012 Annual Report* (Wheaton, IL: 2012), 2; Karla Dial, "Illinois Christian Foster Care Group Loses State Contract," CitizenLink, September 14, 2011, http://www.citizenlink. com/2011/09/14/illinois-christian-foster-care-group-loses-state-contract/; and "Schulz, Craigen, Montague," video uploaded by "Admin," Marriage Anti-Defamation Alliance, December 15, 2011, http://marriageada.org/schulz-craigen-montague/.

34. Justin William Moyer, "Kentucky T-shirt Printer That Wouldn't Make Gay Pride Shirts Vindicated by Court," *Washington Post*, April 28, 2015, http://www.washingtonpost.com/news/morning-mix/wp/2015/04/28/

christian-t-shirt-company-doesnt-have-to-print-gay-pride-festival-shirts-court-says/.

35.   "EMU Student Achieves Final Victory After Court Rules 'Tolerance Is a Two-Way Street,'" press release, Alliance Defending Freedom, December 10, 2012, http://www.adfmedia.org/News/PRDetail/141.

36.   Sonny Bunch, "You Will Be Made to Shut Up," Washington Free Beacon, February 4, 2015, http://freebeacon.com/blog/you-will-be-made-to-shut-up/.

37.   Lawrence Meyers, "Politics Really Is Downstream from Culture," Breitbart, August 22, 2011, http://www.breitbart.com/big-hollywood/2011/08/22/politics-really-is-downstream-from-culture/.

38.   Thomas Paine, "The Crisis," December 23, 1776, available online at http://www.ushistory.org/paine/crisis/c-01.htm.

39.   Kevin DeYoung, *Don't Call It a Comeback: The Old Faith for a New Day* (Wheaton, IL: Crossway, 2011), 23.

CHAPTER 2
THE COMING WILDFIRE

1.   Dawn Stefanowicz, "A Warning from Canada: Same-Sex Marriage Erodes Fundamental Rights," Public Discourse, April 24, 2015, http://www.thepublicdiscourse.com/2015/04/14899/.

2.   "Chastity and Homosexuality," *Catechism of the Catholic Church*, available online at http://www.vatican.va/archive/ccc_css/archive/catechism/p3s2c2a6.htm.

3.   "Statement concerning Mount de Sales Board of Trustees' Recent Personnel Decision," Roman Catholic Diocese of Savannah, May 23, 2014, https://www.diosav.org/news-2014-5-23-statement-mds-personnel.

4.   Amy Leigh Womack, "EEOC Says Mount de Sales Discriminated against Band Director," *Telegraph* (Macon, GA), March 30, 2015, http://www.macon.com/news/local/article30223899.html.

5.   "Quotes about Right and Wrong," Goodreads, no date, https://www.goodreads.com/quotes/tag/right-and-wrong.

6. Thomas L. McDonald, "Evil Talks about Tolerance Only When It Is Weak," *God and the Machine* (blog), Patheos, March 26, 2012, http://www.patheos.com/blogs/godandthemachine/2012/03/evil-talks-about-tolerance-only-when-it-is-weak/.

7. United States v. Windsor, No. 12–307, 570 U.S. ___ (2013) (Scalia, A., dissenting), http://www.supremecourt.gov/opinions/12pdf/12-307_6j37.pdf.

8. Excerpt of Tacitus, *Annals*, trans. Richard Hooker, available online at "Tactitus (c. 55–117 CE): Nero's Persecution of the Christians," excerpt from Paul Brians et al., eds., *Reading about the World*, vol. 1 (New York: Harcourt Brace Custom Books, 1999), http://public.wsu.edu/~brians/world_civ/worldcivreader/world_civ_reader_1/tacitus.html.

9. John Henry Newman, *An Essay on the Development of Christian Doctrine* (London: Basil Montagu Pickering, 1879), 230, https://books.google.com/books?id=RN66gZdNnqoC&pg=PA230&lpg=PA230&dq=tertullian+hostes+humani+generis&source=bl&ots=NYecQ6BhKj&sig=vtZKLWJCGYoH2WDun4y35esKLYY&hl=en&sa=X&ved=0CCYQ6AEwAWoVChMI_oOm5NO9yAIVQSseCh01HgdF#v=onepage&q=tertullian%20hostes%20humani%20generis&f=false.

10. John Granger Cook, *Roman Attitudes toward the Christians: From Claudius to Hadrian* (Tübingen: Mohr Siebeck, 2010), 65, https://books.google.com/books?id=UFa8vXmbRKUC&pg=PA65&lpg=PA65&dq=tertullian+enemies+of+the+human+race&source=bl&ots=CZR_8n4wJ5&sig=cURyDtBWbnshH0LefmSx7MIdyig&hl=en&sa=X&ved=0CB0Q6AEwAGoVChMIsoOm2tK9yAIVzBkeCh3kBA7J#v=onepage&q=tertullian%20enemies%20of%20the%20human%20race&f=false.

11. Newman, *An Essay on the Development*, 230.

12. Frank Bruni, "Bigotry, the Bible and the Lessons of Indiana," *New York Times*, April 3, 2015, http://www.nytimes.com/2015/04/05/opinion/sunday/frank-bruni-same-sex-sinners.html.

13. Ibid.

14. Ibid.

15.   Ibid.

16.   Jason Howerton, "Hillary Clinton: 'Deep-Seated Cultural Codes, Religious Beliefs...Have to Be Changed,'" TheBlaze, April 24, 2015, http://www.theblaze.com/stories/2015/04/24/hillary-clinton-deep-seeded-cultural-codes-religious-beliefshave-to-be-changed/.

17.   J. S. Conway, *The Nazi Persecution of Churches: 1933–1945* (Vancouver: Regent College Publishing, 2001), 77.

18.   Ibid.

19.   "History of Tulips in Holland," Holland.com, no date, http://www.holland.com/us/tourism/article/history-of-tulips-in-holland.htm.

20.   Todd Starnes, "Court: Christian Baker Must Provide Wedding Cakes for Same-Sex Couples," FoxNews.com, August 13, 2015, http://www.foxnews.com/opinion/2015/08/13/court-christian-baker-must-provide-wedding-cakes-for-same-sex-couples.html?intcmp=trending.

21.   "Colo. Cake Artist's Freedom of Belief, Livelihood at Stake," press release, Alliance Defending Freedom, July 6, 2015, http://www.adfmedia.org/News/PRDetail/9704.

22.   Rachel Zoll, "Gordon College President Was Surprised at Reaction to Anti-gay Stance," Associated Press, November 3, 2014, available on the Huffington Post, http://www.huffingtonpost.com/2014/11/03/gordon-college-anti-gay_n_6094652.html.

23.   Stefanowicz, "A Warning from Canada."

24.   Rod Dreher, "Heads LGBTs Win, Tails Christians Lose," American Conservative, May 21, 2015, http://www.theamericanconservative.com/dreher/heads-lgbt-win-tails-christians-lose/.

25.   Ibid.

CHAPTER 3
OUR FIRST FREEDOM

1.   Kristen Waggoner, speech to RedState Gathering, Atlanta, GA, August 7, 2015.

2.   Ryan T. Anderson, "Same-Sex Marriage Trumps Religious Liberty in New Mexico," Daily Signal, August 22, 2013, http://dailysignal. com/2013/08/22/same-sex-marriage-trumps-religious-liberty-in-new-mexico/.

3.   "NM Supreme Court: Price of Citizenship Is Compromising Your Beliefs," press release, Alliance Defending Freedom, August 22, 2013, http://www. adfmedia.org/News/PRDetail/8469.

4.   "Govt Punishment of NM Photographer Stands, Compelled Speech Problem Unresolved... for Now," press release, Alliance Defending Freedom, April 7, 2014, http://www.adfmedia.org/News/PRDetail/5537.

5.   Pinocchio, directed by Norman Ferguson et al. (Los Angeles: Disney, 1943).

6.   Palko v. State of Connecticut, 302 U.S. 319 (1937), decision available online at http://caselaw.findlaw.com/us-supreme-court/302/319. html#sthash.sv4HctCW.dpuf.

7.   "James Madison, Property," in The Founders' Constitution, vol. 1, chapter 16, document 23, available online at http://press-pubs.uchicago. edu/founders/documents/v1ch16s23.html.

8.   Waggoner, speech to RedState Gathering.

9.   Michael Gryboski, "Louie Giglio Withdraws from Obama Inauguration Ceremony," Christian Post, January 10, 2013, www.christianpost.com/ news/louie-giglio-withdraws-from-obama-inauguration-ceremony-88026/#jskQgi5X7K4B4cpi.99.

10. Jurassic World, directed by Colin Trevorrow (Los Angeles: Universal, 2015).

11. Jurassic Park, directed by Steven Spielberg (Los Angeles: Universal, 1993).

12. G. K. Chesterton, "The Ethics of Elflan," chapter 4 of Orthodoxy (Grand Rapids, MI: Christian Classics Ethereal Library, 1908).

13. Thomas H. Crown, "The Empty Joy of Forgetting: Presumably, Confederate War Dead Are Next," T. Crown's Musings (blog), June 23, 2015, http://t-crown.blogspot.com/2015/06/the-empty-joy-of-forgetting-presumably.html.

14. Cain Burdeau, "New Orleans Council Votes to Remove Monument to White Supremacists," Associated Press, September 3, 2015, available on the *Christian Science Monitor*, http://www.csmonitor.com/USA/Society/2015/0903/New-Orleans-council-votes-to-remove-monument-to-white-supremacists.

15. Dan Evon, "Grave Situation," Snopes, July 13, 2015, http://m.snopes.com/2015/07/13/move-forrest-remains/#6SgtbAgBPq1Cc05v.99.

16. Elizabeth Boyd, "Remove the Southern Belle from Her Inglorious Perch," August 21, 2015, https://www.washingtonpost.com/opinions/removing-the-southern-belle-from-her-inglorious-perch/2015/08/14/ea929b2a-3f96-11e5-9561-4b3dc93e3b9a_story.html?wpmm=1&wpisrc=nl_headlines.

CHAPTER 4
THE COMPASSIONATE BULLIES

1. Barronelle Stutzman, personal interview by Bill Blankschaen, Atlanta, GA, August 17, 2015.

2. Ibid.

3. Kristen Waggoner, personal interview by Bill Blankschaen, Atlanta, GA, August 17, 2015.

4. Stutzman, personal interview by Bill Blankschaen.

5. "Wash. Grandmother's Religious Freedom, Livelihood at Stake," press release, Alliance Defending Freedom, December 18, 2014, http://www.adfmedia.org/News/PRDetail/9465.

6. Stutzman, personal interview by Bill Blankschaen.

7. *Monsters, Inc.*, directed by Pete Docter, David Silverman, and Lee Unkrich (USA: Disney Pixar, 2001).

8. "RFRA: Michiana Business Wouldn't Cater a Gay Wedding," ABC57, updated April 1, 2015, http://www.abc57.com/story/28681598/rfra-first-business-to-publicly-deny-same-sex-service.

9. Ibid.

10. Samuel Smith, "Christian Pizza Shop Owners 'in Hiding' amid Death Threats, Close Doors After Indiana HS Coach Threatens to Torch Pizzeria For Saying They 'Won't Cater Gay Weddings,'" *Christian Post*, April 2, 2015, http://www.christianpost.com/news/high-school-coach-threatens-to-torch-indiana-pizzeria-that-wont-cater-gay-weddings-restaurant-closes-down-christian-owners-hiding-after-death-threats-136833/.

11. Ibid.

12. Alix Bryan, Twitter post, April 1, 2015, 4:46 p.m., https://twitter.com/alixbryan/status/583415107188830208.

13. Bryan, Twitter post, April 1, 2015, 4:33 p.m., https://twitter.com/alixbryan/status/583412017433866240.

14. Oliver Darcy, "Fundraiser for Memories Pizza in Indiana Concludes—Here's How Much Was Ultimately Raised," TheBlaze, April 3, 2015, http://www.theblaze.com/stories/2015/04/03/fundraiser-for-memories-pizza-in-indiana-concludes-heres-how-much-was-ultimately-raised/.

15. Andrew T. Walker, personal interview by Bill Blankschaen, Atlanta, GA, August 3, 2015.

16. P. Andrew Sandlin, "Equality: Enemy of Christian Culture," *Doc Sandlin* (blog), August 17, 2015, http://docsandlin.com/2015/08/17/equality-enemy-of-christian-culture/.

17. Ed Morrissey, personal interview by Bill Blankschaen, Atlanta, GA, August 17, 2015.

18. Eugene Volokh, "What Percentage of the U.S. Population Is Gay, Lesbian or Bisexual?," *Volokh Conspiracy* (blog), *Washington Post*, https://www.washingtonpost.com/news/volokh-conspiracy/wp/2014/07/15/what-percentage-of-the-u-s-population-is-gay-lesbian-or-bisexual/.

19. Karissa Bell, "Facebook's New Gender Options Let You Choose Anything You Want," Mashable, February 26, 2015, http://mashable.com/2015/02/26/facebooks-new-custom-gender-options/#S9eAQlaarOk9.

CHAPTER 5
THE ANTIRELIGION RELIGION

1.   Thomas L. McDonald, "Evil Talks about Tolerance Only When It Is Weak," *God and the Machine* (blog), Patheos, March 26, 2012, http://www.patheos.com/blogs/godandthemachine/2012/03/evil-talks-about-tolerance-only-when-it-is-weak/.

2.   Kevin Stormans, personal interview by Bill Blankschaen, Atlanta, GA, August 28, 2015.

3.   Ibid.

4.   Ibid.

5.   Kristen Waggoner, personal interview by Bill Blankschaen, Atlanta, GA, August 28, 2015.

6.   Ed Whelan, "Important Victory for Religious Liberty in Washington State," *Bench Memos* (blog), National Review Online, February 22, 2012, http://www.nationalreview.com/bench-memos/291733/important-victory-religious-liberty-washington-state-ed-whelan.

7.   Waggoner, personal interview by Bill Blankschaen.

8.   "Court Strikes Down Law Requiring Pharmacies to Dispense the Morning-After Pill," press release, Becket Fund for Religious Liberty, February 22, 2012, http://www.becketfund.org/court-strikes-down-law-requiring-pharmacies-to-dispense-the-morning-after-pill/.

9.   Meghan Ross, "Pharmacists Can't Refuse to Fill Based on Religion in Washington State," Pharmacy Times, August 5, 2015, http://www.pharmacytimes.com/news/pharmacists-cant-refuse-to-fill-based-on-religion-in-washington-state#sthash.eXFwSzwm.dpuf.

10. Russell Moore, personal interview by Bill Blankschaen, Atlanta, GA, July 16, 2015.

11. William Shakespeare, *Julius Caesar*, act 3, scene 1, line 273.

12. *Oxford Advanced Learner's Dictionary*, s.v. "religion," http://www.oxforddictionaries.com/us/definition/american_english/religion.

13. Bill Blankschaen, *A Story Worth Telling: Your Field Guide to Living an Authentic Life* (Nashville, TN: Abingdon Press, 2015), 24.

14. Ibid., 29.

15. *Oxford Advanced Learner's Dictionary*, s.v. "religion."

16. Joseph Gales, ed., *The Debates and Proceedings in the Congress of the United States*, vol. 1 (Washington: Gales & Seaton, 1834), 27–29.

17. "Charlie Hebdo," *Wikipedia*, accessed September 23, 2015, https://en.wikipedia.org/wiki/Charlie_Hebdo.

18. John Daniel Davidson, "Charlie Hebdo Teaches Us Terrorism Does Work," The Federalist, July 21, 2015, http://thefederalist.com/2015/07/21/charlie-hebdo-teaches-us-terrorism-does-work/.

19. Brian Mattson, personal interview by Bill Blankschaen, Atlanta, GA, July 14, 2015.

CHAPTER 6
FAITH IN A BOX

1. Michael Stone, "Leading Scientist E.O. Wilson: Religious Faith Harms Humanity," *Progressive Secular Humanist* (blog), Patheos, January 30, 2015, http://www.patheos.com/blogs/progressivesecularhumanist/2015/01/leading-scientist-e-o-wilson-religious-faith-harms-humanity.

2. Billy Hallowell, "Christian Minister Reportedly Banned from Juvenile Jail After He Refused to Sign a Form Promising Not to Call Homosexuality 'Sinful,'" TheBlaze, July 29, 2015, http://www.theblaze.com/stories/2015/07/29/christian-minister-reportedly-banned-from-juvenile-jail-after-he-refused-to-sign-a-form-promising-not-to-call-homosexuality-sinful/.

3. "Pastor Barred from Juvenile Jail for Biblical Beliefs," CBN News, August 18, 2015, http://www.cbn.com/cbnnews/us/2015/August/Pastor-Barred-from-Juvenile-Jail-for-Biblical-Beliefs/.

4. "Policy Manual," Department of Juvenile Justice, http://djj.ky.gov/Pages/Policy-Manual.aspx.

5. Ibid.

6. John Cheves, "Religious Group Threatens Lawsuit over Kentucky Policy Banning Anti-gay Comments at Juvenile Jails," *Lexington (KY) Herald Leader*, July 27, 2015, http://www.kentucky.com/2015/07/27/3961792_religious-group-threatens-lawsuit.html?rh=1.

7. Bob Unruh, "State Defends Firing For Calling Homosexuality 'Sinful,'" WND, July 27, 2015, http://www.wnd.com/2015/07/state-defends-firing-for-calling-homosexuality-sinful.

8. Bertrand Russell, *Freedom and Organization, 1814–1914* (Bertrand Russell Peace Foundation), excerpt available online at https://www.big-lies.org/bertrand-russell-peace-tribunal/bertrand-russell-e-d-morel-belgian-congo.html.

9. "Vivid Lecture on Congo," *Harvard Crimson*, February 28, 1908, http://www.thecrimson.com/article/1908/2/28/vivid-lecture-on-congo-prev-joseph/.

10. "Campaigning with a Camera: Capturing Abuse in the Congo," Anti-Slavery International *Reporter* (Fall 2010): http://www.antislavery.org/includes/documents/cm_docs/2012/9/9_autumn_2010_history.pdf.

11. Aaron Blake, "Why Obama Invoked the Crusades—and What It Says about How He Views Terrorism," *The Fix* (blog), *Washington Post*, February 6, 2015, http://www.washingtonpost.com/news/the-fix/wp/2015/02/06/why-obama-invoked-the-crusades-in-re-islam-and-terrorism/.

12. "Black Liberation Theology, in Its Founder's Words," NPR, July 17, 2011, http://www.npr.org/templates/story/story.php?storyId=89236116.

13. "Obama: 'They Cling to Guns or Religion,'" Christianity Today, April 13, 2008, http://www.christianitytoday.com/gleanings/2008/april/obama-they-cling-to-guns-or-religion.html.

14. Charles Colson, "How William Wilberforce Changed the World," CBN, no date, http://www.cbn.com/spirituallife/churchandministry/churchhistory/Colson_Wilberforce_Birthday.aspx.

15. Dinesh D'Souza, *What's So Great about Christianity* (Carol Stream, IL: Tyndale House Publishers, 2008), 73.

16.   Friedrich Nietzsche, *The Will to Power* (New York: Vintage Books, 1968),
      401.

17.   D'Souza, *What's So Great About Christianity*, 79.

18.   The Obama administration argued that churches have a ministerial
      exception only for "freedom of worship." The Supreme Court unanimously
      disagreed, arguing that freedom of worship is included in freedom of
      religion and that the ministerial exception is broader than just worship and
      goes to expressions of faith. See Justice Samuel Alito's concurring opinion
      in *Hosana-Tabor Evangelical Lutheran Church and School v. Equal
      Employment Opportunity Commission*, 565 U.S. ___ (2012), available
      online at https://www.law.cornell.edu/supremecourt/text/10-
      553#writing-10-553_CONCUR_5.

19.   Ashley Samelson, "Why Freedom of Worship Is Not Enough," *First
      Things*, February 22, 2010, http://www.firstthings.com/web-
      exclusives/2010/02/why-ldquofreedom-of-worshiprdquo-is-not-enough.

20.   *"Pirates of the Caribbean: The Curse of the Black Pearl* (2003) Quotes,"
      IMDB, http://www.imdb.com/title/tt0325980/quotes.

21.   J. S. Conway, *Nazi Persecution of Churches: 1933–1945* (Vancouver:
      Regent College Publishing, 2001), 113.

22.   Ibid.

23.   Ibid., 114.

24.   Ibid.

CHAPTER 7
WHAT THE HELL ARE THEY THINKING?

1.   "C.S. Lewis > Quotes > Quotable Quote," Goodreads, http://www.
      goodreads.com/quotes/19967-of-all-tyrannies-a-tyranny-sincerely-
      exercised-for-the-good.

2.   Russell Moore, "Same-Sex Marriage and the Supreme Court: What Now
      for the Church?," RussellMoore.com, October 6, 2014, http://www.

russellmoore.com/2014/10/06/same-sex-marriage-and-the-supreme-court-what-now-for-the-church/.

3. Os Guinness, *A Free People's Suicide: Sustainable Freedom and the American Future* (Downer's Grove, IL: IVP Books, 2012), 153.

4. Nancy Pearcey, personal interview by Bill Blankschaen, Atlanta, GA, August 25, 2015.

5. Ibid.

6. Pearcey, *Finding Truth: Five Principles for Unmasking Atheism, Secularism, and Other God Substitutes* (Colorado Springs, CO: David C. Cook, 2015), 115.

7. Pearcey, personal interview by Bill Blankschaen.

8. Pearcey, *Finding Truth*, 118.

9. Steve Smothermon, *Big Problems, Bigger God* (Eugene, OR: Harvest House Publishers, 2015), 122.

CHAPTER 8
PASTORS, PRIESTS, AND POWERLESS PULPITS

1. Bryan Fischer, "Separation of Church and State: Straight from the Mind of Hitler," RenewAmerica.com, January 19, 2008, http://www.renewamerica.com/columns/fischer/080119.

2. Sarah Pulliam Bailey, "Could Religious Institutions Lose Tax-Exempt Status over Supreme Court's Gay Marriage Case?," *Washington Post*, April 28, 2015, https://www.washingtonpost.com/news/acts-of-faith/wp/2015/04/28/could-religious-institutions-lose-tax-exempt-status-over-supreme-courts-gay-marriage-case/.

3. Allahpundit, "9–0: Supreme Court Finds 'Ministerial Exception' to Job Discrimination Laws for Religious Organizations," *Hot Air* (blog), January 11, 2012, http://hotair.com/archives/2012/01/11/9-0-supreme-court-finds-ministerial-exception-to-job-discrimination-laws-for-religious-organizations/.

4. Brian Mattson, personal interview by Bill Blankschaen, Atlanta, GA, July 14, 2015.

5. Ed Morrissey, personal interview by Bill Blankschaen, Atlanta, GA, August 17, 2015.

6. David McNeely, personal interview by Bill Blankschaen, Atlanta, GA, July 9, 2015.

7. Russell Moore, personal interview by Bill Blankschaen, Atlanta, GA, July 17, 2015.

8. Eric Connor, "First Baptist Opens Its Doors to Same-Sex Couples," Greenville Online, August 3, 2015, http://www.greenvilleonline.com/story/news/local/2015/08/03/first-baptist-greenville-sex-couples/31071697/.

9. Ibid.

10. Ibid.

11. Lawrence Farley, "Another Jesus," Orthodox Christian Network, April 3, 2015, http://myocn.net/another-jesus/.

12. McNeely, personal interview by Bill Blankschaen.

CHAPTER 9
RAINBOW STICKERS AND SUPREME SILLINESS

1. Obergefell v. Hodges, 576 U.S. ___ (2015), available online at http://www.supremecourt.gov/opinions/14pdf/14-556_3204.pdf.

2. Jaime Fuller, "Kentucky County Clerk Who Refused to Issue Marriage Licenses Sent to Jail [Updated]," New York, September 3, 2015, http://nymag.com/daily/intelligencer/2015/09/kim-davis-sent-to-jail-in-kentucky.html.

3. Ibid.

4. Gabe Gutierrez and Jon Schuppe, "Rowan County Clerk Kim Davis Isn't Kentucky's Only Gay Marriage Holdout," NBC News, September 9, 2015, http://www.nbcnews.com/news/us-news/why-arent-other-defiant-kentucky-clerks-joining-kim-davis-jail-n423496.

5. "Mayor Defends Same-Sex Marriages," CNN, February 22, 2004, http://www.cnn.com/2004/LAW/02/22/same.sex/.

6. Associated Press, "Obama: DOMA Unconstitutional, DOJ Should Stop Defending in Court," Huffington Post, February 23, 2011, updated May 25, 2011, http://www.huffingtonpost.com/2011/02/23/obama-doma-unconstitutional_n_827134.html.

7. Obergefell v. Hodges.

8. Planned Parenthood of Southeastern Pa. v. Casey, 505 U.S. 833 (1992), available online at https://supreme.justia.com/cases/federal/us/505/833/.

9. Walt Whitman, "Song of Myself," available online at http://whitmanarchive.org/published/LG/1891/poems/27.

10. Shane Ferro, "This Scalia Zinger Is the Funniest Footnote to Come Out of the Supreme Court This Term," Business Insider, June 26, 2015, http://www.businessinsider.com/this-scalia-zinger-is-funniest-footnote-to-come-out-of-the-supreme-court-this-term-2015-6.

11. Hugh Hewitt, personal interview by Bill Blankschaen, Atlanta, GA, July 14, 2015.

12. Charles LiMandri, personal interview by Bill Blankschaen, Atlanta, GA, August 18, 2015.

13. Michael J. New, "In the Wake of Obergefell, Three New Polls Show Reduced Support for Same-Sex Marriage," The Corner (blog), National Review Online, July 21, 2015, http://www.nationalreview.com/corner/421443/obergefell-same-sex-marriage-poll-reduced-support.

14. Obergefell v. Hodges.

15. The Ten Commandments, directed by Cecil B. DeMille (USA: Paramount Pictures: 1956).

16. Hewitt, personal interview by Bill Blankschaen.

CHAPTER 10
WHAT DIFFERENCE DOES IT MAKE?

1. Andrew T. Walker and Eric Teetsel, *Marriage Is: How Marriage Transforms Society and Cultivates Human Flourishing* (Nashville: B&H Publishing, 2015), Kindle edition.

2. "Hillary Clinton at Benghazi Hearing: 'What Difference, Does It Make?,'" YouTube video, from January 23, 2013, testimony, posted by "Joe Bunting," May 13, 2013, https://www.youtube.com/watch?v=Ka0_nz53CcM.

3. Walker and Teetsel, *Marriage Is*.

4. American Chesterton Society, "Taking a Fence Down," Chesterton.org, no date, https://www.chesterton.org/taking-a-fence-down/.

5. Hugh Hewitt, personal interview by Bill Blankschaen, Atlanta, GA, July 14, 2015.

6. Robert P. George, *Conscience and Its Enemies: Confronting the Dogmas of Liberal Secularism* (Wilmington, DE: ISI Books, 2013), 126.

7. Ryan T. Anderson, Robert P. George, and Sherif Girgis, *What is Marriage? Man and Woman: A Defense* (New York: Encounter Books, 2012), 1.

8. Ibid., 55.

9. Brian Mattson, personal interview by Bill Blankschaen, Atlanta, GA, July 14, 2015.

10. Anderson, George, and Girgis, Sherif. *What is Marriage?*, 26.

11. Ibid., 30.

12. Sean McDowell and John Stonestreet, *Same Sex Marriage: A Thoughtful Approach to God's Design for Marriage* (Grand Rapids, MI: Baker Books, 2014), 47.

13. Russell Moore, personal interview by Bill Blankschaen, Atlanta, GA, July 16, 2014.

14. Maggie Gallagher, personal interview by Bill Blankschaen, Atlanta, GA, August 26, 2015.

15. "Marriage from a Child's Perspective: How Does Family Structure Affect Children, and What Can We Do about It?," *Child Trends Research Brief*

(Washington, DC: Child Trends, 2002), http://www.childtrends.org/wp-content/uploads/2013/03/MarriageRB602.pdf.

16. Brian Mattson, personal interview by Bill Blankschaen, Atlanta, GA, July 14, 2015.

17. Peter Sprigg, "Homosexual Parent Study: Summary of Findings," *Issue Brief* (Washington, DC: Family Research Council, 2012), http://downloads.frc.org/EF/EF12H47.pdf.

18. Cheryl Wetzstein, "Study Suggests Risks from Same-Sex Parenting," *Washington Times*, June 10, 2012, http://www.washingtontimes.com/news/2012/jun/10/study-suggests-risks-from-same-sex-parenting/?page=all.

19. Sprigg, "Homosexual Parent Study."

20. Mark Regnerus, "A Married Mom and Dad Really Do Matter: New Evidence from Canada," Public Discourse, October 8, 2013, http://www.thepublicdiscourse.com/2013/10/10996/.

21. Ibid.

22. "Why Children Need Both a Mom and a Dad," Focus on the Family, no date, http://www.focusonthefamily.com/socialissues/marriage/teach-your-children-about-marriage/mom-and-dad-children-need-both.

CHAPTER 11
ABOLISHING MARRIAGE

1. Mike Opelka, "Lesbian Activist's Surprisingly Candid Speech: Gay Marriage Fight Is a 'Lie' to Destroy Marriage," TheBlaze, April 29, 2013, http://www.theblaze.com/stories/2013/04/29/lesbian-activists-surprisingly-candid-speech-gay-marriage-fight-is-a-lie-to-destroy-marriage/.

2. Patrick Lee and Robert P. George, *Conjugal Union: What Marriage Is and Why It Matters* (New York, NY: Cambridge University Press, 2014), 107.

3. George, *Conscience and Its Enemies: Confronting the Dogmas of Liberal Secularism* (Wilmington, DE: ISI Books, 2013), 127.

4.   Matthew Schmidt, "N. T. Wright on Gay Marriage," *First Things*, June
     11, 2014, https://www.firstthings.com/blogs/firstthoughts/2014/06/n-t-
     wrights-argument-against-same-sex-marriage.

5.   Maggie Gallagher, personal interview by Bill Blankschaen, Atlanta, GA,
     August 26, 2015.

6.   Luis Ritto, "The Wrong Side of History," *ISPD News* (blog), August 4,
     2014, https://ispdnews.wordpress.com/2014/04/08/the-wrong-side-of-
     history/.

7.   Opelka, "Lesbian Activist's Surprisingly Candid Speech."

8.   Leo Hohmann, "LGBT Activists: Marriage Was Never the 'End Game,'"
     WND, June 30, 2015, http://www.wnd.com/2015/06/lgbt-activists-
     marriage-was-never-the-end-game/#GlxIv7CTE82Xqodq.99.

9.   John Bresnahan, "Clinton: Believing Petraeus and Crocker Requires
     'Willing Suspension of Disbelief,'" *Politico Now* (blog), *Politico*,
     September 11, 2007, http://www.politico.com/blogs/politico-
     now/2007/09/clinton-believing-petraeus-and-crocker-requires-willing-
     suspension-of-disbelief-003088.

10. Opelka, "Lesbian Activist's Surprisingly Candid Speech."

11. Matthew Lee Anderson, "Naive Young Evangelicals and the Illiberal
     DNA of the Gay Rights Movement," *Mere Orthodoxy*, April 8, 2015,
     http://mereorthodoxy.com/naive-young-evangelicals-illiberal-dna-gay-
     rights-movement/.

12. "*Jurassic Park* Quotes," IMDB, no date, http://www.imdb.com/title/
     tt0107290/quotes.

13. "G.K. Chesterton > Quotes > Quotable Quote," Goodreads, no date,
     https://www.goodreads.com/quotes/44015-when-men-choose-not-to-
     believe-in-god-they-do.

14. "G.K. Chesterton > Quotes > Quotable Quote," Goodreads, no date,
     https://www.goodreads.com/quotes/461990-it-is-always-simple-to-fall-
     there-are-an-infinity.

15. Ravi Zacharias, personal interview by Bill Blankschaen, Atlanta, GA,
     September 14, 2015.

16. "Leo Tolstoy > Quotes > Quotable Quote," Goodreads, no date, https://www.goodreads.com/quotes/106513-wrong-does-not-cease-to-be-wrong-because-the-majority.

CHAPTER 12
REDEFINING GENDER

1. American Chesterton Society, "When Man Ceases to Worship God," Chesterton.org, http://www.chesterton.org/ceases-to-worship/.

2. Charles LiMandri, personal interview by Bill Blankschaen, Atlanta, GA, August 18, 2015.

3. Ibid.

4. Ibid.

5. Ibid.

6. David Jackson, "Spokesman: Obama Praises Caitlyn Jenner's Courage," *USA Today*, June 2, 2015, http://www.usatoday.com/story/theoval/2015/06/02/obama-caitlyn-jenner-vanity-fair-bruce-jenner/28357535/.

7. David French, "Yes, ESPN Did Pick Caitlyn Jenner Ahead of Iraq War Vet and Amputee Noah Galloway for the ESPY Courage Award," *The Corner* (blog), National Review Online, June 3, 2015, http://www.nationalreview.com/corner/419254/yes-espn-did-pick-caitlyn-jenner-ahead-iraq-war-vet-and-amputee-noah-galloway-espy.

8. Ibid.

9. Patrick Howley, "Caitlyn Jenner Is the Greatest Female Athlete of All Time," Daily Caller, June 1, 2015, http://dailycaller.com/2015/06/01/caitlyn-jenner-is-the-greatest-female-athlete-of-all-time/#ixzz3lvAxzdav.

10. "Why Caitlyn Jenner Is More Than a Name," video, *Washington Post*, June 2, 2015, https://www.washingtonpost.com/posttv/editorial/why-caitlyn-jenner-is-more-than-a-name/2015/06/02/25e48b20-0950-11e5-951e-8e15090d64ae_video.html.

11. Charles Curtis, "Ex-Jet Brett Favre Called Out by Jenn Sterger over Caitlyn Jenner Reaction," NJ.com, July 16, 2015, http://www.nj.com/

jets/index.ssf/2015/07/ex-jet_brett_favre_called_out_by_jenn_sterger_
over.html.

12. Justine Harman, "So, What Does 'Authentic Self' Really Mean?," *Elle*,
July 27, 2015, http://www.elle.com/culture/movies-tv/a29486/authentic-
self/.

13. CBMW, "Emerson University Follows Disturbing Trend By Making
Restrooms Gender-Neutral to Accommodate 'Transgender' Students,"
CBMW.org, September 5, 2007, http://cbmw.org/uncategorized/emerson-
university-follows-disturbing-trend-by-making-restrooms-gender-neutral-
to-accommodate-transgender-students/.

14. Samuel Smith, "Billy Graham's Hometown Rejects Transgender Bathroom
Ordinance, Still Permits Businesses to Refuse Service Based on Religious
Belief Opposing Homosexuality," *Christian Post*, March 4, 2015, http://
www.christianpost.com/news/billy-grahams-hometown-rejects-
transgender-bathroom-ordinance-still-permits-businesses-to-refuse-
service-based-on-religious-belief-opposing-homosexuality-135127/.

15. Sam Brodey and Julia Lurie, "Get Ready for the Conservative Assault on
Where Transgender Americans Pee," *Mother Jones*, March 9, 2015, http://
www.motherjones.com/politics/2015/03/transgender-bathroom-
discrimination-bills.

16. "University of California Offers Six Choices for 'Gender Identity,'"
FoxNews.com, July 28, 2015, http://www.foxnews.com/us/2015/07/28/
university-california-offers-six-choices-for-gender-identity/.

17. Ibid.

18. Chris McKee, "UNM to Accept 'Preferred Names' for Transgender
Students," KRQE News 13, November 26, 2014, http://krqe.
com/2014/11/26/unm-to-accept-preferred-names-for-transgender-
students/.

19. Laura Ungar, "Transgender People Face Alarmingly High Risk of
Suicide," *USA Today*, August 16, 2015, http://www.usatoday.com/story/
news/nation/2015/08/16/transgender-individuals-face-high-rates--suicide-
attempts/31626633/.

20.   Char Adams, "Students Walk out of School After Transgender Classmate Is Allowed to Use Girls' Locker Room: 'I Am a Girl. I Am Not Going to Be Pushed Away to Another Bathroom,'" *People*, September 2, 2015, updated September 5, 2015, http://www.people.com/article/transgender-student-backlash-girls-restroom.

21.   Jon Street, "Transgender Student Refuses to Use Private Bathroom After Girls Say They Are Uncomfortable—Here's How Over 100 Students Responded," TheBlaze, September 1, 2015, http://www.theblaze.com/stories/2015/09/01/transgender-student-refuses-to-use-private-bathroom-after-girls-say-they-are-uncomfortable-heres-how-over-100-students-responded/.

22.   Doug Moore, "Hillsboro High Students Walk Out over Transgender Dispute," *St. Louis (MO) Post-Dispatch*, September 1, 2015, http://www.stltoday.com/news/local/education/hillsboro-high-students-walk-out-over-transgender-dispute/article_be488fab-d239-5944-9733-32f569dcdc32.html.

23.   Petula Dvorak, "Shame On Parents Fighting against Transgender Kids in School Bathrooms," *Washington Post*, May 11, 2015, https://www.washingtonpost.com/local/shame-on-parents-fighting-against-transgender-kids-in-school-bathrooms/2015/05/11/8cc005f8-f808-11e4-a13c-193b1241d51a_story.html.

24.   Ibid.

25.   Paul McHugh, "Transgender Surgery Isn't the Solution," *Wall Street Journal*, June 12, 2014, http://www.wsj.com/articles/paul-mchugh-transgender-surgery-isnt-the-solution-1402615120.

CHAPTER 13
DISCRIMINATING AGAINST TRUTH

1.   "Isaac Newton > Quotes > Quotable Quote," Goodreads, no date, https://www.goodreads.com/author/show/135106.Isaac_Newton.

2.   "About Marquette: Catholic and Jesuit," Marquette University, no date, http://www.marquette.edu/about/catholic-jesuit.php.

3.   Conor Friedersdorf, "Stripping a Professor of Tenure over a Blog Post,"
      Atlantic, February 9, 2015, http://www.theatlantic.com/education/
      archive/2015/02/stripping-a-professor-of-tenure-over-a-blog-
      post/385280/.

4.   Cheryl Abbate, "Recent Controversy," *Cheryl Abbate* (blog), updated
      February 11, 2015, https://ceabbate.wordpress.com/recent-controversy/.

5.   Friedersdorf, "Stripping a Professor of Tenure."

6.   Ibid.

7.   John McAdams, "Marquette Philosophy Instructor: 'Gay Rights' Can't
      Be Discussed in Class Since Any Disagreement Would Offend Gay
      Students," *Marquette Warrior* (blog), November 9, 2014, http://
      mu-warrior.blogspot.in/2014/11/marquette-philosophy-instructor-gay.
      html.

8.   Friedersdorf, "Stripping a Professor of Tenure."

9.   Emily Brooker v. the Governors of the Missouri State University, United
      States District Court, Western District of Missouri, Southern Division,
      available online at http://adfwebadmin.com/resources/Files/Brooker%20
      v.%20Franks,%20et%20al._Complaint.pdf.

10.   Emily Brooker, personal interview by Bill Blankschaen, Atlanta, GA,
      August 7, 2015.

11.   Ibid.

12.   Karen M. Sowers and Michael Patchner, "School of Social Work Site Visit
      Report," Office of the Provost, Missouri State University, March 28,
      2007, https://www.thefire.org/pdfs/ff16c8943c91efd4f7e5b73f44fed324.
      pdf.

13.   Brooker, personal interview by Bill Blankschaen.

14.   Jennifer Keeton, personal interview by Bill Blankschaen, Atlanta, GA,
      August 7, 2015.

15.   Ruth Malhotra, personal interview by Bill Blankschaen, Atlanta, GA,
      August 7, 2015.

16.   Ibid.

17.   Ibid.

18. Ibid.

19. Ibid.

CHAPTER 14
YOU HAVE THE RIGHT TO REMAIN SILENT

1. "Martin Niemöller: 'First They Came for the Socialists ... ,'" United States Holocaust Memorial Museum, updated August 18, 2015, http://www.ushmm.org/wlc/en/article.php?ModuleId=10007392.

2. Mathew D. Staver, "On Marriage, We Will Not Render to Caesar What Is God's," BarbWire, April 22, 2015, http://barbwire.com/2015/04/22/0900-on-marriage-we-will-not-render-to-caesar-what-is-gods/.

3. "Edmund Burke Quotes," Brainy Quote, no date, http://www.brainyquote.com/quotes/quotes/e/edmundburk377528.html.

4. Kelsey Harkness, "State Says Bakers Should Pay $135,000 for Refusing to Bake Cake for Same-Sex Wedding," Daily Signal, April 24, 2015, http://dailysignal.com/2015/04/24/state-says-bakers-should-pay-135000-for-refusing-to-bake-cake-for-same-sex-wedding/.

5. Harkness, "Emails Raise Questions of Bias in Case against Bakers Who Denied Service for Same-Sex Wedding," Daily Signal, June 1, 2015, http://dailysignal.com/2015/06/01/emails-raise-questions-of-bias-in-case-against-bakers-who-denied-service-for-same-sex-wedding/.

6. Aaron and Melissa Klein, personal interview by Bill Blankschaen, Atlanta, GA, August 13, 2015.

7. Frederick E. Allen, "Howard Schultz to Anti-gay-marriage Starbucks Shareholder: 'You Can Sell Your Shares,'" Forbes.com, March 22, 2013, http://www.forbes.com/sites/frederickallen/2013/03/22/howard-schultz-to-anti-gay-marriage-starbucks-shareholder-you-can-sell-your-shares/.

8. PennLive Editorial Board, "The Supremes Got It Right—It's No Longer 'Gay Marriage.' It's 'Marriage.' And We're Better for It: Editorial," PennLive, June 26, 2015, http://www.pennlive.com/opinion/2015/06/gay_marriage_anthony_kennedy_o.html.

9. Lisa Respers France, "Benham Brothers Lose HGTV Show after 'Anti-gay' Remarks," CNN, May 9, 2014, http://www.cnn.com/2014/05/08/showbiz/tv/benham-brothers-hgtv/.

10. Associated Press, "Mozilla CEO Resignation Raises Free-Speech Issues," *USA Today*, April 4, 2014, http://www.usatoday.com/story/news/nation/2014/04/04/mozilla-ceo-resignation-free-speech/7328759/.

11. Tish Harrison Warren, "The Wrong Kind of Christian," Christianity Today, August 27, 2014, http://www.christianitytoday.com/ct/2014/september/wrong-kind-of-christian-vanderbilt-university.html.

12. Aaron Smith, "Denver Puts Chick-fil-A's Restaurant Bid on Back Burner," CNNMoney, August 24, 2015, http://money.cnn.com/2015/08/24/news/companies/chick-fil-a-denver/.

13. Emanuella Grinberg, "Planet Fitness Revokes Woman's Membership after Transgender Complaint," CNN.com, March 9, 2015, http://www.cnn.com/2015/03/07/living/feat-planet-fitness-transgender-member/.

14. Paul Milo, "N.J. Teacher Suspended for Anti-gay Facebook Posts Still Getting Paid, Diocese Says," NJ.com, March 20, 2015, updated March 21, 2015, http://www.nj.com/somerset/index.ssf/2015/03/nj_teacher_suspended_for_anti-gay_facebook_posts_s.html.

15. Tobias Salinger, "N.J. Catholic High School Teacher Who Spewed Anti-gay Rhetoric on Facebook Reinstated after Uproar," *New York Daily News*, April 12, 2015, http://www.nydailynews.com/news/national/catholic-teacher-spewed-anti-gay-rhetoric-reinstated-article-1.2182104.

16. Charles LiMandri, personal interview by Bill Blankschaen, Atlanta, GA, August 18, 2015.

17. Maggie Gallagher, personal interview by Bill Blankschaen, Atlanta, GA, August 26, 2015.

18. Ed Morrissey, personal interview by Bill Blankschaen, Atlanta, GA, August 17, 2015.

19. "Rick Warren > Quotes > Quotable Quote," Goodreads, no date, https://www.goodreads.com/quotes/601712-our-culture-has-accepted-two-huge-lies-the-first-is.

20.	"*The Dark Knight* Quotes," IMDB, no date, http://www.imdb.com/title/tt0468569/quotes.

21.	"*The Dark Knight* Joker Quotes," Daily Movie Quotes, no date, https://dailymoviequotes.wordpress.com/the-dark-knight-joker-quotes/.

CHAPTER 15
THE RESURGENT COMMUNITY

1.	Jason Dohm, "A Sifting Time Ahead," *Jason Dohm Online* (blog), May 26, 2013, http://jasondohm.com/tag/martin-niemoller/.

2.	Sarah Pulliam Bailey, "Is Polygamy Next in the Marriage Debate?," *Washington Post*, July 10, 2015, https://www.washingtonpost.com/news/acts-of-faith/wp/2015/07/10/heres-why-people-are-arguing-over-whether-polygamy-is-the-next-gay-marriage-debate/.

3.	Russell Moore, personal interview by Bill Blankschaen, Atlanta, GA, July 16, 2015.

4.	Charles LiMandri, personal interview by Bill Blankschaen, Atlanta, GA, August 18, 2015.

5.	Steve Smothermon, personal interview by Bill Blankschaen, Atlanta, GA, August 11, 2015.

6.	Ravi Zacharias, personal interview by Bill Blankschaen, Atlanta, GA, September 14, 2015.

7.	Napp Nazworth, "Russell Moore to Parents: Don't Be Ashamed of Your Gay Kids, Don't Throw Them Out; That Is Pride," *Christian Post*, June 18, 2015, http://www.christianpost.com/news/russell-moore-to-parents-dont-be-ashamed-of-your-gay-kids-dont-throw-them-out-that-is-pride-140568/.

CHAPTER 16
THE RESURGENT BELIEVER

1.	"The American Proposition," *Commonweal* 73 (January 20, 1961): transcript of *Catholic Hour* interview, available online at http://www.library.georgetown.edu/woodstock/murray/1961a.

2. "Thinking and Feeling," *The History of Rome* (podcast), March 15, 2010, http://thehistoryofrome.typepad.com/the_history_of_rome/2010/03/index.html.

3. "Winston S. Churchill > Quotes > Quotable Quote," Goodreads, no date, https://www.goodreads.com/quotes/717228-never-let-a-good-crisis-go-to-waste.

4. Russell Moore, personal interview by Bill Blankschaen, Atlanta, GA, July 16, 2015.

5. *"The Lord of the Rings: The Fellowship of the Ring* Quotes," IMDB, no date, http://www.imdb.com/title/tt0120737/quotes.

6. "Dietrich Bonhoeffer > Quotes > Quotable Quote," Goodreads, no date, https://www.goodreads.com/quotes/695194-if-we-want-to-be-christians-we-must-have-some.

7. Kevin DeYoung, personal interview by Bill Blankschaen, Atlanta, GA, September 17, 2015.

8. Charles Dunahoo, "John Calvin: The Reformer and Educator," CDM, no date, http://www.pcacdm.org/john-calvin-the-reformer-and-educator/.

9. This phrase comes from the subtitle of Nancy Pearcey's book *Total Truth: Liberating Christianity from Its Cultural Captivity.*

10. Bill Blankschaen, *A Story Worth Telling: Your Field Guide to Living an Authentic Life* (Nashville, TN: Abingdon Press, 2015).

11. *"Skyfall* Quotes," IMDB, no date, http://www.imdb.com/title/tt1074638/quotes.

12. DeYoung, personal interview by Bill Blankschaen.

13. Brian Mattson, personal interview by Bill Blankschaen, Atlanta, GA, July 14, 2015.

14. Nancy Pearcey, personal interview by Bill Blankschaen, Atlanta, GA, August 25, 2015.

15. David McNeely, personal interview by Bill Blankschaen, Atlanta, GA, July 9, 2015.

CHAPTER 17
THE RESURGENT FAMILY

1. "John Adams > Quotes > Quotable Quote," Goodreads, no date, https://www.goodreads.com/quotes/534874-the-foundations-of-national-morality-must-be-laid-in-private.

2. Shaunti Feldhahn, e-mail interview by Bill Blankschaen, August 23, 2015.

3. Feldhahn, "The Numbers," Shaunti.com, no date, http://www.shaunti.com/research-good-news-about-marriage/numbers/#sthash.chwBWa6a.dpuf.

4. Andrew T. Walker, personal interview by Bill Blankschaen, Atlanta, GA, August 3, 2015.

5. Maggie Gallagher, personal interview by Bill Blankschaen, Atlanta, GA, August 26, 2015.

6. Andrew T. Walker and Eric Teetsel, *Marriage Is: How Marriage Transforms Society and Cultivates Human Flourishing* (Nashville: B&H Publishing, 2015), Kindle Edition.

7. Os Guinness, *A Free People's Suicide: Sustainable Freedom and the American Future* (Downer's Grove, IL: IVP Books, 2012), 83.

8. Joe Gelonesi, "Is Having a Loving Family an Unfair Advantage?," *The Philosopher's Zone*, ABC Radio, May 1, 2015, http://www.abc.net.au/radionational/programs/philosopherszone/new-family-values/6437058.

9. Ravi Zacharias, personal interview by Bill Blankschaen, Atlanta, GA, September 14, 2015.

CHAPTER 18
THE RESURGENT CHURCH

1. Dietrich Bonhoeffer, *The Cost of Discipleship* (New York: Simon and Schuster, 1959), 118.

2. David McNeely, personal interview by Bill Blankschaen, Atlanta, GA, July 9, 2015.

3. Ravi Zacharias, personal interview by Bill Blankschaen, Atlanta, GA, September 14, 2015.

4. Kevin DeYoung, personal interview by Bill Blankschaen, Atlanta, GA, September 17, 2015.

5. Zacharias, personal interview by Bill Blankschaen.

6. Bonhoeffer, *Life Together* (New York: Harper and Row, 1954), 11.

7. Nancy Pearcey, personal interview by Bill Blankschaen, Atlanta, GA, August 25, 2015.

8. Andrew T. Walker, personal interview by Bill Blankschaen, Atlanta, GA, August 3, 2015.

9. Russell Moore, personal interview by Bill Blankschaen, Atlanta, GA, July 16, 2015.

10. Antonia Blumberg, "'God Loves Sex' Billboard Turns Heads on Pennsylvania Highway," Huffington Post, August 29, 2014, http://www.huffingtonpost.com/2014/08/29/god-loves-sex-billboard_n_5732038.html.

11. DeYoung, personal interview by Bill Blankschaen.

12. Ibid.

13. Bonhoeffer, *The Cost of Discipleship*, 119.

CHAPTER 19
THE RESURGENT CITIZEN

1. "Quote DB :: Authors :: Daniel Webster," Quote DB, no date, http://www.quotedb.com/quotes/2522.

2. Russell Moore, personal interview by Bill Blankschaen, Atlanta, GA, July 16, 2015.

3. Hugh Hewitt, personal interview by Bill Blankschaen, Atlanta, GA, July 14, 2015.

4. Os Guinness, *A Free People's Suicide: Sustainable Freedom and the American Future* (Downer's Grove, IL: IVP Books, 2012), 107.

5. Guinness, "The Golden Triangle of Freedom," RZIM, August 21, 2012, http://rzim.org/just-thinking/the-golden-triangle-of-freedom.

6.   "Apple Rejects 'Manhattan Declaration' App for Second Time," MacNN, December 29, 2010, http://www.macnn.com/articles/10/12/29/company. believes.app.promotes.intolerance/.

7.   Daniel Schuman, "Religious Freedom Restoration Act: An Overview of Gonzales v. O Centro Espirita Beneficente Uniao do Vegetal," Congressional Research, no date, http://congressionalresearch.com/ RS22392/document.php?study=Religious+Freedom+Restoration+Act+A n+Overview+of+Gonzales+v.+O+Centro+Espirita+Beneficente+Uniao+ do+Vegetal.

8.   David Johnson and Katy Steinmetz, "This Map Shows Every State with Religious-Freedom Laws," *Time*, April 2, 2015, http://time.com/3766173/ religious-freedom-laws-map-timeline/.

9.   From *Imprimis* 44, no. 4 (April 2015), adapted from a speech delivered on April 25, 2015, at Hillsdale College's Allan P. Kirby, Jr., Center for Constitutional Studies and Citizenship, in Washington, D.C.

10.   Maggie Gallagher, personal interview by Bill Blankschaen, Atlanta, GA, August 26, 2015.

11.   Andrew T. Walker, personal interview by Bill Blankschaen, Atlanta, GA, August 3, 2015.

12.   *"The Weight of Glory* Quotes," Goodreads, no date, https://www. goodreads.com/work/quotes/1629232-the-weight-of-glory.

13.   Dietrich Bonhoeffer, "Letter to Family and Conspirators, 1942," in *Dietrich Bonhoeffer Works*, vol. 16 (Minneapolis: Augsburg Fortress, 2006).

14.   "Rediscovering 'Calling' Will Revitalize Church and Society," *Religion & Liberty* 8, no. 4 (Summer 1998): http://www.acton.org/sites/v4.acton. org/files/pdf/rl_v08n4.pdf.

CONCLUSION
YOU ARE NOT ALONE

1. Chelsea Clinton, "Jason Collins: The NBA Player Who Went First," *Time*, April 23, 2014, http://time.com/70898/jason-collins-2014-time-100/.

2. Ibid.

3. Ryan Parker, "Michael Sam: I'd Still Be in the NFL If I Hadn't Come Out," *Hollywood Reporter*, September 25, 2015, http://www.hollywoodreporter.com/news/michael-sam-still-nfl-he-827287.

4. Jared Dubin, "Michael Sam, First Openly Gay Player, Retires for Mental Health Reasons," CBS Sports, August 14, 2015, http://www.cbssports.com/nfl/eye-on-football/25270305/michael-sam-walks-away-from-football-cites-mental-health.

5. Matt Baume, "Peyton Manning Supports Michael Sam and Antigay Politicians," Queerty, May 15, 2014, http://www.queerty.com/peyton-manning-supports-michael-sam-and-antigay-politicians-20140515.

6. Ibid.

7. Reuters, "Wahlberg Raises Eyebrows as Host of the Philadelphia Pope Concert," Yahoo! News, September 26, 2015, https://ca.news.yahoo.com/wahlberg-raises-eyebrows-host-philadelphia-pope-concert-012122044.html.

8. Charlie Spiering, "Obama Warns Christians: Gay Rights More Important Than Religious Freedom," Breitbart, September 28, 2015, http://www.breitbart.com/big-government/2015/09/28/obama-warns-christians-gay-rights-important-religious-freedom/.

9. "Transcript: Obama's Speech during a Visit from Pope Francis," *Washington Post*, September 23, 2015, https://www.washingtonpost.com/local/social-issues/transcript-obamas-speech-during-a-visit-from-pope-francis/2015/09/23/0762e80c-620d-11e5-9757-e49273f05f65_story.html.

INDEX